Art Director
Michel Durand
Computer Editing
Michel Durand and Carole Berthélemy
Photoengraving
Euresys
Text Coordination
Sylvie Girard and Gérard Guicheteau
Recipe Translation
Charles Pierce
Text Translation
Paul Rankin

GEORGES BLANC

THE FRENCH VINEYARD TABLE

PHOTOGRAPHS BY CHRISTOPHER BAKER

UNDER THE DIRECTION OF PHILIPPE LAMBOLEY

CLARKSON POTTER / PUBLISHERS
NEW YORK

FOREWORD

FOOD AND WINE ARE PART OF OUR CULTURE, OF OUR HERITAGE, AND OF THE FRENCH ART OF LIFE, WHICH MAKES THE WHOLE WORLD DREAM. ALLIES OF BOTH THE HEART AND REASON, THEY HAVE BEEN HONORED FROM THE BEGINNING OF OUR CIVILIZATION. FOR CENTURIES THEY HAVE BEEN AT THE CENTER OF POETIC AND PHILOSOPHICAL EVOCATIONS; THEY HAVE FED CONVERSATION AND NOURISHED CONVIVIALITY. NO DOUBT THEY WILL CONTINUE TO PLAY THIS ROLE FOR A VERY LONG TIME.

MY PROFESSION AS A CHEF HAS LED ME QUITE NATURALLY TO DISCOVER THE WORLD OF WINE AND TO EXPLORE IT WITH A CONSTANT DESIRE TO PERFECT MY KNOWLEDGE. IT IS A SOURCE OF INSPIRATION FOR AN EXCITING PROFESSION WHOSE CALLING IS TO ENRICH THE PLEASURE OF CELEBRATION BY EXCITING TASTE.

THE IDEA FOR THIS BOOK, A CELEBRATION OF THE MARRIAGE OF FOOD AND WINE, WAS BORN FROM A DISCUSSION WITH THE PHOTOGRAPHER, CHRISTOPHER BAKER, DURING WORK ON THE ILLUSTRATIONS OF A PREVIOUS BOOK, *THE NATURAL CUISINE OF GEORGES BLANC*. AFTER SEVERAL YEARS—ALWAYS WITH THE SAME ENTHUSIASM—WE ONCE AGAIN TRAVELED THROUGHOUT FRANCE TO MEET THE MOST ENGAGING PEOPLE IN THE WINE REGIONS. WE WANTED TO HELP YOU DISCOVER THROUGH THE VARIETY OF RECIPES THE TASTIEST WAY OF SHARING THE BEST OF OUR REGIONS. EACH DISH PRESENTED IS COMPOSED IN THE SPIRIT OF ONE OF THE THIRTEEN GREAT WINE-GROWING REGIONS OF FRANCE, WHICH IT HONORS BY COMBINING THE LOCAL PRODUCTS AND THE WINES.

THIS BOOK MAY BE CONSIDERED A HOMAGE TO ALL THE ARTISTS OF WINE WHO IN THEIR RESPECTIVE REGIONS MAINTAIN THE GREAT TRADITIONS AND STRIVE TO DEVELOP QUALITY IN DIVERSITY. THUS, THEY GLORIFY THE EXPRESSION OF CULINARY ART OF WHICH WINE WILL ALWAYS BE THE FAITHFUL COMPANION.

GEORGES BLANC

CONTENTS

THE SAGA OF THE BLANC FAMILY

THE INN AT VONNAS.

It all began well before the French Revolution in the heart of the Bresse region where the Blanc family had farmed for several generations, in Marboz, in Cruet near Montrevel, then in Saint-Didier d'Aussiat. Jean-Louis Blanc and his wife were the first innkeepers to settle in Vonnas near the marketplace. The main clientele of the time were egg merchants who, arriving for market by horse-drawn carriage on Thursdays, warmed themselves with soup. Their purchases completed, they sat down to a hearty snack. The soup was good, and word eventually traveled from market to market. In 1902, their son Adolphe Blanc, who had married Élisa Gervais, succeeded his parents. It was Élisa, installed in the kitchen, who made famous the name of La Mère Blanc. Élisa inherited from her mother, Virginie, the secrets of a culinary art rich in butter; she then perfected her skills during an apprenticeship with an innkeeper in Vonnas, Madame Lambert-Peney, of whom one still speaks with respect. Curnonsky, Prince of Gastronomes, wrote in 1933 that La Mère Blanc was the "best cook in

ABOVE: The first innkeeper around 1885: Jean-Louis Blanc, his wife, Rosalie, and their children Cécile, Adolphe, and Frédéric.
OPPOSITE: The second generation: Adolphe Blanc and Élisa, "La Mère Blanc."
BELOW: Jean Blanc, born in 1906, and his brother Paul, born in 1908, a cook in Thoissy until the eighties.

THE WORLD," BUT SHE WAS NOT WHAT ONE CALLS A GREAT CHEF. FAR FROM THE COOKS OF THE GREAT PALACES OF THE ERA, SHE NEVER RECEIVED ANY TRAINING IN CULINARY THEORY AND LEARNED EVERYTHING BY INSTINCT AND BY TASTE. SHE CREATED A CUISINE OF THE *TERROIR*, SIMPLE, OF GREAT HONESTY, PREPARED WITH LOVE AND TO PERFECTION, EXCLUSIVELY USING FRESH LOCAL PRODUCTS OF THE HIGHEST QUALITY. WITH THE IMPROVEMENT OF COMMUNICATION, PEOPLE CAME FROM FARTHER AND FARTHER AWAY TO TASTE HER "FROGS LEGS FROM DOMBES WITH HERBS" AND "BRESSE CHICKEN IN CREAM SAUCE WITH VONNAS-STYLE CRÊPES," WHICH WAS ESPECIALLY APPRECIATED BY PRIME MINISTER ÉDOUARD HERRIOT. SUNDAYS THE RAILROAD BROUGHT FAMILIES FROM MÂCON AND GROUPS OF FRIENDS. BUSINESS PROSPERED.

AWARDS FOR LA MÈRE BLANC.

THE AUTOMOBILE ACCELERATED THE SPREAD OF THIS RENOWN. IN 1930, THE TOURING CLUB OF FRANCE AWARDED FIRST PRIZE IN ITS CULINARY COMPETITION TO LA MÈRE BLANC. THE BEST GASTRONOMIC WRITERS OF THE TIME HONORED IT IN THE PRESS, AS DID THE CLUB DES CENT (THE ACADEMY OF GASTRONOMES). IN 1934, JEAN BLANC, THE ELDEST SON, TOOK OVER. HIS WIFE, PAULINE, DAUGHTER OF A BAKER, TOOK RESPONSIBILITY FOR THE KITCHEN. GUIDED BY HER MOTHER-IN-LAW, WHO WAS TO DIE IN 1949, SHE RETAINED THE TRADITIONAL SPECIALTIES THAT HAD MADE THE INN FAMOUS. AFTER THE DIFFICULT PERIOD OF THE SECOND WORLD WAR, THE HOUSE FOUND ITSELF IN EVER GREATER FASHION. IN 1965, THEIR SON

TOP: Georges Blanc, born January 2, 1943, and the menu for a memorable baptism.
ABOVE: Jean Blanc, a lover of fine automobiles, at the wheel of his Citroën in the thirties.
ABOVE RIGHT: Élisa Blanc at the stove around 1932. Behind her, in the typical headdress of the Bresse region, her mother, Virginie, born in 1860.
RIGHT: Marie, Juliette, Andrée, and Claudette, the waitresses of the inn in 1930.
FAR RIGHT: The Blancs' inn, around 1900.

THE SAGA OF THE BLANC FAMILY

CAFÉ-RESTAURANT

FABRIQUE DE LIMONADES

A. Blanc

Vonnas *Ain*

NOTE

TOP: Pauline Blanc at the stove.
ABOVE: A check from a meal in 1911.
LEFT: Alexandre, Georges, and Frédéric Blanc.

THE SAGA OF THE BLANC FAMILY

GEORGES, AFTER STUDY AT THE HOTEL SCHOOL OF THONON-LES-BAINS AND A PERIOD OF TRAINING IN VARIOUS ESTABLISHMENTS, ENTERED THE FAMILY BUSINESS TO WORK BESIDE HIS MOTHER, WHO YIELDED HER PLACE IN 1968. AT THE AGE OF TWENTY-FIVE, HE FOUND HIMSELF AT THE HEAD OF THE FAMILY BUSINESS.

GEORGES BLANC, THE INNOVATOR.

FROM 1970 ONWARD, IMPORTANT WORK COMPLETELY TRANSFORMED THE ESTAB-LISHMENT. THE SIMPLE INN BECAME A JEWEL IN THE PRESTIGIOUS RELAIS ET CHÂTEAUX CHAIN. WITHOUT DISAVOWING HIS ATTACHMENT TO TRADITION, GEORGES BLANC GRADUALLY EVOLVED IN A SIGNIFICANT WAY AS THE GASTRONOMIC WORLD OPENED TO NEW IDEAS. IN 1981, HE OBTAINED THREE STARS IN THE MICHELIN GUIDE. AT THE SAME TIME HE WAS AWARDED THE COVETED "CHEF OF THE YEAR" TITLE FROM GAULT MILLAUT. A TRUE BUSINESSMAN, GEORGES BLANC HAS SINCE SOUNDLY DIRECTED THE HUNDRED-ODD PEOPLE WHO WORK WITH HIM. HIS TWO SONS, FRÉDÉRIC AND ALEXANDRE, ARE PREPARING TO FOLLOW IN HIS FOOTSTEPS.

**ABOVE: A Sunday in 1955, Jean and Pauline surrounded by their entire staff.
BELOW: Today's kitchen staff gathered around the chef.**

A PASSION FOR WINE.

NOT CONTENT WITH OWNING ONE OF THE FINEST WINE CELLARS IN THE WORLD (120,000 BOTTLES IN MORE THAN 2,500 DIFFERENT APPELLATIONS), GEORGES BLANC REALIZED AN OLD DREAM IN 1985 AND CREATED HIS OWN VINEYARD FROM FALLOW LAND. FORTY TWO ACRES OF CHARDONNAY WERE PLANTED IN THE MIDDLE OF AN APPELLATION AREA ON A SITE PARTICULARLY WELL EXPOSED TO AZE EN MÂCONNAIS, THUS GIVING BIRTH TO THE DOMAINE D'AZENAY. THE FIRST VINTAGES, WHICH WON MEDALS IN SEVERAL COMPETITIONS, EXPERIENCED A RAPID SUCCESS IN FRANCE AS WELL AS ABROAD. GEORGES BLANC ALSO OPENED THE CELLIER D'AZENAY IN VONNAS, A PRESTIGIOUS WINE SHOP THAT SHOWS OFF THE BEST PROPRIETARY WINES OF FRANCE.

BURGUNDY

THIS FRENCH PROVINCE IS A FORMER EUROPEAN STATE OF THE MIDDLE AGES WHOSE
POSSESSIONS EXTENDED AS FAR AS BELGIUM. BURGUNDY HAS PRESERVED A SPLENDOR,
AN ARCHITECTURAL RICHNESS, AND A ROYAL TASTE FOR FOOD AND WINE.
THROUGHOUT THE WORLD THE NAMES DIJON, BEAUNE, AND CLOS VOUGEOT
HOLD A DOUBLE MEANING AS BOTH TOURISTIC AND GASTRONOMIC WONDERS.

MODERN BURGUNDY STRETCHES FROM CHAMPAGNE TO THE MASSIF CENTRAL
AND FROM THE SAÔNE RIVER PLAIN TO THE BANKS OF THE UPPER LOIRE RIVER. IT IS
A LAND OF LARGE HILLS, GREEN MOUNTAINS, NARROW VALLEYS, DEEP FORESTS, AND
OPEN FIELDS. IT BEGINS AT THE GATES OF PARIS IN THE YONNE AND CLIMBS, LITTLE
BY LITTLE, THE SPLENDID HILLS THAT ROUND OFF THE PARISIAN BASIN TO THE
SOUTHEAST. AS IN CHABLIS, THE GRAPEVINE MUST VIE WITH GRAIN AND FORESTS.
AT THE EDGE OF THE LIMESTONE PLATEAU THAT STEEPLY BREAKS OFF ABOVE THE
SAÔNE RIVER, BURGUNDY HAS PLACED ITS HEART: THE CÔTE D'OR AND ITS TWO
GREAT CAPITALS, ITS APPROXIMATELY THIRTY ODD *GRANDS CRUS*, ITS HUNDREDS OF
"CLIMATES," AND THE MOTHER ABBEY OF GREAT CISTERCIAN ART. TO THE SOUTH
THE SAÔNE-ET-LOIRE, AND MOST PARTICULARLY THE CHALONNAIS, STRETCH OUT.
TO THE WEST THE MORVAN AND THE NIÈVRE ROUND OFF THIS REGION.

THE BURGUNDIAN DUKES WERE NO SIMPLE LORDS. AS DID THE KINGS OF FRANCE
OR ENGLAND WITH WHOM THEY WERE SOMETIMES ALLIES, SOMETIMES ADVERSARIES,
THEY LIVED IN TOWN WHERE THEY BUILT SPLENDID PALACES SUCH AS THOSE OF
DIJON OR BEAUNE.

THANKS TO THEM, AND TO THE MONKS THEY PROTECTED, BURGUNDY IS RICH
IN DWELLINGS, ABBEYS, AND HOSPICES, OF A GRAND, FLAMBOYANT STYLE THAT SO
DELICATELY UNITES PALE STONE, BRICK, WOOD, AND WINDOWS IN A SINGULAR
HARMONY.

A GLIMPSE AT TRADITION

Eggs Poached in Red Wine Sauce

—

Cut 4 ounces slab bacon into small dice and blanch for a
minute or two in boiling water. Drain well and pat dry. Peel
and finely chop 2 garlic cloves, 2 shallots, and 1 onion.

Melt 2 tablespoons unsalted butter in a large saucepan and
add the bacon. Cook over medium-high heat, stirring, until lightly
browned. Add the garlic, shallots, and onion. Cook until the
bacon is golden brown and the vegetables are softened. Sprinkle
with a little flour and cook 2 minutes longer. Whisk in 2 cups
hearty red wine and 1 cup chicken stock. Season lightly with salt,
reduce the heat to medium-low, and simmer until the sauce has
reduced by half, about 30 minutes. Meanwhile, finely chop a
small bunch of parsley.

After the sauce has been cooking for 15 minutes, break 8 large
eggs, one at a time, into a saucer and add to the sauce. Gently
poach for 3 to 4 minutes. Several eggs can be poached at once.
Simply remember the order in which they were added so that they
can removed at the appropriate time. (Do not overcook the eggs.)
Carefully remove the eggs with a slotted spoon and drain on paper
towels. Using a small knife, trim the rough edges of the eggs.

Toast 16 thick slices of crusty bread and place 2 on each of 8
individual serving plates. Top with the poached eggs. Whisk ½
cup unsalted butter into the sauce to enrich it. Season the sauce
with salt and freshly ground black pepper and spoon over the eggs.
Sprinkle liberally with chopped parsley and serve at once.

At the edge of the Burgundian plateau across from the Saône plain, the slopes spread out or grow narrower according to the deep movements of the limestone of the mother-rock. In winter, in the silence of the snow-covered earth, the sap prepares to rise that will set in motion the pruning of the branches.

OPPOSITE: The harvest of Pinot Noir grapes is set to macerate in these vats: The "chapeau" is regularly reimmersed in the fermentation liquid by "pigeage" which is carried out by pressing down the grapes by foot.

ABOVE LEFT: Burgundian roofs decorated with designs in glazed tile express the character of the old province from Dijon to Chagny.

ABOVE RIGHT: Entrance to the Château de Chamirey in Mercurey, property of the Maison Antonin Rodet.

ABOVE: Typical land-
scape of the Côte with,
at the top of the slope,
the forest which stops
neatly where the vine-
yards begin. Sometimes
it is just a matter of
inches. This limit has
been established from
the dawn of time as has
the delineation of the
land below, the clear
lines of the *clos*,
hemmed in by low walls,
the fixing of the bound-
aries of the *crus*, great
and lesser, which are
called "climates" in
Burgundy.

RIGHT: In the exact
geometry of the rows of
grapevines, the decision
as to the times of opti-
mal ripening and the
harvest is a delicate
operation.

Burgundian dwellings of the golden age reflect the magnificence of a state that was at the time of the Grand Dukes of Valois rival to France and England. The ribs of figured wood, the warm color of the faience tiles, and the elegance of the glass are harmonious.

Bertrand Devillard is one of the dominant individuals in Burgundian wine growing. A great wine lover once said that he had "reconciled him to Burgundy," which implies that this same connoisseur could once have had doubts about one of the great wines of the world!

Leading a remarkable team, Bertrand Devillard, head of the Maison Antonin Rodet, has a great passion for the fine wines of Burgundy, of which his is one of the most respected names. Founded in 1875, the house of Antonin Rodet has its roots in the marvelous Côte Chalonnaise at the Château de Chamirey in Mercurey. The Marquis de Jouennes, heir to Antonin Rodet, and Bertrand Devillard, his son-in-law, have worked together to give a magnificent élan to their wine growing and trading house while making prestigious acquisitions. With 395 acres, the house of Antonin Rodet is present in several of the better "climates" of the Côte de Nuit (Chambertin, Clos de Vougeot), of the Côte de Beaune (Corton-Charlemagne, Volnay, Meursault, Montrachet), as well as the Côte Chalonnaise (Mercurey, Rully). The combination of these estates is unique and the most important in Burgundy.

Under an ideal autumn sun, the harvest of the Pinot Noir grape has begun. The gathering is done by hand and the grapes must not be damaged by handling. Depending on the year, one needs from two to three clusters of grapes for one bottle of wine.

BERNARD L'OISEAU

La Côte d'Or
Saulieu
Côte d'Or

———

Preparation: 40 minutes

Cooking time: 50 minutes

Serves 4

●

1 LARGE PIKE PERCH OR STRIPED BASS,
6 TO 8 POUNDS, SCALED (SEE NOTE)

3 MEDIUM CARROTS, PEELED AND
COARSELY CHOPPED

1 CUP (2 STICKS) UNSALTED BUTTER

18 TO 20 MEDIUM SHALLOTS, ABOUT
1 POUND, THINLY SLICED

3 CUPS POMMARD OR SIMILAR HEARTY
RED WINE

COARSE SALT AND FRESHLY GROUND
BLACK PEPPER TO TASTE

1 TABLESPOON OLIVE OIL

PIKE PERCH WITH SHALLOT CONFIT AND POMMARD

Have the fishmonger remove 4 large fillets (with skin intact) from the fish. Keep the fillets chilled in the refrigerator until just before preparing them.

Bring a large pot of salted water (1 tablespoon coarse salt per 1 quart water) to a boil. Add the carrots, bring back to a boil, and cook rapidly until very tender, 20 to 25 minutes. Drain well, transfer to a food processor, and process until smooth. Set the purée aside.

Meanwhile, melt half of the butter in a large heavy saucepan. Add the shallots and cook over medium-low heat, stirring often, until softened, 20 to 25 minutes. Watch the shallots carefully; regulate the heat and stir frequently to prevent scorching. Drain the shallots on paper towels and gently pat with additional paper towels to remove as much fat as possible. Wipe out the saucepan and return the shallots to it. Set aside.

Pour the wine into a large nonreactive saucepan. Bring to a boil over high heat, then flame the wine. Let the flames die out and continue to boil until the wine has reduced by one-third.

Whisk the carrot purée into the reduced wine and mix well. Strain the carrot mixture and return to the pan used to reduce the wine. Set the pan over low heat. Cut the remaining ½ cup butter into small pieces and whisk it, one or two pieces at a time, into the sauce. Continue until all of the butter is incorporated. Season the sauce with salt and pepper and keep warm over very low heat.

Gently reheat the shallot confit over low heat. Pour the olive oil into a large non-stick skillet and heat over high heat. Season the fish fillets with salt and pepper and then place them skin side down in the skillet. Cook for 4 to 5 minutes, until the skin is very crisp.

Pour over enough of the sauce to cover the bottom of 4 well-heated serving plates. Place a large spoonful of the shallot confit in the center of the plates and top with the fish, skin side up. The heat of the plate will finish cooking the flesh side of the fish fillets. Serve at once. If desired, garnish with a crouton fried in butter and dipped in chopped parsley.

NOTE: The original recipe calls for a type of fish called *sandre*. This delicacy is difficult to find outside of France. Striped bass makes a wonderful substitute.

During fermentation, the "chapeau," or crust of Pinot Noir, is broken up by "pigeage."

JEAN-MICHEL LORAIN

La Côte St. Jacques
Joigny

Marinade: 6 hours before preparation

Preparation: 50 minutes

Cooking time: 45 minutes

Serves 4

●

8 SMALL RED SNAPPER FILLETS WITH SKIN
INTACT, ABOUT 4 OUNCES EACH
(SEE NOTE)

½ CUP THINLY SLICED ONION

½ CUP THINLY SLICED CARROTS

1 FRESH THYME SPRIG

1 FRESH BAY LEAF

1 TABLESPOON COARSELY GROUND
WHITE PEPPER

1 CUP LIGHT RED WINE, PREFERABLY
IRANCY (A RED BURGUNDY FROM THE
AREA AROUND AUXERRE)

SALT AND FRESHLY GROUND BLACK
PEPPER TO TASTE

4 TABLESPOONS (½ STICK) UNSALTED
BUTTER

¼ CUP FINELY CHOPPED SHALLOTS

2 CUPS FISH STOCK

FRESH HERBS AND TENDER SALAD
GREENS, FOR GARNISH

FISH FILLETS
IN RED WINE CHAUD-FROID SAUCE

The morning before serving, trim the fillets into attractive serving pieces and make sure that all the bones and scales have been removed. In a medium nonreactive bowl, combine the onion, carrots, thyme, bay leaf, white pepper, and wine. Season the fillets with salt and black pepper. Add the fish to the marinade and refrigerate for 6 hours.

To prepare the dish, transfer the fish with the marinade to a large saucepan. Bring to a simmer over medium heat and cook for 3 minutes, until the fish is firm and cooked through. Carefully remove the fillets to a plate and refrigerate until ready to serve.

Strain the marinade through a fine sieve. Reserve the liquid and solids separately. Discard the thyme and bay leaf.

In a small saucepan, melt 1 tablespoon of the butter and add the shallots. Cook over medium heat, stirring often, for 2 to 3 minutes or until softened but not browned. Add the liquid from the marinade, increase the heat to high, and boil until reduced by three-quarters. Pour in the fish stock, return to a boil, and cook again until reduced by half. Strain through a fine sieve and set aside.

In a small skillet, combine 1 tablespoon of the remaining butter, 2 tablespoons of the wine reduction, and the reserved carrots and onions from the marinade. Cover and cook over medium-low heat, stirring often, until all of the liquid has evaporated. Remove the vegetables to a large plate and refrigerate until ready to serve.

In a small nonreactive saucepan, bring the remaining wine reduction to a boil. Remove from the heat and whisk in the last 2 tablespoons butter. Season the sauce with salt and pepper.

To serve, coat the bottom of 4 flat serving plates with equal amounts of the sauce. Place in a cool area until set. The sauce should have a soft, "trembling" jelly consistency.

Place 2 fish fillets on each plate. (The fish should be chilled but not ice cold when served.) Arrange the carrots and onions attractively around the fish and garnish with fresh herbs and tender greens.

NOTE: The original recipe calls for *rougets*, a small rockfish popular in France. Red snapper is a colorful and flavorful alternative.

The pruning of the vines is done in winter during the fall of the sap.

A Friend's Recipe

MARC MENEAU

L'Esperence
Saint-Père-sous-Vézelay
Yonne

———

For the Marinade: start the day before

Preparation: 1 hour 30 minutes

Cooking time: 2 hours

Serves 4

◖

1 BOTTLE LIGHT RED WINE, PREFERABLY IRANCY (A RED BURGUNDY FROM THE AREA AROUND AUXERRE)

1 SADDLE OF RABBIT, CUT INTO 2 PIECES

2 RABBIT THIGHS, EACH CUT INTO 2 PIECES

SALT AND FRESHLY GROUND BLACK PEPPER TO TASTE

1 SMALL ONION, THINLY SLICED

1 SMALL CARROT, THINLY SLICED

½ CELERY RIB, THINLY SLICED

SEVERAL SPRIGS FRESH THYME

1 FRESH BAY LEAF

SEVERAL JUNIPER BERRIES

6 TABLESPOONS OLIVE OIL

1 SMALL LAMB SWEETBREAD, 4 TO 6 OUNCES

1 10-INCH PUFF PASTRY SHELL, PARTIALLY COOKED

2 OUNCES UNCOOKED PUFF PASTRY, FOR DECORATION

1 LARGE EGG, LIGHTLY BEATEN

¼ CUP HEAVY CREAM (SEE NOTE)

RABBIT TART WITH WINE

Bring the wine to a boil in a large nonreactive saucepan, then flame the wine. Let the flames die out, remove from the heat, and cool. Season the pieces of rabbit with salt and pepper and place in a large nonreactive bowl. Add the onion, carrot, celery, thyme, bay leaf, and juniper berries. Drizzle with 2 tablespoons of the olive oil and mix well. Pour in the wine, cover with plastic wrap, and refrigerate overnight.

The next day, fill a small saucepan with cold water. Add the sweetbread, bring to a boil, reduce the heat, and simmer for 3 minutes until cool enough to handle. Remove the skin and outer pieces of membrane. Refrigerate until ready to assemble the tart.

Remove the rabbit from the marinade and pat dry with paper towels, reserving the marinade ingredients. Heat 2 of the remaining tablespoons oil in a large skillet. Add the rabbit and cook over medium-high heat, turning often, until browned. Transfer to paper towels and pat to remove as much of the fat as possible.

Use a slotted spoon to remove the onion, carrot, and celery from the marinade. Heat the remaining 2 tablespoons oil in a small skillet. Add the vegetables and cook over medium-high heat, stirring often, until lightly browned. Transfer to paper towels and pat to remove as much of the fat as possible.

Combine the rabbit and the vegetables in a large pan. Pour in the wine marinade and bring almost to a boil over high heat. Immediately reduce the heat to medium and simmer until the rabbit is very tender, about 1 hour. Transfer the rabbit to a plate or platter and let stand until cool enough to handle. Remove the meat from the bones of the rabbit and use forks to shred it into small pieces. Add about a quarter of the cooked vegetables to the rabbit and set aside.

Strain the cooking liquid through a fine sieve into a large saucepan. Bring to a boil over high heat and cook rapidly until reduced by half. Remove from the heat and cover to keep the sauce warm.

Preheat the oven to 375°F. Fill the tart shell with the shredded rabbit mixture. Cut the sweetbread into 3 or 4 thin slices and arrange on top of the rabbit. Make ⅜-inch-wide strips with the uncooked puff pastry and arrange in a lattice design over the filling. Using a pastry brush, lightly paint the bands with the egg to give a nice color to the finished tart. Bake the tart for about 20 minutes, until the pastry is golden brown.

Warm the sauce over medium-high heat. Stir in the cream and season with salt and pepper. Just before serving, spoon a small amount of the sauce over the tart, without touching the pastry lattice. Serve the tart with the remaining sauce on the side.

NOTE: The original recipe calls for chicken blood (or pork blood if the chicken blood is not available), which often acts as a rich thickener for wine sauces. We've substituted heavy cream with good results.

These wheelbarrows are used for branches that are burned after pruning.

JACQUES LAMELOISE

Lameloise
Chagny
Saône et Loire

Preparation: 35 minutes

Cooking time: 1 hour 20 minutes

Serves 4

━

for the flans:
2 POUNDS FRESH FLAT-LEAF PARSLEY,
TOUGH STEMS REMOVED

3 LARGE EGGS

1 CUP HEAVY CREAM

SALT AND FRESHLY GROUND BLACK
PEPPER TO TASTE

for the sauce:
2 SHALLOTS, MINCED

2 CUPS RED BURGUNDY WINE

SALT AND FRESHLY GROUND BLACK
PEPPER TO TASTE

14 TABLESPOONS UNSALTED BUTTER,
COLD, CUT INTO SMALL PIECES

for the snails:
2 TABLESPOONS UNSALTED BUTTER

4 DOZEN SMALL SNAILS,
RINSED AND DRIED

1 SHALLOT, MINCED

1 SMALL BUNCH FRESH CHIVES

1 SMALL BUNCH FRESH CHERVIL

SALT AND FRESHLY GROUND BLACK
PEPPER TO TASTE

SNAILS IN RED WINE SAUCE WITH SMALL PARSLEY FLANS

To prepare the flans, preheat the oven to 300°F. Bring a large pot of salted water to a boil over high heat. Add the parsley, return to a boil, drain, and rinse under cold running water. Squeeze out the excess moisture from the parsley and transfer to a food processor. Process until finely puréed. In a small bowl, beat the eggs with the cream until well blended. Add ¼ cup of the parsley purée and season with salt and pepper. Divide between 4 buttered small molds. Transfer the molds to a large baking dish and pour in enough hot water to come within an inch of the tops. Bake for about 1 hour, until firm and set in the middle.

To make the sauce, combine the shallots and wine in a large nonreactive saucepan. Season lightly with salt and pepper. Place over medium-high heat and cook until reduced to about 3 tablespoons. The consistency should be thick and syrupy. Add the butter a few pieces at a time, whisking constantly and working on and off the heat, until the sauce is slightly thickened and smooth. Correct the seasoning and keep warm over hot, not boiling, water, until ready to serve. Do not let the sauce boil.

To prepare the snails, melt the butter in a large sauté pan over medium-high heat. Add the snails and cook, stirring often, until warmed through, 5 to 10 minutes. Stir in the shallot. Snip a small amount of the chives and chervil into the pan with scissors.

To serve, arrange the parsley flans in the center of 4 warmed plates. Surround with snails and ladle over a small amount of the sauce. Garnish with several sprigs of chives and fine leaves of chervil and serve at once.

Grape carrier near Mercurey.

Preparation: 30 minutes

Cooking time: 1 hour 30 minutes

Serves 4

—

2 SMALL EGGPLANTS,
ABOUT 6 OUNCES EACH

3 OR 4 SMALL ZUCCHINI,
ABOUT 4 OUNCES EACH

2 SMALL RIPE TOMATOES,
6 TO 8 OUNCES EACH

1 MEDIUM RED BELL PEPPER,
ABOUT 8 OUNCES

½ MEDIUM GREEN BELL PEPPER,
ABOUT 4 OUNCES

ABOUT 2 CUPS OLIVE OIL

2 MEDIUM YELLOW ONIONS, FINELY
CHOPPED

4 GARLIC CLOVES, MINCED

1 HEAPING TEASPOON TOMATO PASTE

1 BOUQUET GARNI

SALT AND FRESHLY GROUND BLACK
PEPPER TO TASTE

4 DOZEN LARGE SNAILS, PREFERABLY
COOKED IN CHABLIS-BASED COURT
BOUILLON (SEE NOTE)

1 CUP CHABLIS

1 TABLESPOON FINELY CHOPPED FRESH
PARSLEY

SNAIL RATATOUILLE CHABLISIENNE

Rinse the eggplants and wipe dry. Use the tip of a vegetable peeler to cut long, thin strips along the length of the eggplants to make decorative stripes in the skin. Do the same with the zucchini. Remove the cores from the tomatoes. Turn the tomato over and lightly cross-hatch the bottom. Plunge into boiling water and boil for 1 minute. Drain and rinse under cold running water. Slip off the peel and cut each tomato horizontally in half. Squeeze each half and gently scrape away the seeds. Slice the peppers in half, cut away the membranes, and scrape out the seeds. Cut the eggplants, zucchini, tomatoes, and peppers into ⅜-inch dice. Reserve each separately.

In a large, heavy, ovenproof sauté pan, heat a small amount of the olive oil. Add the onions and cook, stirring, over medium-high heat until lightly colored, about 5 minutes. Add half of the garlic, the tomato paste, diced tomatoes, and bouquet garni. Season with salt and pepper. Reduce the heat to medium and cook uncovered, stirring often, until the liquid that the tomatoes gives off has evaporated.

Preheat the oven to 400°F. Heat more of the olive oil in a large, heavy sauté pan. Add the zucchini and cook over medium heat until tender. Transfer to a colander to drain. Cook and drain the eggplants and the peppers separately in the same manner. Add the drained zucchini, peppers, and eggplants to the tomato mixture and stir gently to blend.

Cut the snails in half and add to the ratatouille. Pour in the Chablis and gently blend, being careful not to crush the vegetables. Cover the sauté pan and bake for 15 minutes. Remove and discard the bouquet garni.

Just before serving, heat about ½ cup of olive oil in a small saucepan. Add the remaining garlic and the parsley. Drizzle this mixture over the ratatouille. Serve very hot in small individual casseroles or warmed shallow bowls.

NOTE: For the court bouillon, combine 1 quart water, 1 peeled and thinly sliced carrot, 1 thinly sliced onion, 1 bouquet garni, 8 whole black peppercorns, 1 teaspoon salt, and 1 cup Chablis or other dry white wine in a large nonreactive saucepan. Bring to a boil, reduce the heat to medium-low, and simmer, partially covered, for 30 minutes. Strain, cool to room temperature, and refrigerate.

5 TABLESPOONS UNSALTED BUTTER

12 OUNCES CHICKEN NECKS, WINGS, OR
CARCASS, COARSELY CHOPPED

1 SMALL CARROT, FINELY CHOPPED

1 SMALL WHITE ONION, FINELY CHOPPED

1 SMALL LEEK, WHITE PART ONLY,
HALVED AND THINLY SLICED

2 SHALLOTS, MINCED

½ CELERY RIB, FINELY CHOPPED

2 GARLIC CLOVES, MINCED

1 FRESH BAY LEAF

1 FRESH THYME SPRIG

1 WHOLE CLOVE

1 TABLESPOON ALL-PURPOSE FLOUR

4 CUPS HEARTY RED WINE, PREFERABLY
MARSANNAY

1 CUP RICH VEAL STOCK

SALT AND FRESHLY GROUND BLACK
PEPPER TO TASTE

3 ENVELOPES UNFLAVORED GELATIN

½ CUP COLD WATER

3 POUNDS SKINNED EEL FILLETS

5 TO 6 MEDIUM YELLOW ONIONS,
1½ POUNDS, THINLY SLICED

2 MEDIUM RED BELL PEPPERS, ROASTED
AND PEELED

1 LARGE BUNCH FRESH CURLY PARSLEY,
ABOUT 4 OUNCES

8 SMALL FIRM-FLESHED YELLOW
POTATOES

1 CUP THICK REDUCED BEEF STOCK

DIJON MUSTARD TO TASTE

OLIVE OIL TO TASTE

RED WINE VINEGAR TO TASTE

1 BUNCH BABY ARUGULA, FOR GARNISH

TERRINE OF PARSLIED EEL AND RED WINE ASPIC

Melt 3 tablespoons of the butter in a large saucepan over medium-high heat. Add the chicken parts and cook, stirring, until lightly browned, about 5 minutes. Stir in the carrot, white onion, leek, shallots, celery, garlic, bay leaf, thyme, and clove. Sprinkle in the flour and cook, stirring, until well combined and warmed through, about 5 minutes. Pour in the wine, increase the heat to high, and bring to a boil. Carefully ignite to flame the wine, and stir until the flames subside. Pour in the veal stock, reduce the heat to medium, and season with salt and pepper. Cook, uncovered, until reduced and concentrated, about 1 hour. Strain the sauce through a fine sieve. Discard the solids.

Meanwhile, sprinkle the gelatin over the cold water in a small saucepan. Leave for 5 minutes to soften, then heat gently, stirring, over very low heat until completely dissolved. Remove from the heat and stir into the strained sauce.

Preheat the oven to 425° F. Place the eel fillets on large nonstick baking sheets and season with salt and pepper. Bake until white and firm to the touch. Remove from the oven and cool completely.

Melt the remaining 2 tablespoons butter in a large sauté pan. Add the yellow onions and cook over medium heat, stirring often, until very soft but not browned. Season with salt and pepper and set aside.

Cut the peppers into small, uniform-shaped cubes. Reserve any scraps for the final sauce.

Rinse the parsley and dry well. Chop the leaves very fine and set aside. Save the stems for another use.

Line a terrine mold with a sheet of parchment and let the ends of the paper hang over each side. Alternate with layers of the jellied wine aspic, eels, parsley, and cooked onions. Repeat with layers of chopped parsley and the red bell peppers. Fill the terrine with the jellied wine aspic and fold over the paper. Cover the terrine tightly and refrigerate for 24 hours.

Cook the potatoes in salted water until tender. Cool, peel, and slice ⅜ inch thick.

Combine the beef stock, any scraps from the red bell peppers, the mustard, olive oil, vinegar, salt, and pepper in a food processor. Blend until smooth.

Arrange slices of the terrine on individual serving plates. Garnish with arugula leaves and 3 slices of potato. Spoon over a small amount of the beef sauce and serve at once.

for the tulip cookie shells:
1 CUP GRANULATED SUGAR

9 TABLESPOONS ALL-PURPOSE FLOUR

2 TEASPOONS GRATED ORANGE ZEST

JUICE OF 1 ORANGE

⅓ CUP MELTED UNSALTED BUTTER

for the meringues:
4 EGG WHITES

½ CUP GRANULATED SUGAR

½ CUP CONFECTIONERS' SUGAR

for the frozen bombes:
1 CUP HAZELNUTS

¾ CUP PLUS 2 TABLESPOONS
GRANULATED SUGAR

½ CUP MILK

3 LARGE EGG YOLKS

½ CUP MARC DE BOURGOGNE
(SEE NOTE)

¾ CUP CRÈME FRAÎCHE, WHIPPED STIFF

for serving:
1 POUND RIPE STRAWBERRIES

3 TABLESPOONS SUGAR

JUICE OF ONE LEMON

1 BUNCH FRESH MINT

½ CUP CRÈME FRAÎCHE, WHIPPED STIFF

FROZEN BOMBE WITH MARC DE BOURGOGNE AND STRAWBERRY COMPOTE

To make the tulip cookie shells, preheat the oven to 400°F and butter 2 baking sheets. In a large bowl, combine the sugar, flour, orange zest, orange juice, and melted butter. Stir rapidly to form a smooth batter. Use the back of a spoon to spread out thin, 4-inch rounds of the batter on the cookie sheets. Bake until lightly browned around the edges, 3 to 4 minutes. Remove from the oven and immediately transfer to upside-down coffee cups. While still warm, press lightly to form the shape of an opened tulip. Cool completely and store in airtight containers.

To make the meringues, beat egg whites until stiff peaks form, add a pinch of granulated sugar. With a wooden spoon, lightly fold in both sugars. Transfer to a pastry bag fitted with a large tip. Pipe out 8 small rounds that will fit into the center of the tulip cookies and 8 small or "kisses" to use as garnish (see photo). Bake the meringues at 200°F for about 3 hours. Store in an airtight container.

To make the bombes, combine the hazelnuts and ¾ cup sugar in a small, heavy saucepan. Cook over medium heat, stirring often, until the sugar melts. Reduce the heat to low and continue cooking until lightly caramelized (330°F on a candy thermometer). Pour out onto an oiled marble slab or baking sheet and spread out with a spatula. Cool until hardened. Crack the praline into pieces and grind to a powder in a food processor. Transfer to a large saucepan and pour in the milk. Bring to a boil. Meanwhile, in a large bowl, beat the yolks with 2 tablespoons sugar until light and lemon colored. Pour in the hot milk with praline, stir well, and return to the saucepan. Bring back to a boil, stirring. Transfer to the bowl of an electric mixer and beat until the mixture has completely cooled. Fold the marc and the whipped crème fraîche. Fill 8 small ramekins with this mixture and freeze until very firm, at least 5 hours.

To serve, dip the ramekins into a bowl of cold water for a few seconds and unmold onto large plates. Return to the freezer. Wash the strawberries and drain well. Slice 8 strawberries and decorate the outsides of the bombes. Cut 8 more strawberries into wedges and decorate the tops of the bombes. Slice 16 of the strawberries. Crush the remaining strawberries with a fork, add a pinch of sugar and the lemon juice. Mix well.

Place the tulips cookies off to the side of the plate and fill each one with a meringue round. Spoon in a small amount of the crushed strawberries and garnish with a meringue "kiss." On the other side of the plate, add a spoonful of the whipped crème fraîche. Arrange slices of strawberries on top, overlapping. Garnish with mint and serve at once.

NOTE: The original recipes calls for red pralines, popular with many modern French pastry chefs. These are not available in the U.S. due to a ban on certain red food colorings. The chef has suggested using the hazelnut praline above.

Marc is brandy made from grape pressings left in the press after the wine (or juice from white wines) has been extracted.

CHAMPAGNE

CHAMPAGNE IS A VENERABLE REGION OF FRANCE. WITH THE ORLÉANAIS, IT WAS THE BASE OF THE KINGDOM, BORN IN THE ILE-DE-FRANCE, THAT BECAME FRANCE. FOR CENTURIES THE COUNTS OF CHAMPAGNE WERE THE GUARANTORS OF ROYAL POWER AND PROMOTERS OF HIGH CULTURE AND PROTECTORS OF COMMERCE. THE KINGS OF FRANCE CAME TO REIMS—FOLLOWING THE STEPS OF CLOVIS, THE FIRST CHIEF OF THE FRANCS—FOR THE CORONATION THAT ESTABLISHED THEIR LEGITIMACY.

EARLY ON, THE WINES OF CHAMPAGNE HAD A GREAT REPUTATION. THE DISCOVERY IN THE BEGINNING OF THE EIGHTEENTH CENTURY OF A WAY OF CONTROLLING THIS EFFERVESCENCE WAS THE POINT OF DEPARTURE FOR THE CHAMPAGNE WE KNOW TODAY. THE MOST POWERFUL ABBEYS AND PRINCES CONTROLLED THE TRADE, WHICH DEVELOPED EVEN MORE WHEN THE USE OF A PARTICULAR BOTTLE PERMITTED THE CAPTURING OF THE PROVERBIAL EFFERVESCENCE.

THE GASTRONOMY ASSOCIATED WITH CHAMPAGNE HAS ITS ORIGINS IN A RURAL WORLD WHERE TILLING AND PASTURING WERE COMMON. TO THIS WAS ADDED A CUISINE DESTINED FOR THE DAILY LABORERS IN THE VINEYARDS AND THE HARVESTERS. IN CITIES SUCH AS REIMS, EPERNAY, OR EVEN CHALONS, THE CUISINE OF THE MERCHANTS AND *NÉGOCIANTS* REFLECTS EVEN MORE DISTANT INFLUENCES SUCH AS THOSE OF LORRAINE, THE ARDENNES, ALSACE, BURGUNDY, OR PARIS. EARLY SOPHISTICATION TRANSFORMED FOWL, PORK, VARIOUS ORGAN MEATS, GAME, AND LAMB INTO NATIONAL GLORIES. FRUITS, HARVESTED ON THE HILLSIDES, WERE ESSENTIAL TO THESE COMPOSITIONS WHERE DISTILLATIONS OBVIOUSLY HOLD A VERY IMPORTANT PLACE. THE INTERNATIONAL TRADE ROUTES THAT CROSSED CHAMPAGNE (SUCH AS THOSE OF THE FAIRS OF THE MIDDLE AGES) GAVE AN EXOTIC TOUCH TO DESSERTS AS WELL AS TO THE DISHES OF THE GRAND AND NOBLE TABLES. TODAY, GLORIFIED BY TODAY'S WINES (WHERE STILL WINES PLAY A LARGE PART), THE GASTRONOMIC PAST OF CHAMPAGNE HAS INSPIRED AN UNFLAGGING TRADITION.

A GLIMPSE AT TRADITION

Oyster Gratin with Champagne

—

Shuck 4 dozen oysters over a bowl. Strain the liquid through a fine sieve. Remove the oysters from their shells and set aside.

Cut 10 ounces fresh mushrooms into matchsticks and toss lightly with lemon juice. Cook in a little salted water with 1 tablespoon unsalted butter. Clean 8 ounces wild mushrooms. Sauté quickly in 1 tablespoon unsalted butter, then cut into thin julienne. Remove the leaves from a head of Boston lettuce and blanch in boiling salted water. Drain, rinse, and set aside in cold water. Clean 2 zucchini and cut into thin julienne. Cook 1 minced shallot in 1½ teaspoons butter in a large sauté pan until softened, then add all the mushrooms. Drain the lettuce and add along with the zucchini. Cook over medium-high heat until the vegetables are cooked and the liquid they give off has reduced by half. Stir in ¾ cup thick crème fraîche and season to taste with salt and pepper.

Melt 1 cup butter and cool. Drain the oysters and cook the oyster liquid in a small saucepan with ¾ cup Champagne over high heat until reduced by one-third. Whisk in 3 or 4 large egg yolks, a pinch of ground black pepper, and 1 tablespoon water. Cook in a double boiler, whisking constantly, until thickened. Gradually add the melted butter, whisking constantly until incorporated. Season to taste with salt and pepper. Cover the bottoms of small gratin dishes with the mushroom mixture and top with oysters. Spoon the sauce over each and broil until browned on top.

LEFT: The vineyards of Champagne stretch out over 86,000 acres of chalky soil, thickly planted with Pinot and Chardonnay.

LEFT: The landscape of the Montagne de Reims is one of the most celebrated in wine growing. The Verzenay windmill, which one spies from the A4 autoroute, spreads its sails at the beginning of the last spur of the "cliffs" of the Ile-de-France facing the Vesle, the little river of Reims that winds through what was once an immense plain of wheat. Verzenay and the villages crowning the edge of the mount are among the better *crus*.

ABOVE: To the southeast of Mount Sinai, the highest point, an authentic lighthouse stands watch over the ocean of vines.

The sparkling marvel rests in the peaceful galleries of the caves carved out of the mother rock.

Each year between 230 and 260 million bottles of all types are sold. The stock represents a reserve of about four years.

Chef de cave of the world leader in Champagne, Dominique Foulon has mastered the tradition as well as the modern imperatives of the trade.

A house of Champagne is judged above all on the quality of its nonvintage wine," Dominique Foulon is fond of repeating. Mr. Foulon is responsible for the wine making and the blends of Moët & Chandon. This historic house was created in 1749. It is the owner, among others, of the vineyards of the Abbey of Hautvilliers whose bursar, Dom Pierre Pérignon, invented the method of trapping bubbles in wine. Annually it sends out some 25 million bottles both in France and abroad. The group also includes the Mercier and Ruinart Champagne houses. The nonvintage wine is blended from wines of the best vineyards of the Montagne de Reims, the Marne Valley, and the Clos des Blancs. The vintage wine, the "absolute of Champagne," is made according to the quality of the harvest. The best wines of thirteen *grands crus* of Champagne are blended in order to highlight them.

GÉRARD BOYER

Les Crayères
Reims

Preparation: 1 hour

Cooking time: 1 hour

Serves 8

●

2 TABLESPOONS UNSALTED BUTTER

1 TABLESPOON VEGETABLE OIL

1 LARGE FREE-RANGE CHICKEN, 4 TO 5
POUNDS, CUT INTO 8 PIECES

SALT AND FRESHLY GROUND BLACK
PEPPER TO TASTE

2 SHALLOTS, MINCED

1½ CUPS DRY CHAMPAGNE

4 OUNCES THIN GREEN BEANS (*HARICOTS
VERTS*), CUT LENGTHWISE IN HALF

4 OUNCES CARROTS, PEELED AND CUT
INTO LONG, THIN JULIENNE STRIPS

4 OUNCES CELERY ROOT, PEELED AND
CUT INTO THIN JULIENNE STRIPS

1 SMALL BLACK TRUFFLE, CUT INTO THIN
PIECES (OPTIONAL)

1 CUP CRÈME FRAÎCHE

3 LARGE EGG YOLKS

FREE-RANGE CHICKEN WITH CHAMPAGNE

Melt the butter with the vegetable oil in a large heavy skillet. Season the chicken with salt and pepper and add it to the skillet. Cook over medium-high heat, turning often, until browned on all sides, about 10 minutes. Remove the chicken and pour off the fat from the skillet. Add the shallots and cook, stirring constantly, until softened but not browned, 3 to 4 minutes. Return the chicken to the skillet and pour in the Champagne. Reduce the heat to medium, cover, and cook for 20 to 25 minutes.

Meanwhile, cook the beans, carrots, and celery root separately in a large pot of boiling salted water until tender yet firm. Drain each one and rinse under cold running water.

Remove the chicken to a large platter and cover loosely with foil to keep warm. Increase the heat under the skillet to high and reduce the pan juices until thickened and syrupy. Add blanched vegetables, truffle, and crème fraîche. Cook for 5 minutes. With a slotted spoon, remove the vegetables and the truffle and scatter over the top of the chicken.

In a small heavy saucepan, combine the egg yolks with about 3 tablespoons of the cooking liquid from the skillet. Cook over low heat, whisking constantly, until thickened. Slowly pour in the remaining cooking liquid, while whisking constantly, and cook until incorporated. Season with salt and pepper. Spoon a small amount of the sauce over each piece of chicken and serve at once.

A pigeon house installed in the lodge of a vineyard in Champagne.

Preparation: 55 minutes

Cooking time: 30 minutes

Serves 4

—

for the peppers:
2 LARGE RED BELL PEPPERS

¼ CUP OLIVE OIL

½ CUP WATER

2 GARLIC CLOVES,
UNPEELED AND CRUSHED

SEVERAL FRESH THYME SPRIGS

for the tapenade:
4 OUNCES PITTED BLACK OLIVES,
PITTED AND COARSELY CHOPPED

2 GARLIC CLOVES, PEELED AND CRUSHED

10 TO 12 ANCHOVY FILLETS, DRAINED

1 TEASPOON CAPERS, CHOPPED

¾ CUP OLIVE OIL

SALT AND FRESHLY GROUND BLACK
PEPPER TO TASTE

for the sauce:
5 TABLESPOONS UNSALTED BUTTER,
CUT INTO SMALL PIECES

1 SHALLOT, MINCED

1 CUP CHAMPAGNE,
PREFERABLY *BLANC DE BLANCS*

2 TABLESPOONS CRÈME FRAÎCHE

for the sea bass:
4 FRESH SEA BASS FILLETS,
WITHOUT SKIN

SALT AND FRESHLY GROUND BLACK
PEPPER TO TASTE

1 TABLESPOON OLIVE OIL

SEVERAL FRESH BASIL LEAVES,
FOR GARNISH

SEA BASS WITH SWEET PEPPERS, TAPENADE, AND CHAMPAGNE

To prepare the peppers, preheat the oven to 300° F. Halve each pepper lengthwise and remove the seeds. Place the halves in a baking dish large enough to hold them in a single layer. Add the olive oil, water, garlic, and thyme. Bake until the peppers are tender to the touch, about 15 minutes. Peel the peppers and keep them covered in their cooking liquid until ready to use.

To make the tapenade, combine the olives, garlic, anchovy fillets, and capers in a food processor. With the machine running, gradually add the olive oil to make a smooth paste. Season with salt and pepper and set aside.

To prepare the sauce, heat 1 tablespoon butter in a small saucepan. Add the shallot and cook over medium-high heat, stirring often, until softened. Add ¾ cup Champagne and increase the heat to high. Cook until all but about 1 tablespoon of the liquid has boiled off. Whisk in the crème fraîche. Working on and off the heat, whisk in the remaining butter, a few pieces at a time, until the sauce is thick and emulsified. Keep warm in a double boiler over warm, not boiling, water.

To cook the fish, season the fillets with salt and pepper. Heat the oil in a large non-stick skillet. Add the fish and cook over medium-high heat until cooked through and firm to the touch, 3 to 5 minutes.

To assemble the dish, heat the tapenade in a small saucepan over low heat and stir the remaining ¼ cup Champagne into the sauce. Cut the peppers into uniform diamond shapes and arrange in a harlequin pattern on top of each fillet. Fill the in-between spaces with the tapenade. Place the decorated fish on warmed serving plates and surround with a small amount of the sauce. Serve at once, garnished with the fresh basil leaves.

The Abbey of Hautvilliers near Epernay where Dom Pérignon discovered the method of controlling the effervescence of Champagne.

—

20 ASPARAGUS SPEARS,
CUT INTO 3-INCH PIECES

4 SMALL LOBSTERS,
ABOUT 1 POUND EACH

1 FRESH TRUFFLE, ABOUT 2 OUNCES

½ CUP (1 STICK) UNSALTED BUTTER

2 SHALLOTS, MINCED

1¼ CUPS CHAMPAGNE

2 TABLESPOONS CRÈME FRAÎCHE

SALT AND FRESHLY GROUND BLACK
PEPPER TO TASTE

SEVERAL SPRIGS FRESH CHIVES,
FOR GARNISH

LOBSTER AND TRUFFLES WITH CHAMPAGNE

Preheat the oven to 425°F. Bring a small saucepan of salted water to a boil and add the asparagus. Bring back to a boil and cook until slightly softened, 1 to 2 minutes. Rinse under cold running water and drain well.

Bring a lobster pot full of salted water to a boil. Add the lobsters, bring back to a boil, and cook for 3 minutes. Drain well, transfer to large roasting pans, and bake until done, about 4 minutes. Quickly remove the meat from the shells. Cut the lobster tail meat lengthwise in half and set aside, unrefrigerated. Reserve the remaining lobster for another use.

Cut the truffle into razor-thin slices and reserve.

Melt 1 tablespoon of the butter in a small saucepan. Add the shallots and cook over medium-high heat, stirring often, until softened but not browned, about 3 minutes. Pour in 1 cup of the Champagne and increase the heat to high. Boil until the liquid has reduced by three-quarters. Add the crème fraîche and bring back to a boil. Working on and off the heat, add 5 tablespoons of the remaining butter to the sauce, a little at a time, whisking constantly until thick and emulsified. Season with salt and pepper. Keep the sauce warm in a double boiler over warm, not boiling, water.

Melt the remaining 2 tablespoons butter in a large sauté pan. Add the lobster tails and cook, turning carefully, until warmed through, 2 to 3 minutes. Remove to a work surface. Add the slices of truffle to the pan. Cook, turning carefully, until warmed through, 1 to 2 minutes. Remove to a plate and cover to keep warm. Add the asparagus spears to the pan and sauté quickly to warm through.

Cut the lobster tail into thick slices and arrange on individual plates, alternating the slices with a slice of truffle. Place a few asparagus spears at the top of the each plate and garnish with chives. Add the remaining ¼ cup Champagne to the sauce and spoon a small amount over the lobster and truffles. Season the plate with a grind of pepper and serve at once with any remaining sauce on the side. Oven-roasted tomatoes are a delicious accompaniment.

After the harvest, several late-ripening "conscripts" remain on the vine.

Preparation: 55 minutes

Cooking time: 30 minutes

Serves 4

—

for the peppers:

2 LARGE RED BELL PEPPERS

¼ CUP OLIVE OIL

½ CUP WATER

2 GARLIC CLOVES,
UNPEELED AND CRUSHED

SEVERAL FRESH THYME SPRIGS

for the tapenade:

4 OUNCES PITTED BLACK OLIVES,
PITTED AND COARSELY CHOPPED

2 GARLIC CLOVES, PEELED AND CRUSHED

10 TO 12 ANCHOVY FILLETS, DRAINED

1 TEASPOON CAPERS, CHOPPED

¾ CUP OLIVE OIL

SALT AND FRESHLY GROUND BLACK
PEPPER TO TASTE

for the sauce:

5 TABLESPOONS UNSALTED BUTTER,
CUT INTO SMALL PIECES

1 SHALLOT, MINCED

1 CUP CHAMPAGNE,
PREFERABLY *BLANC DE BLANCS*

2 TABLESPOONS CRÈME FRAÎCHE

for the sea bass:

4 FRESH SEA BASS FILLETS,
WITHOUT SKIN

SALT AND FRESHLY GROUND BLACK
PEPPER TO TASTE

1 TABLESPOON OLIVE OIL

SEVERAL FRESH BASIL LEAVES,
FOR GARNISH

SEA BASS WITH SWEET PEPPERS, TAPENADE, AND CHAMPAGNE

To prepare the peppers, preheat the oven to 300°F. Halve each pepper lengthwise and remove the seeds. Place the halves in a baking dish large enough to hold them in a single layer. Add the olive oil, water, garlic, and thyme. Bake until the peppers are tender to the touch, about 15 minutes. Peel the peppers and keep them covered in their cooking liquid until ready to use.

To make the tapenade, combine the olives, garlic, anchovy fillets, and capers in a food processor. With the machine running, gradually add the olive oil to make a smooth paste. Season with salt and pepper and set aside.

To prepare the sauce, heat 1 tablespoon butter in a small saucepan. Add the shallot and cook over medium-high heat, stirring often, until softened. Add ¾ cup Champagne and increase the heat to high. Cook until all but about 1 tablespoon of the liquid has boiled off. Whisk in the crème fraîche. Working on and off the heat, whisk in the remaining butter, a few pieces at a time, until the sauce is thick and emulsified. Keep warm in a double boiler over warm, not boiling, water.

To cook the fish, season the fillets with salt and pepper. Heat the oil in a large non-stick skillet. Add the fish and cook over medium-high heat until cooked through and firm to the touch, 3 to 5 minutes.

To assemble the dish, heat the tapenade in a small saucepan over low heat and stir the remaining ¼ cup Champagne into the sauce. Cut the peppers into uniform diamond shapes and arrange in a harlequin pattern on top of each fillet. Fill the in-between spaces with the tapenade. Place the decorated fish on warmed serving plates and surround with a small amount of the sauce. Serve at once, garnished with the fresh basil leaves.

The Abbey of Hautvilliers near Epernay where Dom Pérignon discovered the method of controlling the effervescence of Champagne.

Preparation: 50 minutes

Cooking time: 30 minutes

Serves 6

━

4½ TO 5 POUNDS LEEKS, WHITE PARTS
ONLY, THICKLY SLICED

6 LARGE SCALLIONS, TRIMMED OF ALL
BUT 1 INCH GREENS

SALT AND FRESHLY GROUND BLACK
PEPPER TO TASTE

14 TABLESPOONS (1¾ STICKS)
UNSALTED BUTTER

4 OUNCES SALT PORK, CUT INTO
1 × ¼-INCH STRIPS

12 THIN PIKE FILLETS

1 SHALLOT, MINCED

1½ CUPS PLUS 2 TABLESPOONS
CHAMPAGNE

8 TABLESPOONS CRÈME FRAÎCHE

1 TEASPOON DIJON MUSTARD

12 THIN FRESH CHIVES

COARSE SEA SALT

PIKE FILLETS *À LA RÉMOISE*

Bring a large saucepan of salted water to a boil. Add the leeks and cook until tender. Drain well, transfer to a food processor, and process until smooth. Set aside.

Place the scallions in a large saucepan. Add cold water to cover, season with salt, and add 2 tablespoons of the butter. Bring to a boil over high heat and cook until the scallions are tender. Drain well and set aside.

Bring a large saucepan of water to a boil. Add the salt pork and return to a boil. Boil for 2 minutes, then drain and rinse under cold running water. Pat the pieces dry and transfer to a small skillet. Add 1 tablespoon of the butter. Cook over medium-high heat, stirring often, until lightly browned. Drain on paper towels.

Trim the fish and remove any bones. Place the fillets on a large nonstick baking sheet and keep covered in the refrigerator.

To prepare the sauce, melt 2 tablespoons of the butter in a large saucepan. Add the shallot and cook, stirring often, until softened but not browned, 3 to 5 minutes. Add 1½ cups Champagne, increase the heat to high, and boil until reduced to less than a tablespoon. Add 2 tablespoons of the crème fraîche and return to a boil. Working on and off the heat, whisk in 7 tablespoons of the butter, a little at a time, until well incorporated. Season with salt and pepper to taste.

To prepare the fish, preheat the oven to 450° F. Melt the remaining 2 tablespoons butter in a small saucepan. Cook the butter over medium-high heat until golden brown. Brush the fish fillets with the browned butter and season with salt and pepper. Transfer to the oven and bake until tender to the touch, about 5 minutes.

Meanwhile, reheat the leek purée and season with salt and pepper. Place a tablespoonful in the center of warmed plates. Stir the remaining 2 tablespoons Champagne into the sauce and spoon a small amount over the leeks.

Remove the fish from the oven. In a small bowl, stir the mustard into the remaining 6 tablespoons crème fraîche. Spoon a small amount over each fillet.

Using a large spatula, top the leek purée with 2 fish fillets. Surround with the salt pork pieces and season with sea salt and pepper. Garnish each plate with 1 cooked scallion and 2 chives crossed to form an X. Serve at once.

40 SCALLOPS (ABOUT ½ POUND)

1½ POUNDS LEAN FISH BONES
(SOLE, TURBOT, BASS, OR SNAPPER),
COARSELY CHOPPED

32 OYSTERS

8 TABLESPOONS (1 STICK) UNSALTED
BUTTER

2 TABLESPOONS PLUS 1 TEASPOON
VEGETABLE OIL

1 SMALL ONION, FINELY CHOPPED

1 LEEK, GREENS ONLY, CHOPPED

½ CARROT, FINELY CHOPPED

½ CELERY RIB, FINELY CHOPPED

1 GARLIC CLOVE, MINCED

2 BOUQUETS GARNIS

2 TEASPOONS ALL-PURPOSE FLOUR

4 CUPS DRY WHITE WINE, PREFERABLY
CHARDONNAY

½ CUP BASMATI RICE

1 SHALLOT, MINCED

1½ CUPS BOILING WATER

SALT AND FRESHLY GROUND BLACK
PEPPER TO TASTE

1 BELGIAN ENDIVE

PINCH OF CONFECTIONERS' SUGAR

RISOTTO OF OYSTERS AND SCALLOPS WITH CHARDONNAY

Pick over the scallops and cut away any tough connective tissue. Set aside.

Place the chopped fish bones in a large bowl. Fill the bowl with cold water and let the water continue to flow for several minutes to flush out all impurities.

Shuck the oysters, reserving juices and discarding the shells. Trim away any connective tissue on the oysters and gently rinse in cold water. Strain the juices to remove any sand. Chop 12 of the oysters and set aside in a small bowl with a little of the strained juices. Reserve the 20 whole oysters in the remaining juices.

To prepare the sauce, heat 2 tablespoons of the butter with 2 tablespoons vegetable oil in a large saucepan. Add the fish bones and cook, stirring, over medium-high heat for 2 minutes. Add the onion, leek greens, carrot, celery, garlic, and a bouquet garni. Cook, stirring, until all liquid has evaporated. Sprinkle with the flour and stir to blend. Add the wine and increase the heat to high. Bring to a boil, skimming off any impurities that rise to the surface. Reduce the heat slightly and simmer for 25 to 30 minutes, until the liquid has reduced by half. Strain into a large saucepan, discard the solids, and set the sauce aside.

In a large saucepan, melt 2 more tablespoons of the butter. Add the rice and cook over medium heat, stirring constantly, for about 1 minute, until the grains are transparent. Add the shallot and the remaining bouquet garni. Add to the rice the boiling water and 6 tablespoons oyster juice. Season with salt and pepper. Stir well, cover, and cook over low heat until the rice is tender, 16 to 20 minutes. Remove from the heat and stir in the chopped oysters with their juices. Cover to keep warm.

Meanwhile, melt 2 more tablespoons of the butter in a large skillet. Separate the leaves of the endive and add to the skillet. Cook over medium-high heat, stirring often, until heated through. Season with salt and pepper. Add the sugar and cook until the leaves are lightly browned around the edges. Keep warm.

Transfer the whole oysters with any juices to a small saucepan. Warm gently over low heat.

Bring the sauce to a boil and whisk in the remaining 2 tablespoons butter. Season with salt and pepper. Keep warm.

Pat the scallops dry.

Heat 1 teaspoon oil in a nonstick skillet over high heat. Add the scallops and quickly cook until golden brown. Season with salt and pepper.

Arrange 5 endive leaves in a star pattern on each of 4 warmed plates. Place 5 warmed oysters between the leaves on each plate. Place a metal ring in the center of the plate that measures 2 inches in diameter and ¾ inch high. Fill the ring with the rice mixture. Place the scallops on top and spoon over a small amount of the sauce. Remove the metal rings and serve at once.

for the dried fruit:

12 DRIED FIGS

12 PRUNES

12 DRIED APRICOTS

JUICE OF 2 GRAPEFRUIT

JUICE OF 2 ORANGES

JUICE OF ½ LEMON

for the pastry:

14 TABLESPOONS (1¾ STICKS)
UNSALTED BUTTER, CUT INTO SMALL
PIECES

¾ CUP CONFECTIONERS' SUGAR

2½ CUPS ALL-PURPOSE FLOUR

PINCH OF SALT

1 TO 2 TABLESPOONS COLD WATER

for the pastry cream:

1 CUP MILK

½ VANILLA BEAN, SPLIT LENGTHWISE

2 TABLESPOONS UNSALTED BUTTER

3 LARGE EGG YOLKS

⅓ CUP SUGAR

2 TABLESPOONS CORNSTARCH

for the sabayon:

4 LARGE EGG YOLKS

FINELY CHOPPED ZEST OF ½ ORANGE

PINCH OF VANILLA SUGAR

¾ CUP SUGAR

1¼ CUPS CHAMPAGNE, PREFERABLY
BLANC DE NOIRS

DRIED FRUIT TART WITH CHAMPAGNE SABAYON

To prepare the dried fruit, place the figs, prunes, and apricots in a small bowl. Pour in the grapefruit, orange, and lemon juices. Cover and refrigerate overnight.

To make the pastry, combine the butter and sugar in a food processor. Process until blended. Add the flour and salt. Pulse quickly to mix. With the machine running, add 1 tablespoon of the water. Process until the dough forms a ball around the blades, adding the remaining water as needed. Turn the dough out onto a floured work surface and knead lightly into a ball. Refrigerate, covered, for 1 hour.

To make the pastry cream, combine the milk, vanilla bean, and butter in a small saucepan. Bring to a boil over medium-high heat. In a small bowl, whisk the egg yolks and sugar until light and lemon colored. Whisk in the cornstarch. Remove the vanilla bean from the boiling milk and pour the milk into the egg mixture. Whisk until smooth. Return this mixture to the saucepan and bring to a boil, whisking frequently. Cook, whisking constantly, until the cream is thickened, about 2 minutes. Work the mixture through a fine sieve into a bowl and let cool. Refrigerate until ready to use.

To assemble the tart, drain the dried fruit, pat dry with paper towels, and cut each piece crosswise in half.

Preheat the oven to 425°F. Roll the pastry out thin and cut into 8 large rectangles, triangles, or rounds. Transfer to floured baking sheets. Bake until lightly colored, 10 to 15 minutes. Remove from the oven and cool completely. Cover with a thin layer of the pastry cream. Arrange the figs, prunes, and apricots decoratively over the pastry cream. Reduce the oven temperature to 350°F and bake the tarts for 8 to 10 minutes.

To prepare the sabayon, combine the egg yolks, orange zest, vanilla sugar, and sugar in a small heatproof bowl. Whisk until light and foamy. Place the bowl over simmering, but not boiling, water in a saucepan. Whisking constantly, gradually add the Champagne. Whisk until the mixture is well thickened, then remove the bowl from the water and reserve.

As soon as the tarts come from the oven, place them on ovenproof plates. Preheat the broiler and set the rack about 4 inches from the source of heat. Spoon about 3 tablespoons of the sabayon around each tart and cover the tart with foil that has been cut to fit the shape of the tart. Place the plates under the broiler and broil, watching carefully, until the sauce is lightly browned on top. Serve at once.

When disease threatens, roses are first affected. The wine growers therefore have time to treat the vines.

In Vouvray, the estate of
Gaston Huet proudly
displays its ancient
press.

Ever since wine existed
in the Vouvray area, the
art of making sparkling
wines has been known to
wine makers. The wine
makers of Vouvray
devote some 105,000
gallons of their annual
harvest to these wines.

Created in 1928, the domaine Gaston Huet has been a model of wine growing that respects the soil, the vine, and the environment.

As with its neighbor Anjou, the Touraine is a mixture of appellations of reds (Chinon, Bourgeuil), of whites (Vouvray, Mont-Louis), and of rosés.

In the heart of the AOC Vouvray, the Gaston Huet estate brings together three properties: the Haut-Lieu, the Mont, and the Clos du Bourg—each of which is representative of the potentials of the vineyards of Vouvray. Gaston Huet, who for decades has preferred tradition to the enthusiasms of fashion, has always had the greatest respect for Chenin, the varietal of the great white wines of the Loire Valley. Half of his vineyards are between thirty and fifty years old; fifteen percent are young or very young vines. The "biodynamic" method which the Huet wine growers practice rests on a mechanical maintenance of the earth and the use of organic fertilizers. All chemically synthesized products are forbidden. The harvest, which is accomplished in successive pickings, is pressed under light pressure and made without adding yeast, taking into consideration the year's climatic conditions.

JEAN BARDET

Tours
Indre et Loire

—————

Preparation: 30 minutes

Cooking time: 25 minutes

Serves 4

◗

for the shellfish:

1 MEDIUM LOBSTER, 2 TO 3 POUNDS

8 LARGE LANGOUSTINES (SEE NOTE)

SALT AND FRESHLY GROUND BLACK
PEPPER TO TASTE

4 LARGE CRAYFISH

for the sauce:

¼ CUP THINLY SLICED, PEELED FRESH
GINGER

½ CUP SWEET VOUVRAY WINE

2 TABLESPOONS HEAVY CREAM

14 TABLESPOONS (1¾ STICKS) UNSALTED
BUTTER, CUT INTO SMALL PIECES

JUICE OF ½ LIME, OR TO TASTE

SALT AND FRESHLY GROUND BLACK
PEPPER TO TASTE

for the garnish:

4 BABY CARROTS, BLANCHED

12 BABY TURNIPS, BLANCHED

4 SMALL SPRING ONIONS, COOKED

LIME ZEST CUT INTO JULIENNE STRIPS

SEVERAL FRESH CHERVIL SPRIGS

SEVERAL FRESH DILL SPRIGS

LOBSTER AND CRAYFISH IN GINGER AND SWEET VOUVRAY SAUCE

To prepare the shellfish, steam the lobster for 8 minutes. Remove the tail from the body and steam the claws 2 minutes longer. Cool, then remove the meat from the shells. Cut the meat into 16 pieces. Remove the tails of the langoustines and place them in a small buttered baking dish. Season with salt and pepper. Cook the crayfish in boiling salted water and drain. Remove the shells from around the tails but leave attached to the heads.

To prepare the sauce, combine the ginger and half of the Vouvray in a small saucepan. Boil over high heat until the liquid has reduced by half. Add the cream and return to a boil. Working on and off the heat, whisk in the butter, a few pieces at a time, until the sauce is smooth and thickened. Season with the lime juice and salt and pepper. Strain through a fine sieve and keep warm.

Preheat the oven to 450°F. Combine the lobster pieces and the crayfish in a baking dish with the remaining Vouvray. Bake until firm to the touch. Bake the langoustines in the hot oven for 1 minute. Divide the lobster, lanqoustines, and crayfish between 4 serving plates. Heat the carrots, turnips, and onions in a steamer and arrange decoratively on the plates. Spoon over equal amounts of the sauce. Garnish with the lime zest, chervil, and dill.

NOTE: Langoustines are sometimes available in specialty fish markets but are extremely rare. Fresh large shrimp, peeled and deveined, can be used instead.

Beautiful vegetables in a market in Touraine.

—

1 HARE, ABOUT 5 POUNDS

2½ POUNDS HARE TRIMMINGS (SMALL
BONES, SCRAPS OF MEAT—AVAILABLE
FROM SOME SPECIALTY BUTCHERS)

⅔ CUP PLUS 1 TABLESPOON GOOSE FAT
OR VEGETABLE OIL

5 OUNGES WHOLE SHALLOTS

1 TEASPOON SUGAR

1½ CUPS DRY WHITE LOIRE VALLEY
WINE, PREFERABLY SAUMUR BLANC

2½ CUPS DRY LIGHT RED LOIRE VALLEY
WINE, PREFERABLY CHINON

½ CUP BEST QUALITY VINEGAR,
PREFERABLY VINAIGRE D'ORLEANS

12 OUNCES SALT PORK, CUT INTO LARGE
PIECES, BLANCHED AND RINSED

1 BOUQUET GARNI

4 OUNCES LEAN GROUND BEEF

2 LARGE EGG WHITES

2 MEDIUM CARROTS, PEELED AND DICED

2 MEDIUM LEEKS, COARSELY CHOPPED

1 ENVELOPE UNFLAVORED GELATIN

¼ CUP COLD WATER

8 OUNCES COOKED FOIE GRAS TERRINE

2 CUPS HEAVY CREAM

SALT AND FRESHLY GROUND BLACK
PEPPER TO TASTE

SEA SALT TO TASTE

PÂTÉ OF HARE AND FOIE GRAS WITH CHINON

Skin the hare and eviscerate. Separate the carcass into hind legs, forelegs, saddle, and rib cage. Place the hind legs, forelegs, and saddle in a large bowl and refrigerate.

Cut the rib cage and trimmings into 2-inch pieces. Heat ⅔ cup goose fat in a large casserole or Dutch oven. Add the rib cage and trimmings. Cook over medium-high heat, stirring often, until well browned, about 15 minutes. Regulate the heat and stir often so that the liquid that these trimmings give off does not burn.

Meanwhile, peel the shallots and heat the remaining 1 tablespoon goose fat in a large saucepan. Add the sugar and the shallots. Cook over medium-high heat, stirring often, until golden.

Spoon off as much fat as possible from the casserole with the browned trimmings. Add the white wine and increase the heat to high. Boil rapidly until the wine has evaporated. Add the red wine and boil again until the wine has evaporated. Pour in enough cold water to cover the bones and trimmings.

Preheat the oven to 300°F. Pour the vinegar into the pan with the shallots. Cook, stirring to dislodge the browned bits in the bottom of the pan, until the vinegar has evaporated and the shallots are browned. Transfer to the casserole. Add the salt pork and the bouquet garni. Cover and bake 4 hours.

Remove the casserole from the oven and strain into a large saucepan. Discard the solids. Bring to a boil, skimming off all the fat and scum that rises to the surface. Add the hind legs, forelegs, and saddle of the hare and reduce the heat to medium-low. Cook until the flesh is falling off the bones, 45 minutes to 1 hour. Remove the flesh from the bones and place it in a bowl. Reserve the bones. Cover the flesh with some of the cooking liquid to prevent it from drying. Cover and refrigerate. Combine the reserved bones and the remaining cooking liquid in a large saucepan. Bring to a boil, reduce the heat to medium-low, and cook this stock for 30 minutes.

To clarify the stock, mix the ground beef with the egg whites in a large bowl. Stir in the carrots and leeks. Strain the stock into a large saucepan. Whisk the meat mixture into the stock and bring to a boil over high heat. Reduce the heat to medium and simmer for 1½ hours. Strain through a sieve lined with damp cheesecloth. Sprinkle the gelatin over the cold water and let stand for 5 minutes to soften. Stir well and add to the strained liquid. Working over a bowl of cold water, stir the mixture until it starts to thicken.

Line the bottom and sides of a terrine mold with the aspic. Add half the hare meat and more aspic. Arrange half the foie gras along the length of the terrine. Cover with the remaining hare and aspic. Reserve a small amount of the aspic to serve, chopped, as garnish. Refrigerate the terrine for 24 hours.

In a large saucepan, gently warm the remaining foie gras over low heat and incorporate the cream. Season with salt and pepper.

Cut the terrine into thick slices. Serve on individual plates. Garnish with a spoonful of the foie gras sauce and a little of the chopped aspic. Grind over fresh pepper and sprinkle over several grains of sea salt. Serve the remaining sauce on the side.

Begin the day before

Preparation: I hour

Cooking time: 2 hours

Serves 8

━

3 LARGE PINK GRAPEFRUIT

SUGAR

2 ORANGES

½ LEMON

1 BOTTLE SWEET LOIRE VALLEY WINE,
PREFERABLY QUARTS DE CHAUME

28 PITTED PRUNES

3 DRIED FIGS

¾ CUP RAISINS

10 HAZELNUTS

10 ALMONDS

1 CUP CRÈME FRAÎCHE

8 OUNCES BITTERSWEET COATING
CHOCOLATE (COUVERTURE),
FINELY CHOPPED

1½ TEASPOONS UNFLAVORED GELATIN

¼ CUP COLD WATER

STUFFED PRUNES WITH CANDIED FRUIT AND CITRUS-WINE SAUCE

Place the grapefruit on a large work surface. Cut a small slice off the tops and bottoms. Use a sharp knife to cut away the zest and pith, working from top to bottom and following the curve of the grapefruit. Set the flesh aside.

Cut the grapefruit rinds into strips ⅜ inch wide and 2 to 3 inches long. Bring a large pot of water to a boil. Add the grapefruit rind and return to a boil. Boil rapidly for 5 minutes. Repeat this process 5 times. Weigh the blanched rind and place in a large saucepan. Add the same weight of sugar and a little water to start the cooking and to dissolve the sugar. Bring slowly to a boil then reduce the heat to medium and simmer until the rind is transparent, 50 minutes to 1 hour. Transfer the pieces to paper towels and set aside to dry.

Juice the grapefruit flesh by cutting it in half and forcing through a sieve. Juice the oranges and lemon half. Combine all of the citrus juices with the wine.

Place the prunes, figs, and raisins in 3 separate bowls. Cover each generously with the citrus mixture. Cover and refrigerate overnight.

Crush the hazelnuts and almonds. Set aside.

Prepare a ganache by bringing the crème fraîche to a boil in a large saucepan. Remove from the heat and add the chocolate. Stir well to incorporate. Thin with 3 tablespoons of the marinade. Add the hazelnuts and almonds. Drain the figs and raisins. Finely chop 10 pieces of the candied grapefruit rind and dice the figs. Add to the chocolate mixture along with the raisins. Stir gently to blend.

Cook the prunes in marinade for 10 minutes. Drain, reserving the liquid. Cool and halve the prunes.

Using a pastry bag fitted with a large star tip, fill the prune halves with a small amount of the chocolate ganache mixture.

Sprinkle the gelatin over the cold water. Let stand for 5 minutes to soften. Stir well and pour into the liquid used to poach the prunes. Stir over a bowl of cold water until the mixture begins to thicken.

Arrange 7 filled prune halves in a star-shaped pattern on each of 8 individual plates. Spoon over a small amount of the gelatin-thickened sauce and garnish with the remaining pieces of candied grapefruit rind. Refrigerate until very cold and serve.

Preparation: I hour

Cooking time: I hour

Serves 4

━

12 SEA URCHINS

4 WHITING FILLETS, SKIN REMOVED

8 OUNCES FRESH MUSHROOMS

JUICE OF 1 LEMON

12 SMALL POTATOES

1 CUP (2 STICKS) UNSALTED BUTTER

PINCH OF SAFFRON THREADS

2 SHALLOTS

SALT AND FRESHLY GROUND BLACK
PEPPER TO TASTE

½ BOTTLE MUSCADET

1 TABLESPOON WINE VINEGAR

½ CUP PLUS 1 TABLESPOON HEAVY
CREAM

2 TABLESPOONS CHOPPED SEEDED AND
PEELED TOMATO

¼ TEASPOON CURRY POWDER

FRESH CHIVES, FOR GARNISH

WHITING AND POTATO RAGOUT WITH SEA URCHIN ROE

Fresh sea urchins have firm, sharp "thorns" and tightly closed bottoms or mouths. To open, cut from the mouth side of the shell to about halfway up the side with sharp scissors. In a circular movement, cut around the circumference of the shell, like opening a soft-boiled egg. Extract the roe with a spoon and refrigerate it.

Use tweezers to remove all bones from the whiting. Cover the trimmed fillets on a plate with plastic wrap and refrigerate.

Clean and trim the mushrooms. Blanch 1 to 2 minutes in a large amount of boiling salted water that has been acidulated with the lemon juice. Drain and coarsely chop. Set aside.

Peel the potatoes and cut lengthwise in half. Hollow out the center of each half and lightly brown the halves in 6 tablespoons of butter, then cook in salted water with a pinch of saffron until tender. Drain and set aside.

Peel and mince the shallots. Cook the drained mushrooms in a large saucepan with 3 tablespoons of the butter until the water they exude has evaporated. Add half of the shallots and season with salt and pepper.

To prepare the butter sauce, combine the remaining shallot, the Muscadet, vinegar, and a little pepper in a small heavy saucepan. Bring to a boil over high heat and cook rapidly until the amount of liquid has reduced by two-thirds. Stir in 1 tablespoon cream. Add the remaining 7 tablespoons butter, a little at a time, whisking constantly. Work on and off the heat so that the sauce thickens and the butter emulsifies. Season with salt and pepper. Keep warm.

Cut the whiting into 12 thick slices or *goujonettes* and set aside.

Reheat the potatoes in the oven, covered with buttered foil to prevent them from drying.

In a small bowl, combine the chopped tomato and the mushroom mixture. Stir in the curry powder and ½ cup cream. Add the sea urchin roe and 2 tablespoons of the butter sauce. Season with salt and pepper. The ragout should be velvety and neither too thick or too liquid.

Lightly brown the trimmed whiting strips and season with salt and pepper.

Remove the potatoes from the oven. Divide between 4 serving plates and fill the cavities with the ragout. Place 3 pieces of the browned whiting on each plate and season with pepper. Spoon over a small amount of the butter sauce. Garnish with the chives and serve at once.

Preparation: 35 minutes

Cooking time: 50 minutes

Serves 4

—

14 TABLESPOONS (1¾ STICKS)
UNSALTED BUTTER

3 TO 3½ POUNDS FROG'S LEGS

¾ CUP GROS PLANTE OR SIMILAR DRY
WHITE WINE

1 BUNCH FRESH THYME

1 POUND FRESH CÈPE OR PORCINI
MUSHROOMS

SALT AND FRESHLY GROUND BLACK
PEPPER TO TASTE

¾ CUP OLIVE OIL

2 SHALLOTS, MINCED

¼ CUP CRÈME FRAÎCHE

FRESH CHERVIL, FOR GARNISH

BLANQUETTE OF FROG'S LEGS WITH CÈPES AND GROS PLANTE WINE

In a large heavy saucepan, melt the butter. Add the frog's legs and ½ cup of the wine. Cover and cook over low heat until tender but not brown. Carefully debone the legs and discard the bones. Add the thyme to the cooking liquid. Cover and infuse the liquid over very low heat for 15 minutes. Strain and pour over the deboned frog's legs.

Clean and trim the mushrooms. Blanch 1 to 2 minutes in boiling salted water and drain. Thinly slice the mushrooms and season with salt and pepper. Fry quickly in the olive oil in a large skillet over high heat until golden brown. (Do this in several batches if necessary to ensure even browning.) Drain the mushrooms and set aside.

Strain the frogs legs and bring the infused liquid to a boil in a saucepan, add the shallots, and cook rapidly until the liquid is reduced by half. Add the crème fraîche, return to a boil, and cook until slightly reduced and thickened. Add the frog's legs and mushrooms. Season with salt and pepper. Pour in the remaining ¼ cup wine and divide between shallow bowls. Season with freshly ground pepper and garnish with the chervil leaves. Serve at once.

Preparation: I hour

Cooking time: 2¼ hours

Serves 8

—

16 MEDIUM TOMATOES

SALT AND FRESHLY GROUND BLACK
PEPPER TO TASTE

2 TEASPOONS SUGAR

FRESH THYME FLOWERS TO TASTE

2 GARLIC CLOVES, THINLY SLICED

¼ CUP OLIVE OIL

4 SKINLESS SALMON FILLETS,
ABOUT 4 OUNCES EACH

40 SMALL ASPARAGUS SPEARS

½ CUP (1 STICK) UNSALTED BUTTER

2 SHALLOTS, MINCED

1 CUP PLUS 1 TABLESPOON SANCERRE

¾ CUP CRÈME FRAÎCHE

SNIPPED CHIVES, FOR GARNISH

SEA SALT TO TASTE

SALMON WITH ASPARAGUS, OVEN-DRIED TOMATOES, AND SANCERRE

Preheat the oven to 225°F. Peel the tomatoes, cut a ¼-inch slice off the top of each, and gently squeeze to remove the seeds. Season with salt, pepper, and the sugar. Place close together in a baking dish and add the thyme and garlic. Spoon over the olive oil and bake until very soft, 1½ to 2 hours.

Lightly butter 2 large nonstick baking sheets. Use tweezers to remove all the bones from the salmon. Cut each fillet into thin strips. Arrange the strips in 8 circles on the baking sheets, each about 5 inches in diameter.

Peel away the tough outer skins of the asparagus. Cut off the tips and slice the stalks into ¼-inch slices. Bring a large pot of salted water to a boil. Add the tips and sliced stalks, return to a boil, and drain at once, being careful to not crush the tips. Melt 2 tablespoons of the butter in a small sauté pan. Add the blanched asparagus, season with salt and pepper, and set aside until just before serving.

In a small saucepan, melt 2 more tablespoons of the butter. Add the shallots and cook over medium-high heat, stirring often, until tender, 2 to 3 minutes. Add 1 cup Sancerre and increase the heat to high. Boil until reduced to about 2 tablespoons. Add the crème fraîche and boil until slightly thickened. Working on and off the heat, add the remaining 4 tablespoons butter bit by bit, whisking constantly to emulsify it. Season with salt and pepper.

Preheat the oven to 425°F. Sauté the asparagus over medium-high heat until warmed through. Season the salmon circles with salt and pepper and bake just until pale pink around the edges, 2 to 3 minutes. Place a tablespoonful of the sliced asparagus in the center of each plate and top with a circle of salmon. Garnish with the asparagus tips and the tomatoes. Stir the remaining tablespoons of Sancerre into the sauce and spoon a small amount over the salmon. Sprinkle with the chives. Season with sea salt and freshly ground pepper. Serve at once.

Preparation: I hour 30 minutes

Cooking time: I hour 10 minutes

Serves 4

—

for the vegetables and cod:

4 OUNCES SMALL WHITE ONIONS

4 OUNCES SMALL CARROTS

6 ARTICHOKES

JUICE OF 1 LEMON

3 TABLESPOONS UNSALTED BUTTER

1 CUP MUSCADET

1½ CUPS CHICKEN STOCK

1 BOUQUET GARNI

SALT AND FRESHLY GROUND BLACK
PEPPER TO TASTE

1 LARGE COD FILLET,
ABOUT 1¾ POUNDS

for the beurre blanc:

1 LARGE SHALLOT

1 TABLESPOON WHITE WINE VINEGAR

1 TABLESPOON COLD WATER

1 TABLESPOON CRÈME FRAÎCHE

5 TABLESPOONS UNSALTED BUTTER

SALT AND FRESHLY GROUND BLACK
PEPPER TO TASTE

for the beurre monté:

4 TABLESPOONS (½ STICK) UNSALTED
BUTTER

½ CUP COLD WATER

SALT TO TASTE

LEMON JUICE TO TASTE

for the Muscadet sauce:

1 CUP PLUS 1 TABLESPOON MUSCADET

¼ TEASPOON CURRY POWDER,
OR TO TASTE

¼ TEASPOON POWDERED SAFFRON,
OR TO TASTE

SALT AND FRESHLY GROUND BLACK
PEPPER TO TASTE

SEA SALT AND FRESHLY GROUND BLACK
PEPPER

4 FRESH BAY LEAVES (OPTIONAL)

THIN PIECES OF COD WITH SPICED MUSCADET SAUCE

To prepare the vegetables and cod, peel the onions and carrots. Use a channel knife or stripping tool (*canneleur*) to cut thin strips from the outside of the carrots. Thinly slice the carrots. (They should have the shape of a star.) Cut off all the large bottom leaves of the artichokes, leaving a cone of soft small leaves in the center. Cut off the top of the cone and scoop out the fibrous choke. Cut the bottoms in half, then each half into triangles. Set aside in cold water mixed with lemon juice to prevent discoloration.

In a large heavy saucepan, melt the butter. Add the onions and carrots and cook over medium-high heat, stirring often, until slightly softened but not browned. Drain the artichokes and add to the pan. Cook a few minutes longer, until slightly softened. Add the Muscadet, chicken stock, and bouquet garni. Season with salt and pepper and cook, covered, for about 15 minutes. Remove and discard the bouquet garni. Set the vegetables aside.

Trim the cod and remove all bones with tweezers. Cut into 16 wide strips. Keep refrigerated.

To prepare the beurre blanc, finely mince the shallot. In a small saucepan, combine the shallot, vinegar, and cold water. Bring to a boil over high heat. Cook rapidly until all but 1 tablespoon liquid remains. Working on and off the heat, whisk in the crème fraîche and the butter bit by bit until thick and emulsified. Season with salt and pepper. Strain through a fine sieve and keep warm in a double boiler.

To prepare the beurre monté, cut the butter into small pieces and place on a plate. Keep very cold until just before using. Bring the cold water to a boil in a small saucepan. Whisking constantly, add the butter bit by bit, working on and off the heat. Season with salt and lemon juice. Keep warm in a double boiler.

To prepare the Muscadet sauce, combine 1 cup Muscadet, the curry, and saffron in a small saucepan. Boil until reduced by three-quarters. Add the beurre blanc and the *beurre monté.* Season with salt and pepper.

Preheat the oven to 450°F. Arrange the pieces of cod in a single layer on a buttered baking dish and season with salt and pepper. Bake for 5 minutes. Reheat the vegetables.

Arrange the cod on warmed serving plates. Dab the fish with paper towels to absorb excess moisture. Garnish the plates with the carrots, onions, and artichokes. Add 1 tablespoon Muscadet to the sauce and spoon a small amount over the fish. Sprinkle with sea salt and freshly ground black pepper. Garnish with fresh bay leaves.

The flower beds and clipped boxwood of the celebrated gardens of Villandry.

for the meringues:

8 LARGE EGG WHITES

¾ CUP SUGAR

1½ CUPS CONFECTIONERS' SUGAR, SIFTED

for the cookie shells:

1 CUP SUGAR

½ CUP FINELY CHOPPED ALMONDS

½ CUP ALL-PURPOSE FLOUR

JUICE OF 1 MEDIUM ORANGE

⅓ CUP UNSALTED BUTTER, MELTED

2 TEASPOONS FINELY GRATED ORANGE ZEST

for the rhubarb compote:

1 POUND TRIMMED AND PEELED RHUBARB

1¼ CUPS PLUS 1 TABLESPOON BONNEZEAUX OR SIMILAR DESSERT WINE

6 TABLESPOONS SUGAR

2 TABLESPOONS UNSALTED BUTTER

for the strawberry compote:

4 OUNCES RASPBERRIES

3 TABLESPOONS SUGAR

12 OUNCES STRAWBERRIES, HULLED

1 TABLESPOON BONNEZEAUX OR SIMILAR DESSERT WINE

CONFECTIONERS' SUGAR, FOR GARNISH

STRAWBERRY AND RHUBARB COMPOTE WITH BONNEZEAUX

To prepare the meringues, preheat the oven to 200°F and line a large baking sheet with parchment. Beat the egg whites with a pinch of the granulated sugar until firm. With a large spatula, delicately incorporate both sugars. Using a pastry bag fitted with a plain tip, pipe the meringue onto the baking sheet in 8 small circles, about 2 inches in diameter each. Bake until firm, about 3 hours. Store in a dry area or in a tightly covered container.

To make the cookie shells, preheat the oven to 400°F and butter 2 baking sheets. Warm the sheets so that they are tepid before spreading the batter. In a large bowl, combine the sugar, almonds, flour, orange juice, butter, and orange zest. Stir rapidly to form a smooth batter. Use the back of a spoon to thinly spread three-quarters of the batter over one of the baking sheets. With the remaining batter, form 8 thin oval-shaped cookies on the other baking sheet. Place both baking sheets in the oven and bake until slightly browned around the edges, about 5 minutes. While warm, cut ¾-inch-wide strips from the first sheet. Use the strips to line the interior of 8 round or decorative molds, pushing against the sides to adhere. Cool and carefully remove the formed cookie shell. Set aside in a dry spot until ready to assemble the dessert. With the ovals, pinch one side of the still warm cookies to form a "wing" to use as a garnish. Set aside in a dry area.

To make the rhubarb compote, cut the rhubarb stalks into ⅜-inch thick slices. Place in a large bowl, pour in the wine, and stir in the sugar. Set aside in a cool spot to macerate for 1½ hours. Drain the rhubarb and pour the juice into a small saucepan. Bring to a boil and cook until reduced by half. Heat the butter in a small skillet and add the rhubarb. Pour in the reduced juices and cook over medium-low heat for 15 minutes. Remove from the heat and cool completely.

To make the strawberry compote, rinse the raspberries and purée in a food processor. Add the sugar and process until blended. Set aside 8 of the prettiest strawberries. Place the remaining strawberries in a bowl and slightly crush them with a fork. Add the puréed raspberries and the wine.

Fill each of the cookie shells with a meringue round and place on serving plates. Cover the meringue with a small amount of the rhubarb compote. Cut each of the whole strawberries into halves or quarters and place decoratively on top of the compote. Spoon over some of the strawberry compote. Surround the shells with the remaining rhubarb and strawberry compotes. Garnish with the cookie "wings" and confectioners' sugar.

In the vegetable garden, a shed at the side of a pathway.

Alsatian vineyards extend over 32,000 acres in a band, wider in the south and narrower in the north, from Thann to Wissembourg. They have a potential annual yield of 24 million gallons, of which 25 percent is exported. White is the principal wine. Red (Pinot Noir) comes from less than eight percent of the vineyards. Eleven varietals are used in this region.

"Wine growers forever," the Hugel family of Riquewehr are at the heart of a renewal of the reputation of the great wines of Alsace.

Riquewehr is undoubtedly the quintessential Alsatian wine-growing village. To the pleasure of wandering its ancient streets is added the delight of tasting such marvels as Riesling, Tokay-Pinot Gris, or Gewürztraminer.

The first Hugels settled in Riquewehr in 1639 after the disasters of the Thirty Years' War. This family-run enterprise is today directed by the eleventh and twelfth generations. Jean Hugel has revived ancestral practices that had been abandoned. One such was the re-creation with his father of the famous late-harvest wines and "selections of noble grapes." Wine growers and *négociants*, the Hugels have always given preference to the noble varietals (Riesling, Gewürztraminer, Tokay, and Pinot Noir). On their estate at Riquewehr, they practice small yields (two-thirds of the Alsatian average) and natural methods of growing. In their capacity as *négociants*, they buy the harvest of 350 wine growers under contract "only in the form of grapes." All wine that does not meet the criteria of the house is rejected. The prestigious Hugel signature is present in more than one hundred countries and on all the great tables of Europe.

Tradition here dates to before the eighteenth or even the seventeenth centuries. The passerby is reminded of this by several dates on walls.

ROAST SADDLE OF RABBIT WITH A LATE-HARVEST WINE SAUCE

Begin the day before

Preparation: 1 hour

Cooking time: 1 hour 50 minutes

Serves 4

●

1 RABBIT

2½ CUPS LATE-HARVEST WHITE WINE, PREFERABLY VENDAGES TARDIVES (SEE NOTE)

1¼ CUPS (2½ STICKS) UNSALTED BUTTER

1 POUND CARROTS

2 LARGE ONIONS, FINELY CHOPPED

1¼ CUPS DRY WHITE WINE

SALT AND FRESHLY GROUND BLACK PEPPER TO TASTE

PINCH OF SUGAR

2 BUNCHES FLAT-LEAF PARSLEY

2 TABLESPOONS CRÈME FRAÎCHE

1 TABLESPOON GRAINY MUSTARD, PREFERABLY MOUTARDE DE MEDAUX

2 CUPS CHOPPED WALNUTS

CAUL FAT

2 FRESH THYME SPRIGS

1 WHOLE GARLIC HEAD

COARSE SEA SALT TO TASTE

Separate the front and back legs from the rabbit. Remove the saddle. Place the saddle and hind legs in a bowl and add ¾ cup of late-harvest wine. Marinate overnight.

Coarsely chop the front legs and carcass of the rabbit. In a large skillet, melt ½ cup of the butter. Add the bones and cook over medium-high heat until browned. Peel and chop 1 of the carrots and add it with 1 of the chopped onions; cook until lightly browned. Pour in 1 cup of the late-harvest wine and bring to a boil. Cook until the liquid has evaporated. Add the dry white wine and boil again until evaporated. Pour in cold water to cover the bones. Season with salt and pepper. Reduce the heat to medium and simmer for 1 hour. Strain through a fine sieve and set aside.

Finely chop 1 of the remaining carrots and set aside. Peel the rest of the carrots and cut into 1½-inch pieces. Cut out a well in the center of each slice, deep enough to hold a filling. Cook the carrots in a small amount of water with the sugar, 3 tablespoons of the butter, and a pinch of salt until tender. Reserve the carrots in their cooking liquid.

Stem the parsley. Cook the leaves briefly in boiling salted water, then plunge into ice water. Purée in a blender and work through a sieve to obtain a smooth purée. Whisk in 2 tablespoons butter, the crème fraîche, and salt and pepper. Set aside.

Remove the rabbit from the marinade. Bone the leg and cut the meat into strips. Season with salt and pepper. Brush with mustard and sprinkle with half of the walnuts. Shape the mixture and wrap in caul fat to form 8 little sausages.

In a large skillet, melt 2 tablespoons of the butter. Add the saddle and "sausages" and cook over medium-high heat until lightly browned. Add the bones from the legs, the reserved chopped carrot, the remaining chopped onion, and 1 thyme sprig. Mince 1 clove of the garlic and add it as well. Reduce the heat to medium-low and cook until the saddle is tender, about 15 minutes. Set aside.

Glaze the carrots in their own juices over medium-high heat. Fill the cavities with the parsley purée and set aside.

Cook the remaining garlic cloves in boiling salted water until tender and peel. Cut each clove lengthwise in half and brown lightly in 2 tablespoons of the butter.

Remove the two long strips of meat from the saddle. Sprinkle with the remaining walnuts. Heat the skillet that the saddle cooked in over medium-high heat. Pour in the remaining ¾ cup late-harvest wine and bring to a boil. Pour in the strained rabbit stock and boil to reduce slightly. Season with salt and pepper, whisk in the remaining 2 tablespoons butter, and add the remaining thyme sprig.

NOTE: If you cannot find a Vendanges Tardives (a late-harvest wine from Alsace), a German Auslese will work for this recipe.

PERCH FILLETS WITH BUTTERY CABBAGE IN A PINOT GRIS SAUCE

Preparation: 50 minutes

Cooking time: 25 minutes

Serves 4

—

4 PERCH FILLETS

1 GREEN CABBAGE

5 RIPE TOMATOES

1 CUP (2 STICKS) BUTTER

2 OUNCES THICKLY SLICED BACON, DICED

2 GARLIC CLOVES, MINCED

⅓ CUP PINOT GRIS OR OTHER DRY WHITE WINE

SALT AND FRESHLY GROUND BLACK PEPPER TO TASTE

OLIVE OIL

Trim the fillets and carefully remove all small bones with tweezers. Set aside.

Trim the cabbage, removing tough ribs. Blanch quickly in boiling salted water and refresh under cold running water. Drain well and thinly slice the leaves. Set aside.

Peel, seed, and chop the tomatoes. Drain in a colander.

Melt 3 tablespoons of the butter in a large skillet over high heat. Add the cabbage and bacon; cook until the cabbage is soft and the liquid has evaporated. Add the garlic, wine, and the remaining butter, bit by bit, as if you were making a beurre blanc. Stir in the drained tomatoes. Add salt and pepper and keep warm.

Season the fillets. Heat a few drops of olive oil in a nonstick skillet and brown fillets over medium-high heat. They cook very quickly. Spoon the buttery cabbage onto serving plates and set the perch fillets on top.

Preparation: 2 hours

Cooking time: 5 hours

Serves 4

1 POUND SPINACH, TOUGH STEMS
TRIMMED

2 WILD DUCKS

2 TABLESPOONS RED WINE VINEGAR,
PLUS MORE FOR PRESERVING OFFAL

4 TABLESPOONS GOOSE OR DUCK FAT

20 SHALLOTS, PEELED

⅓ CUP PLUS 1 TEASPOON SUGAR

1 SMALL PIECE FRESH PORK RIND, DICED

¾ CUP PLUS 1 TABLESPOON COGNAC

2 CUPS PLUS 2 TABLESPOONS RED WINE,
PREFERABLY PINOT NOIR

1 TABLESPOON TOMATO PASTE

1 BOUQUET GARNI

SALT TO TASTE

4 TABLESPOONS VEGETABLE OIL

4 OUNCES FRESH CHERRIES

¾ CUP SHERRY

3 GOLDEN DELICIOUS APPLES

11 TABLESPOONS UNSALTED BUTTER

FRESHLY GROUND BLACK PEPPER TO
TASTE

1 GARLIC CLOVE, MINCED

3 TABLESPOONS CRÈME FRAÎCHE

FRESHLY GRATED NUTMEG TO TASTE

COARSE SEA SALT TO TASTE

WILD DUCK WITH CHERRIES AND RED WINE

Rinse the spinach in several changes of cold water. Drain well and set aside. Remove all small feathers from the ducks and eviscerate. Save all blood, lungs, heart, and liver in a small bowl covered with a little vinegar. Remove the thighs and keep the breasts on the bone. Keep all duck parts refrigerated.

To prepare the duck stock, coarsely chop the necks, wings, and any scraps from trimming the ducks. Heat 2 tablespoons of the goose fat in a large casserole and add the chopped bones and scraps. Cook over medium-high heat, stirring often, until lightly browned, about 10 minutes. Reduce the heat to medium and cook for 5 minutes longer, being careful to not scorch the contents of the casserole.

Meanwhile, melt the remaining 2 tablespoons goose fat in a small skillet. Add 19 of the shallots and 1 teaspoon sugar. Cook over medium-high heat until golden brown. Pour in 1 tablespoon of the vinegar and cook until the liquid has evaporated.

Preheat the oven to 300° F. Add the diced pork rind to the duck bone mixture. Stir well and skim off all fat. Pour in ¾ cup Cognac and cook until reduced to about 1 tablespoon. Add 2 cups red wine and boil until reduced to about 2 tablespoons. Pour in enough cold water to cover the contents of the casserole. Bring to a boil, skim off any impurities that rise to the surface, and add the browned shallots, the tomato paste and bouquet garni. Season lightly with salt. Cover and bake for 3 hours.

After 3 hours heat 2 tablespoons of the vegetable oil in a large skillet. Add the duck thighs and cook over medium-high heat until golden brown on both sides. Add to the duck stock in the oven and continue baking for 1 hour longer. Remove the thighs and set aside. Strain the contents of the casserole into a large saucepan. Bring to a boil, skim well, and keep warm.

While the stock is cooking, pit the cherries over a bowl to catch all the juices. Keep refrigerated.

In a small heavy saucepan, melt ⅓ cup sugar. Gradually bring to a boil and cook until the sugar reaches a light brown caramel color. Add the cherries and their juice, the sherry, and 1 tablespoon Cognac. Return to a boil, remove from the heat, and set aside.

Peel, seed, and core the apples. Cut into quarters and reserve.

Preheat the oven to 475° F. In a large ovenproof skillet, melt the remaining 2 tablespoons oil with 2 tablespoons of the butter. Season the the breasts (still on the bone) with salt and pepper. Place in the skillet and cook over medium-high heat, turning often, until browned. Transfer to the oven and roast for about 10 minutes. Remove from the oven, cover loosely with foil, and let rest for 15 minutes.

Meanwhile, place the reserved duck blood and offal in the bowl of a food processor. Add a small spoonful of vinegar, the garlic, the remaining shallot, and the remaining 2 tablespoons red wine. Process until puréed and pour into a large bowl. Stir in the crème fraîche. Add about ¾ cup of the duck stock to a small saucepan. Add the creamed purée and warm gently over low heat. Do not boil. Season with salt and pepper and keep warm.

Bring the remaining duck stock to a boil. Add 4 spoonfuls of the cherries and 2 spoonfuls of the cherry cooking juices. Boil until reduced by one-quarter. Whisk in 3 tablespoons of the butter, season with salt and pepper, and keep warm.

Melt 5 tablespoons of the butter in a small saucepan over medium-low heat. Skim off the foam that rises to the top and pour the clear liquid into a large skillet, avoiding the sediment that remains on the bottom. Heat this clarified butter over medium-high heat. Add the quartered apples and cook, turning often, until browned on all sides. Reduce the heat and cook until tender. Transfer to a plate or platter and set aside.

In a large nonreactive skillet, melt 1 tablespoon butter. Add the spinach and season with salt, pepper, and nutmeg. Cook over medium-high heat, stirring constantly, until the water given off by the spinach evaporates. Cook 3 to 5 minutes and stir in the remaining 1 tablespoon butter. Season again with salt and pepper.

Cut the duck breasts from the bones. Remove the skin and slice the meat on a diagonal. Add any accumulated juices to the sauce.

To serve, place the breast fillets on warmed plates. Place a spoonful of the spinach on one side and decoratively fan out the browned apple slices on the other side. Place the thighs on top of the spinach and spoon over some of the creamed sauce. Spoon some of the cherry sauce over the breasts. Season with ground pepper and sea salt. Serve at once.

ALSACE

Preparation: 40 minutes

Cooking time: 50 minutes

Serves 4

—

4 SALMON FILLETS, WITH SKIN INTACT,
5 TO 6 OUNCES EACH

WHOLE BLACK PEPPERCORNS

8 OUNCES (2 MEDIUM) ONIONS

¾ CUP RED WINE, PREFERABLY PINOT
NOIR FROM ALSACE

2 TABLESPOONS VINEGAR

2 CUPS WATER

1 TABLESPOON BUTTER

2 TABLESPOONS HONEY

1 LARGE POTATO

3 TABLESPOONS CLARIFIED BUTTER

SALT AND FRESHLY GROUND BLACK
PEPPER TO TASTE

for the saffron butter:
2 TABLESPOONS MINCED SHALLOTS

1 CUP (2 STICKS) UNSALTED BUTTER,
COLD, CUT INTO SMALL PIECES

¼ CUP WHITE WINE,
PREFERABLY FROM ALSACE

SALT AND FRESHLY GROUND BLACK
PEPPER TO TASTE

PINCH OF SAFFRON THREADS

1 TO 2 TABLESPOONS OLIVE OIL

SEA SALT TO TASTE

FRESH CHIVES, FOR GARNISH

SALMON WITH CRISP POTATO CAKES AND SLOW-COOKED ONIONS

If possible, ask the fishmonger to cut the salmon pieces from the tail end of the fish. With tweezers, carefully remove any bones. Embed a few peppercorns in the flesh. Set aside.

Peel and finely chop the onions; transfer to a heavy saucepan and pour in the red wine and vinegar. Cook over medium-high heat until all the liquid has evaporated. Add the water and cook until all the water has evaporated. Stir in the butter and honey. Set aside.

Peel the potato and grate into a small bowl. Stir in 2 tablespoons of the clarified butter, season with salt and pepper, and mix well. Using a pastry brush, coat the bottom of a large nonstick skillet with the remaining 1 tablespoon clarified butter. With your hands, form the potato mixture into 12 thin patties. Cook over high heat until golden brown on both sides. Set aside in a warm place.

To prepare the saffron butter, in a heavy saucepan, cook the shallots in 1 tablespoon of the butter over medium-low heat until soft and translucent. Pour in the white wine and reduce until 1 to 2 tablespoons liquid remain. Working over medium-low heat, add the butter piece by piece, whisking after each addition. Season with salt and pepper and bring almost to a boil. Add the saffron. Set aside in a warm place while you cook the fish.

To cook the salmon, heat the olive oil in a large skillet over medium heat. Add the salmon fillets skin side down. Cook for 10 to 15 minutes, depending on the thickness; cover the pan once the color of the salmon changes from bright red to a slightly dull reddish orange.

Spoon the saffron butter onto 4 warmed plates. Mound 3 small spoonfuls of onions on each plate and top each with a potato crisp. Set a salmon fillet in the center of each plate, grate a little pepper over the top, and sprinkle with a little sea salt. Decorate each plate with 3 chives and serve.

Autumn is here, adorning the vines with its colors.

5 POUNDS FROG'S LEGS

1¾ CUPS GEWÜRZTRAMINER

⅓ CUP OLIVE OIL

5 GARLIC CLOVES

10 TABLESPOONS UNSALTED BUTTER

SALT (FINE AND COARSE) AND FRESHLY
GROUND BLACK PEPPER TO TASTE

for the batter:

¾ CUP BEER

¼ CUP OIL

1 CUP ALL-PURPOSE FLOUR

2 LARGE EGGS, SEPARATED

PINCH OF SALT

for the parsley purée and garlic butter:

3 BUNCHES FLAT-LEAF PARSLEY, PLUS
¼ CUP FINELY CHOPPED PARSLEY LEAVES

2 TABLESPOONS CRÈME FRAÎCHE OR
HEAVY CREAM

14 TABLESPOONS (1¾ STICKS)
UNSALTED BUTTER

SALT AND FRESHLY GROUND BLACK
PEPPER TO TASTE

5 GARLIC CLOVES, UNPEELED

1 SHALLOT, MINCED

SEVERAL WATERCRESS LEAVES,
FINELY CHOPPED

PINCH OF POWDERED ALMONDS
(OPTIONAL)

PINCH OF GRATED LEMON ZEST

OIL FOR DEEP FRYING

FROG'S LEGS MARINATED IN GEWÜRZTRAMINER WITH PARSLEY AND GARLIC PURÉES

Marinate the frogs legs in the Gewürztraminer, olive oil, and garlic overnight in the refrigerator.

Drain the legs, adding the marinade to a large skillet. Add the butter, salt, and pepper to the skillet as well. Cook—but do not brown—the legs. Drain, reserving the cooking liquid; set the liquid and frogs legs aside to cool.

To prepare the batter, in a bowl, mix the beer, oil, flour, egg yolks, and salt until smooth. Beat the egg whites until soft peaks form and fold into the batter. Let the mixture rest for 15 minutes.

To prepare the parsley purée and garlic butter, stem and rinse the bunches of parsley. Cook in a large quantity of unsalted boiling water. Drain and purée in a food processor. Transfer the purée to a saucepan and dry it over low heat while stirring with a wooden spoon. Stir in 1 tablespoon crème fraîche, 4 tablespoons of the butter, salt, and pepper; set aside.

Cook 4 of the garlic cloves (unpeeled) in boiling salted water until tender; drain and rinse under cold water. Thinly slice to resemble sliced almonds; brown briefly in a little butter and set aside.

Smash and peel the remaining garlic clove and place it in a food processor. Add the ¼ cup chopped parsley, watercress, almond powder, lemon zest, salt, pepper, and remaining 1 cup butter. Pulse just to combine and set aside.

Heat several inches of oil to 360°F in a deep fryer. Dip a few frog's legs at a time in the batter, then quickly transfer to the hot oil. Fry until golden brown, about 2 to 3 minutes.

Just before serving, boil 1 tablespoon crème fraîche and whisk in the garlic butter; add the reserved cooking liquid and cook until reduced by half.

Place a spoonful of the parsley purée in the center of each of 6 shallow bowls. Place a spoonful of the garlic butter on top and arrange the fried frog's legs around the edge. Decorate with the sliced garlic cloves and serve.

Large cask typical of Alsatian cellars, decorated with the arms of its proprietor.

Preparation: 2 hours

Cooking time: 3 hours

Serves 6

━

2 FRESH PINEAPPLES

4 CUPS SUGAR

2½ CUPS WATER

1 PREPARED SPONGE CAKE, MADE WITH 6 LARGE EGGS, 12 TO 13 INCHES SQUARE

for the tartlet shells:

1⅔ CUPS ALL-PURPOSE FLOUR

½ CUP SUGAR

1 LARGE EGG

½ CUP (1 STICK) UNSALTED BUTTER, SLIGHTLY SOFTENED

for the pastry cream:

1¼ CUPS MILK

1 VANILLA BEAN

3 EGG YOLKS

6 TABLESPOONS SUGAR

3 TABLESPOONS CORNSTARCH

for the ice cream and custard sauce:

2½ CUPS MILK

1 CUP HEAVY CREAM

1 FRESH ROSEMARY SPRIG

3 LARGE EGG YOLKS

1 CUP SUGAR

1 VANILLA BEAN

⅓ CUP LATE-HARVEST RIESLING (ALSO KNOWN AS RIESLING GRAINS NOBLES) OR SIMILAR SWEET WINE

for the mousseline cream:

6 TABLESPOONS BUTTER, SOFTENED

to assemble the cake:

⅔ CUP LATE-HARVEST RIESLING (ALSO KNOWN AS RIESLING GRAINS NOBLES) OR SIMILAR SWEET WINE

for the meringue:

3 LARGE EGG WHITES

2 CUP GRANULATED SUGAR

⅔ CUP CONFECTIONERS' SUGAR

6 SMALL FRESH ROSEMARY SPRIGS, FOR GARNISH

A TRIO OF PINEAPPLE DESSERTS WITH LATE-HARVEST RIESLING AND ROSEMARY-SCENTED ICE CREAM

Cut the peel from the pineapples and quarter. Remove the cores and place the pineapples in a large wide pan. Add the sugar and the water. Bring to a boil, reduce the heat to low, and simmer for 2½ to 3 hours.

Trim the sponge cake into 2 rectangles that measure 12 × 6 inches and set aside.

To make the tartlet shells, sift the flour onto a work surface and make a well in the center. In the center of the well, combine the sugar and egg with your fingers. Add the butter to the well and quickly work it with the egg. Gradually blend in the flour. When the dough is smooth, press into a ball, wrap in plastic, and chill for 30 minutes.

Preheat the oven to 400°F. Roll the dough out ¾ inch thick. Cut out twelve 2½-inch circles. Line 6 tartlet pans with 6 of the dough circles. Cut out the centers from the 6 remaining circles to make 6 rings. Transfer the tartlet shells and rings to a baking sheet and bake until golden brown. Set aside.

To make the pastry cream, scald the milk with the vanilla bean. In a large bowl, beat the egg yolks and sugar until light and lemon colored. Whisk in the cornstarch. Remove the vanilla bean and whisk the hot milk into the egg mixture. Mix well and pour into the saucepan used to heat the milk. Cook, whisking, until the pastry cream comes to a boil, about 5 minutes. Cool to room temperature, cover, and chill.

To make the ice cream and custard sauce, pour 1¼ cups of the milk and ½ cup of the cream into a saucepan and bring to a boil. Remove from the heat and add the rosemary. Cover and let infuse for 8 minutes. Discard the rosemary. Beat 3 of the egg yolks and ½ cup of the sugar until light yellow. Pour in the infused milk, stir well, and return to the heat. Cover over low heat, stirring constantly, until the mixture is thick enough to coat the back of a spoon. Pour into an ice-cream maker and freeze according to the manufacturer's instructions.

Make a custard sauce in the same manner as the ice-cream custard with the remaining milk, cream, eggs, and sugar, infusing the milk-cream mixture with the vanilla. Strain, cool, stir in the wine, and chill.

To make the mousseline cream, whisk the butter into the chilled pastry cream until smooth.

To assemble, place one of the sponge cake rectangles on a small baking sheet. Combine ¾ cup of the pineapple cooking liquid with the ⅔ cup Riesling. Use this liquid to moisten the sponge cake. Spread a ⅜-inch-thick layer of mousseline cream on top. Cover with the second cake rectangle and moisten it as well. Spread over another layer of mousseline cream. Refrigerate until well chilled.

To prepare the meringue, beat the egg whites and granulated sugar until stiff. Beat in the confectioners' sugar. Transfer to a pastry bag fitted with a star tip.

Preheat the broiler. Cut 6 of the cooked pineapple quarters into ¼-inch-thick pieces. Cover the cake with the pineapple pieces and pipe the meringue on top. Brown under the broiler.

Thinly slice 1 of the remaining pineapple quarters. Cut the remaining quarter into ½-inch cubes. Set aside.

Cut the sponge cake assembly into 6 little cakes. Set in the center of 6 serving plates. Arrange the thinly sliced pineapple in a circle on one end of the plate. Spoon a tablespoonful or two of the custard sauce into the center of the circle. (Serve any remaining custard sauce on the side.) Set a tartlet shell on the other end of the plate, fill the shell with the pineapple cubes, and top with a scoop of the ice cream. Set a pastry ring on top and garnish with a little sprig of rosemary before serving.

JURA

THE JURA APPEARS AS A SERIES OF TWO GROUPS OF PLATEAUS FACING BURGUNDY, THE HIGHER OF WHICH IS CROWNED BY MEADOWS AND THICK PINE FORESTS. EACH LEVEL IS SEPARATED FROM THE PREVIOUS ONE BY A ONCE INSURMOUNTABLE RIDGE. PASSAGES, OR *CLUSES*, WERE CUT TO TAKE ADVANTAGE OF THE NATURAL BREAKS IN THE ROCKS, ALLOWING STREAMS TO PASS. BEFORE REACHING THESE ROUTES, THE RIVERS FOLLOW THE TERRACES, DRAINING THE WATERS OF SHORT PERPENDICULAR VALLEYS, OR *RECULÉS*, THAT BREAK UP OF THE WALLS OF THE MOUNTAIN RIMS. IT IS IN THESE HIGH VALLEYS AND ON THESE MOUNTAIN RIMS, WELL EXPOSED TO THE NOON-DAY SUN, THAT GRAPEVINES AND FRUIT TREES HAVE BEEN PLANTED FOR CENTURIES. TODAY THEY ARE WISELY CULTIVATED BY DESCENDENTS OF THE ORIGINAL SIMPLE MOUNTAIN FOLK. AN ANCIENT LAND OF WINE GROWERS, HERDSMEN, FORESTERS, AND CRAFTSMEN BEYOND COMPARISON, THE JURA HAS GIVEN THE WORLD SEVERAL OF ITS GREATEST NAMES. ITS WINES, FAMOUS SINCE ANTIQUITY, ARE IN THE MIDST OF A REBIRTH. THE *VIN JAUNE*, MADE JUST AS IN THE TIME OF THE ROMAN EMPEROR WHO HAD HIS VILLA HERE, ALONE PROVES THE SUPERIORITY OF INTUITION OVER MORE RATIONAL PROCEDURES. THE WINES ACCOMPANY A CUISINE WHERE FRESHWATER FISH, GAME, A VARIETY OF MEATS, AND FRUITS FROM THE VINEYARDS OF THE MOUN-TAIN RIMS ABOUND. A LAND OF CATTLE RAISING, THE JURA HAS DISTINGUISHED ITSELF FROM THE DAWN OF TIME BY ITS SPECIAL DAIRY PRODUCTS. INFLUENCES FROM BURGUNDY, GERMANY, SPAIN, AND FRANCE HAVE EACH LEFT THEIR TRACE ON A CUI-SINE THAT IN SEVERAL DOMAINS IS THE MOTHER OF ALL OTHERS. THANKS TO ITS ROCK SALT, THE JURA BECAME FERTILE GROUND FOR MASTERING THE TECHNIQUES OF FOOD CONSERVATION. THE JURA IS ESSENTIAL.

The wine-growing region of the Jura is one of the oldest in France. It spreads out over fifty miles from Saint-Amour to Salins. Arbois (its steeple visible on top of the hill) is one of the best-known appellations. On these typical plots, which resemble ancient breaches in the ramparts of "Revermont," "Bon Pays," or "Vignoble," grow the grapes that produce the most extraordinary palette of wines there is.

A GLIMPSE AT TRADITION

Chicken with Morels and Vin Jaune

Clean a free-range chicken and cut it into 8 pieces. Rub each piece with salt and pepper. Dust with flour. Lightly brown the chicken in ¾ cup butter in a large sauté pan, turning the pieces often. Cover the pan and bake in a 400° F oven until done.

Meanwhile, carefully clean 12 ounces fresh morel mushrooms. Cook for 5 minutes in lightly salted boiling water. Drain the mushrooms, then sauté them in 3 tablespoons butter in a large skil-let for 3 minutes. Set the mushrooms aside.

Take the chicken out of the oven, remove the pieces from the pan, and remove as much fat from the pan as possible. Deglaze the pan with 1¼ cups vin jaune (a deep yellow wine from the Jura region), return the chicken pieces to the pan, add the morels, and 3 cups crème fraîche or heavy cream. Cook, uncovered, over medium heat until the sauce has thickened. Adjust the seasoning and trans-fer to a warmed serving bowl.

The Cuisance River in the heart of Arbois— among the old houses where Louis Pasteur conducted his research on the alcoholic fermentation of grapes and its control. But the true patron of Arbois is Saint Just to whom in autumn is offered the *biou*, an enormous cluster of grapes comparable to that which the Hebrew scouts brought back to Moses from the Promised Land.

Passing through the mountain rims, the rivers of the Jura become torrents. They are responsible for the *cluses* and the erosion that has formed the landscape of the vineyards. Only 3,700 acres remain in appellation wines. The annual production is approximately one million gallons, but, depending on the year, it can be reduced to nothing or tripled. The varietals used by the wine makers of the Jura are among the oldest, such as the Savagnin for white wines or the Trousseau or Poulsard for red wines. The production of *vin jaune* and *vin de paille* has never flagged since the high Middle Ages.

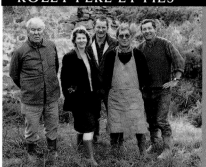

For decades, the Rolet family has offered lovers of the wines of the Jura a range of wines superbly representative of the land and its varietals.

When the *domaine* Rolet was created, one sole passion excited Désiré Rolet: to obtain the best possible balance among soil, subsoil, and varietals. Henceforth in AOC Arbois and in the Côte de Jura, the 136 acres have been distributed between light clay, which bears the 34 percent of Chardonnay (white); gray clay, the 21 percent of Savagnin (the varietal of the extraordinary *vin jaune*); red and blue clays, the 21 percent of Poulsard (the traditional red of the Jura); and rich gravel, the 10 percent of Trousseau. This studied balance of the varietals has permitted the Rolet estate to become a pioneer in the Jura of single-varietal red wines such as Arbois, Poulsard, Arbois Trousseau, and Arbois Pinot. The children of Désiré Rolet have inherited the passion of the founder: to obtain the quintessence of the grape harvested at the peak of maturity. Their dogma: Wine is already made on the vine.

JEAN-PAUL JEUNET

Arbois

Jura

Preparation: 50 minutes

Cooking time: 1¾ hours

Serves 6

●

6 CRAYFISH

1½ CUPS PLUS 2 TABLESPOONS
UNSALTED BUTTER, SOFTENED

1 ONION, CHOPPED

1 CARROT, CHOPPED

2 SHALLOTS, CHOPPED

¾ CUP CHÂTEAU CHALON OR OTHER
DRY WHITE WINE

1 TABLESPOON TOMATO PURÉE

1 BOUQUET GARNI

2 POUNDS TROUT FILLETS, SKINNED,
PIN BONES REMOVED

5 LARGE EGGS

4 CUPS CRÈME FRAÎCHE OR
HEAVY CREAM

SALT AND FRESHLY GROUND BLACK
PEPPER TO TASTE

1 CUP GRATED COMTÉ OR
GRUYÈRE CHEESE

2 TABLESPOONS FLOUR

1 BUNCH FRESH TARRAGON

TROUT SOUFFLÉS WITH CRAYFISH SAUCE

Clean the crayfish. Cook in boiling salted water for 10 minutes. Remove the meat from the tails and set aside for garnish.

Sauté the crayfish bodies, claws, and shells in ¼ cup of the butter and crush with a mallet. Stir in the onion, carrot, shallots, wine, tomato purée, and bouquet garni. Cook over low heat for 1 hour.

Meanwhile, pound the trout fillets and purée through a drum sieve or other fine sieve. Whisking the purée, work in 1¼ cups butter, followed by the eggs, adding them one by one. The mixture should be well blended. Chill for 15 minutes.

Whip 1 cup of the crème fraîche and gently fold into the trout mixture. Add salt and pepper to taste. Transfer to a pastry bag without a tip. Pipe into 6 buttered ramekins and cook, covered, in a water bath on top of the stove for 15 minutes. Remove from the water bath, sprinkle with grated cheese, and bake for 15 minutes.

While the soufflés are in the oven, work the crayfish mixture through a fine sieve set over a saucepan. Set the pan over medium heat. Knead together the remaining 2 tablespoons butter and the flour, add to the pan, and whisk until the sauce is thick. Stir in the remaining 3 cups crème fraîche and season to taste.

Make a pool of sauce on individual plates. Unmold the soufflés on the sauce. Garnish with the reserved crayfish tails and sprigs of tarragon and serve.

QUAIL IN ASPIC AU VIN JAUNE WITH A KITCHEN-GARDEN SALAD

Preparation: 2 hours

Cooking time: 4 hours 40 minutes

Serves 4

◆

4 QUAIL (SEE NOTE)

2 WHOLE GARLIC HEADS, CLOVES SEPARATED BUT NOT PEELED

2 POUNDS COARSE SALT

1 SPRIG THYME

1 BAY LEAF

4 CUPS GOOSE FAT (SEE NOTE)

20 BABY CARROTS

8 SMALL ASPARAGUS SPEARS, WOODY PART REMOVED

3 PEARL ONIONS

4 TINY FENNEL BULBS

2 POUNDS MESCLUN

for the aspic:

¾ CUP GOOSE FAT

2 POUNDS CHICKEN NECKS AND BONES

3 CUPS JURA WHITE WINE, SUCH AS VIN DE L'ETOILE, OR OTHER DRY WHITE WINE

2 CUPS CHICKEN STOCK OR WATER

1 LARGE ONION

2 SMALL CARROTS

1 LEEK, GREENS ONLY

1 CELERY RIB

2 CALVES' FEET

2 SMALL PIECES SLAB BACON RIND

1 BOUQUET GARNI

SALT AND FRESHLY GROUND BLACK PEPPER TO TASTE

1 TO 2 TEASPOONS UNFLAVORED GELATIN IF NEEDED

1 CUP COLD CHICKEN STOCK, IF NEEDED

for the vinaigrette:

1 TABLESPOON WINE VINEGAR

2 TABLESPOONS PEANUT OIL

1 TABLESPOON OLIVE OIL

1 TEASPOON DIJON MUSTARD

SALT AND FRESHLY GROUND BLACK PEPPER TO TASTE

Clean the quail and trim the wing tips. Smash one or two of the garlic cloves and rub over the quail. Set the quail in a deep dish and cover with all but ¼ cup of the coarse salt. Embed the thyme, bay leaf, and remaining garlic cloves in the salt and refrigerate for 4 hours.

Meanwhile, prepare the aspic: heat the goose fat in a Dutch oven or heavy casserole and lightly brown the chicken necks and bones and the quail wing tips. Pour off the fat, deglaze the pan with the wine, and cook until almost all the liquid has evaporated. Add 2 cups chicken stock, bring to a boil, and skim any impurities that rise to the surface. Add the onion, carrots, leek, celery, calves' feet, bacon rind, and bouquet garni. Simmer slowly for 4 hours, skimming often. Strain the stock into another pan and cook rapidly to reduce by one-third. Season to taste and let cool. To check the setting quality of the stock, spoon a little onto a cold plate. If it does not set, sprinkle the gelatin over the cold stock in a small saucepan and let stand 5 minutes to soften. Dissolve the gelatin over low heat and stir into the large pan of stock. Check the setting quality once again and add more gelatin if necessary. Set the aspic aside.

Remove the quail from the salt, wiping away all traces of it. Melt 4 cups goose fat in a large skillet and cook the quail in the simmering oil for 5 minutes. Take the skillet off the heat and set aside.

Peel the baby carrots and cook in boiling salted water; refresh under cold running water. Peel the asparagus and halve the stalks lengthwise; cook in boiling salted water and refresh. Peel and cook the onions in the same manner; quarter and set aside. Cook the fennel in the same manner and set aside. Rinse the mesclun, dry, and set aside.

Whisk the vinaigrette ingredients together in a small bowl. Set aside.

Remove the quail from the goose fat and wipe clean with paper towels. Cut off the legs and remove skin. Remove the bone from the thigh portion. Remove the skin from their breasts and remove the meat from each half in one piece. Set the legs and breasts on a large, deep plate and spoon aspic over to cover. Chill until set. Pour the remaining aspic into a baking dish and chill; when the aspic is set, cut into small dice.

Toss the mesclun with the vinaigrette. Garnish plates with a mound of salad and distribute the baby vegetables on top. Set 2 quail breasts and 2 thighs on each plate. Spoon the diced aspic around them. Grind a little black pepper over the top, sprinkle with a little salt, and serve.

NOTE: This recipe can also be made with pigeon. The salad ingredients may vary according to the season.

Rendered goose fat is available in cans in France. You can use rendered duck or chicken fat if you cannot find goose fat.

For an even more extravagant presentation, garnish the quail with thin rounds of black truffle.

Preparation: 50 minutes

Cooking time: 25 minutes

Serves 4

—

12 OUNCES WILD MUSHROOMS,
PREFERABLY *MOUSSERONS* OR SMALL
CREMINI MUSHROOMS

3 POUNDS FROG'S LEGS

¾ CUP (1½ STICKS) UNSALTED BUTTER

1 CUP JURA WHITE WINE, PREFERABLY
PUPILLIN

2 SHALLOTS, MINCED

¾ CUP CRÈME FRAÎCHE

1 LARGE BUNCH CHERVIL, MINCED

SALT AND FRESHLY GROUND BLACK
PEPPER TO TASTE

SOUP OF FROG'S LEGS WITH PUPILLIN WINE, FIELD MUSHROOMS, AND CHERVIL

Clean and trim the mushrooms. Heat 2 tablespoons of butter in a skillet, add the mushrooms, and sauté over medium-high heat. Season with salt and pepper and set aside.

Salt and pepper the frog's legs. Heat ½ cup of the butter in a large skillet, add the frog's legs, and cook, covered, over medium heat for 8 to 10 minutes; do not allow to brown. Halfway through the cooking, moisten with a little of the wine. Remove the legs from the pan, let cool, and remove the meat from the bones. Add the remaining wine to the skillet and cook until reduced by one-third; set aside.

Just before serving, heat the remaining 2 tablespoons butter in a saucepan, add the shallots, and cook over medium heat. Add the reduced wine, bring to a boil, and whisk in the crème fraîche; cook until reduced by half. Add the frog meat, mushrooms, and chervil. Serve in deep plates.

Near Arbois, the cellars of the Château de Montigny-les-Arsures.

4 OUNCES DRIED FIGS, HALVED

4 OUNCES DATES, PITTED

4 OUNCES CANDIED GRAPEFRUIT

3 OUNCES RAISINS

4 CUPS MACVIN (SEE NOTE)

for the sweet pie pastry:

14 TABLESPOONS UNSALTED BUTTER

¾ CUP CONFECTIONERS' SUGAR

2½ CUPS ALL-PURPOSE FLOUR

PINCH OF SALT

1 TABLESPOON WATER

for the almond cream:

1¼ CUPS (2½ STICKS) UNSALTED
BUTTER, SOFTENED

⅔ CUP CONFECTIONERS' SUGAR

⅔ CUP POWDERED ALMONDS

⅓ CUP MACVIN (SEE NOTE)

4 LARGE EGGS

for the nougatine:

1 POUND SUGAR

2 POUNDS GLUCOSE
(AVAILABLE IN SOME PHARMACIES)

1 POUND CHOPPED ALMONDS

BEGGARS TART WITH NOUGATINE AU MACVIN

Macerate the dried fruits in the Macvin for 15 to 30 minutes, until softened and slightly puffed.

To make the pastry, combine the butter and confectioners' sugar. Work in the flour, salt, and water. Form into a disk, wrap in plastic, and chill for 1 hour.

To make the almond cream, combine the butter and confectioners' sugar; stir in the powdered almonds. Beat until light and well mixed. Stir in the Macvin, then the eggs, one by one. Stir continuously for 15 minutes.

To make the nougatine, combine the sugar and glucose in a heavy-bottomed saucepan. Cook over high heat until amber. Stir in the almonds with a wooden spoon and pour onto a buttered baking sheet. When the nougatine has hardened, crush it to a powder with a rolling pin.

Preheat the oven to 350° F. Roll the pastry out to a 10-inch circle. Line a 7- or 8-inch tart pan with the pastry. Combine the almond cream, drained macerated fruits, and nougatine and spread in the pastry shell—it should come to the brim. Sprinkle with sugar and bake for 20 to 25 minutes. Let cool before serving.

NOTE: Macvin is a liqueurlike drink from the Arbois region; it is a mixture of wine and spirits that has been macerated with herbs, spices, and other flavorings. You can substitute equal parts of Pinot des Charentes and a dry white wine from Jura.

Preparation: I hour 40 minutes

Cooking time: I hour 20 minutes

Serves 4

—

3 GARLIC CLOVES

12 BABY CARROTS OF EQUAL SIZE,
WITH TOPS

6 TABLESPOONS (¾ STICK) UNSALTED
BUTTER

SALT

PINCH OF SUGAR

12 SMALL YELLOW-FLESHED POTATOES

1¼ CUPS CHICKEN STOCK

PINCH OF SAFFRON THREADS

24 SNOW PEAS

4 LIVE LOBSTERS, ABOUT 1¼ POUNDS
EACH

2 TABLESPOONS CRÈME FRAÎCHE OR
HEAVY CREAM

for the beurre blanc:

2 SHALLOTS, MINCED

1 TABLESPOON WHITE VINEGAR

⅓ CUP WATER

2 TABLESPOONS CRÈME FRAÎCHE OR
HEAVY CREAM

4 TABLESPOONS (½ STICK) UNSALTED
BUTTER, COLD, CUT INTO PIECES

SALT AND FRESHLY GROUND BLACK
PEPPER TO TASTE

for the whipped butter:

4 TABLESPOONS UNSALTED BUTTER

SALT TO TASTE

1 LEMON

for the savagnin sauce:

⅔ CUP SAVAGNIN OR SIMILAR
FULL-BODIED WHITE WINE

PINCH OF CURRY POWDER

PINCH OF SAFFRON THREADS

⅓ CUP CRÈME FRAÎCHE OR HEAVY CREAM

SALT AND FRESHLY GROUND BLACK
PEPPER TO TASTE

for serving:

BUTTER

OLIVE OIL

ROAST LOBSTER WITH SAUCE SAVAGNIN

Cook 3 garlic cloves (unpeeled) in boiling water until tender. Peel, push through a sieve, and set aside.

Peel the carrots, leaving 1 inch of their tops. Place in a skillet with 1 tablespoon butter, pinch of salt, and the sugar. Add cold water to cover and cook, covered, over medium-low heat until almost all the liquid has evaporated. Once the carrots are cooked and the cooking liquid is syrupy, uncover and shake the pan to glaze the carrots. Set aside.

Peel the potatoes and trim the ends. Hollow out the centers to form little boats. Melt 1 to 2 tablespoons of the butter in a skillet and cook the potatoes briefly. Bring the chicken stock to a boil with the pinch of saffron. Add the potatoes and cook over medium heat until they are tender and a pretty yellow color. Drain and set aside.

String the peas and cook in boiling salted water. Refresh under cold running water.

Preheat the oven to 425°F. In plenty of boiling water in a lobster pot, boil the lobsters for 5 minutes. Remove from the water, transfer to the oven, and bake for 5 minutes. Separate the lobster tails and large claws from the bodies. Crack the claws and remove the meat; keep under a damp towel along with the tails. Remove the meat from the legs and heads. Cook in 1 to 2 tablespoons butter, then add the crème fraîche and 1 teaspoon garlic purée. Adjust the seasonings. Stuff the potatoes with this filling.

To make the beurre blanc, in a small heavy-bottomed saucepan, cook the shallots, vinegar, and the water. Boil until the liquid has evaporated. Add the crème fraîche and bring to a boil. Whisk in the butter piece by piece. Season with salt and pepper. Strain through a fine sieve. Set aside in a warm place.

To make the whipped butter, spread the butter on a plate with a table knife and chill. Bring the water to a boil in a saucepan over high heat and whisk in the cold butter bit by bit. Add salt and a squeeze of lemon. Keep warm in a water bath.

To make the savagnin sauce, bring the wine to a boil with the curry and saffron. Add the crème fraîche and bring to a boil, then whisk in the whipped butter and beurre blanc. Adjust the seasonings and keep warm.

To serve, cut the lobster tails lengthwise in half and remove the intestinal vein. Place on a heatproof plate along with the claw meat and dot with butter and a drizzle of olive oil. Place in the oven to warm. Rewarm the vegetable garnishes separately.

Arrange the lobster and vegetables on deep dinner plates. Stir the Savagnin into the sauce and spoon the sauce in the center of the plates. Serve.

NOTE: Savagnin is one of the Arbois region's noted *vins jaunes.* These wines are yellow in color, generally at least seven years old, and have a rich sherrylike character. They are hard to find in the United States, but an older Gewürztraminer will do.

Preparation: 1 hour

Cooking time: 1¼ hours

Serves 8

●

4½ TO 5 POUNDS FISH BONES FROM
MILD, WHITE-FLESHED FISH

1 ONION

1 LEEK, GREENS ONLY

¾ CUP (1½ STICKS) UNSALTED BUTTER

3 CUPS RED WINE, PREFERABLY FROM
ARBOIS

⅔ CUP REDUCED VEAL STOCK
(OPTIONAL)

5 OUNCES MUSHROOMS

1 BOUQUET GARNI

COARSE SALT

1 WHOLE SALMON, 2 TO 2¼ POUNDS

3 POUNDS DAIKON RADISHES

SALT AND FRESHLY GROUND BLACK
PEPPER TO TASTE

OLIVE OIL

1 BUNCH FRESH HERBS

4 TABLESPOONS GRAINY DIJON
MUSTARD

SALMON WITH MUSTARD, DAIKON RADISH, AND RED WINE SAUCE

Chop the fish bones and rinse in a bowl under cold running water for 30 minutes. Drain well. Mince the onion and leek greens. In a large heavy pot, cook in 6 table-spoons of the butter until softened. Add the fish bones and cook for 5 minutes. Pour in the wine and water if necessary to cover the bones completely. Add veal stock if using, the mushrooms, bouquet garni, and a pinch of coarse salt. Bring to a boil, skim-ming impurities from the surface, and simmer gently for 30 minutes. Pour through a fine sieve and chill.

Meanwhile, scale and clean the salmon. Fillet the fish and remove all bones with tweezers. Skin the fillets and cut into 8 pieces about 2 inches wide. Butterfly each piece by slicing it horizontally through the center to within 1 inch of the edge. Open as you would a book. (Reserve any trimmings to use in another recipe such as salmon tartar, a terrine, rillettes, etc.)

Peel the radishes and thinly slice. Sauté in 2 tablespoons of the butter. Season with salt and pepper; set aside.

Season the salmon with salt and pepper. Heat a little olive oil in a large nonstick skillet over medium-low heat. Add the salmon and cook on one side only for 7 to 10 minutes until crispy on the bottom.

Bring the fish stock to a boil and reduce to about ¾ cup; whisk in the remaining 4 tablespoons butter bit by bit. Adjust the seasonings.

Place a salmon piece in the center of each dinner plate. Surround with radish slices. Pour some sauce at one end and place a small bouquet of herbs at the other. Spoon some mustard down the center of the salmon. Sprinkle with coarse salt and pepper before serving.

Preparation: 50 minutes

Cooking time: 30 minutes

Serves 6

●

for the cookie dough:

1 CUP ALL-PURPOSE FLOUR

6 TABLESPOONS (¾ STOCK) UNSALTED
BUTTER

3 TABLESPOONS SUGAR

for the granité:

⅔ CUP *VIN DE PAILLE* OR OTHER SWEET
DESSERT WINE (SEE NOTE)

2 CUPS SUGAR

GRATED ZEST OF 1 ORANGE

JUICE OF ¼ LEMON

¾ CUP FRESH GRAPE JUICE

for the garnish:

3 BANANAS

2 CUPS SUGAR

1 TABLESPOON HONEY

JUICE OF 3 ORANGES

¼ CUP *VIN DE PAILLE* OR OTHER SWEET
DESSERT WINE

CONFECTIONERS' SUGAR

1 BUNCH FRESH MINT

HONEYED BANANAS WITH STRAW WINE GRANITÉ

To make the cookies, combine all the cookie ingredients in a standing electric mixer fitted with a paddle. Mix on low speed until a soft dough forms. Roll the dough out ¾ inch. Cut out 18 to 20 banana-shaped cookies and transfer to a baking sheet lined with parchment paper. Bake 15 to 20 minutes. Keep dry.

To prepare the granité, in a nonreactive saucepan, combine the wine, sugar, and orange zest. Bring to a boil, remove from the heat, and let cool. Add the lemon juice and grape juice and pour through a fine sieve into a large shallow metal pan. Freeze, stirring with a fork every 15 minutes to break up large crystals.

To serve, slice the bananas and cook with the sugar and honey for 3 to 4 minutes until golden brown. Transfer the bananas to dessert plates and sprinkle with the orange juice. Deglaze the skillet with the *vin de paille* and drizzle over the bananas. Set a scoop of granité in the center of the plates and surround by 3 cookies sprinkled with confectioners' sugar. Garnish with mint leaves and serve.

NOTE: *Vin de paille,* or straw wine, is a specialty of the Jura. It is a very sweet wine made from grapes that have been dried on straw mats. It is similar to an Italian *passito* or *vin santo.*

Montigny-les-Arsures.
The white grapes of the
Savagnin dry for several
weeks, hung by wires or
laid out on straw. The
vin de paille will be
extracted by pressing at
the end of the year and
will then ferment for at
least one year.

SAVOY

SAVOY WAS ONCE AN INDEPENDENT STATE THAT STRETCHED OUT ON ALL SIDES OF THE ALPS. THIS HISTORY IS IMPORTANT FOR IT EXPLAINS WHY THE TOWNS AND VILLAGES OF TODAY'S TWO *DÉPARTEMENTS* HAVE MAINTAINED AN ANCIENT CHARACTER WHILE UNDENIABLY ADAPTING TO MODERN TIMES, RESULTING IN A GREAT DEAL OF THE CHARM. THE NATIONAL IDENTITY OF THE SAVOYARDS WAS FORMED IN THE HIGH VALLEYS WHERE FOR CENTURIES THEY LEARNED TO LIVE IN HARMONY AND TO MAKE THE BEST OF AN OFTEN HOSTILE MOUNTAIN BY TAKING ADVANTAGE OF THE RICHNESS OF THE FORESTS. SAVOYARD GASTRONOMY HAS RETAINED FROM ITS PEASANT ORIGINS A KEEN SENSE OF GOOD PRODUCTS, WHILE THE TRADITIONS OF THE DUCAL CUISINE HAS ALWAYS BEEN OPEN TO THE INFLUENCES OF ITS GREAT NEIGHBORS AND FARAWAY COUNTRIES, BRINGERS OF SPICES. THE GLACIAL LAKES LEND A MARITIME IMAGE AND PROVIDE THE FISH, FRESHWATER VERSION. GAME, MUSHROOMS, AND A PARTICULAR ABUNDANCE OF WILD FRUITS COMPLETE THE RANGE OF LOCAL FOODS, WHICH HAPPILY JOINS WITH THE WINES OF A THOUGHTFULLY PARCELLED-OUT VINEYARD, SHELTERED IN A MOSAIC OF PROPERTIES SCATTERED FROM LÉMAN (CRÉPY) TO THE ISÈRE (MONTMÉLIAN). NEIGHBORING BUGEY, WHERE THE SLOPES DROP OFF INTO THE VERY ROMANTIC LAC DU BOURGET, NOURISHED THE FATHER OF MODERN GASTRONOMY, BRILLAT-SAVARIN. THERE IS NO LAND ON EARTH WHERE THE PRIMORDIAL FLAVORS ARE MORE PRECISELY PRESERVED.

A GLIMPSE AT TRADITION

Hare Stew à la Mondeuse

—

*S*kin the hare taking care not to cut the skin of the belly. Gut it, collecting the blood in a bowl; add a dash of vinegar and refrigerate. Cut the hare into pieces and set in a deep dish, sprinkle with a bottle of Mondeuse (a vigorous red wine of the region) and 2 tablespoons oil, add a quarter of an onion pierced with a whole clove, some chopped onion, 2 carrots, 2 garlic cloves, a bouquet garni, and a few cracked peppercorns. Marinate overnight in the refrigerator.

Remove the pieces of hare from the marinade, dry them, and dust with flour. Transfer the marinade and vegetables to a large saucepan, bring to a boil, and cook for 10 minutes.

Blanch a 6-ounce piece of salt pork or country bacon. Cut into small dice and brown in a pot along with 1½ tablespoons lard. Increase the heat slightly, add the pieces of hare, and brown on all sides. Add 2 minced onions, and salt and pepper to taste, and cook until the onion is softened. Strain the marinade into the pot. Add 2 carrots in chunks and cook, covered, for 2 hours. Halfway through the cooking, turn the pieces and check the seasoning. At the end of cooking, stir the blood in the bowl and add ⅓ cup crème fraîche. Remove the pieces of hare from the stew, place on a platter, and keep warm. Pour the blood mixture into the stew in a thin stream, whisking the entire time; gently simmer, until thickened. Pour the sauce through a fine sieve over the hare. Serve immediately with polenta, fresh pasta, or potatoes.

108

No fewer than twenty-three varietals may be used to make the wines of Savoy. The grapevines adorn the slopes up to an altitude of about 1,600 feet. Sunny autumns compensate for the delays in flowering and other hazards of springtime.

The mosaic of vineyards in Savoy extends from Léman to Chapareillan (Isère), passing by Crépy, Le Bugey, Seyssel, and the banks of the Lac du Bourget. It covers more than 3,700 acres in all, the greatest part of which is located in Savoy. The most homogenous part is found to the south of Chambéry around Mont Granier (Apremont, Les Abymes) and just opposite around the *cru* of Chignin (ABOVE), thickly planted with Jacquère, the varietal of most white vines from Savoy, and with Roussanne, here called "Bergeron."

Léman, Lac du Bourget, Lac d'Annecy . . . the traces of Quaternary glaciations bring an almost maritime element to the peaceful and infinitely romantic land-scapes of Savoy.

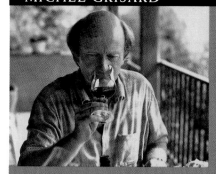

On land that formerly squeezed out the "allobrogica" so dear to the Romans, Michel Grisard rejoins pure tradition with the love of wine.

The people of these lakeside regions have long fished with a consummate art that might be envied by their far-off seaside colleagues. The region abounds in freshwater fish: trout, perch, char, pike, carp, tench, and the whitebait that ends up fried and accompanied by a sharp white wine. This is not to overlook the crayfish, those delicious crustaceans of these shores that have become more and more rare due to a longstanding desire for them and an overeager harvest.

Listening to Michel Grisard at his estate of Prieuré Saint-Christophe in Fréterive in Savoy, it is impossible to forget that wine is first of all a historical product, fruit of the joint influences of a centuries-old tradition, of the soil, and of a skill much closer to alchemy than to chemistry. Michel Grisard favors two typical and original varietals on stony land exposed south-southeast and sheltered behind the wall of the alpine massif of the Bauges. These varietals, Mondeuse (red) and Altesse (white), belong to very ancient indigenous species. The red wine of Mondeuse, from a restricted harvest, can be laid down for a long time and can compete with the greatest wines of the world. The Altesse is made like wines in Burgundy, by fermenting in a barrel and *batonnage,* or the stirring of the lees in the barrel, which create a fine, tender, and elegant white wine of a great complexity of aromas.

CHEF MARC VEYRAT

L'Auberge de l'Eridan
Veyrier du Lac
Annecy
Haute-Savoie

Preparation: 2½ hours

Cooking time: 50 minutes

Serves 4

◆

for the salt crust:
2 CUPS ALL-PURPOSE FLOUR

2 CUPS COARSE SALT,
PREFERABLY SEL DE GUÉRANDE

6 CUPS WATER

for the vegetable bouillon:
3 CUPS WATER

2 ONIONS, CHOPPED

3 CARROTS, CHOPPED

1 SHALLOT

1 GARLIC CLOVE

1 BOUQUET GARNI

2 SUGAR CUBES

PINCH OF SALT

for the Chignin Bergeron sauce:
1 SHALLOT

1 TEASPOON BUTTER

¾ CUP CHIGNIN BERGERON OR SIMILAR
LIGHT WHITE WINE FROM SAVOY

⅓ CUP HALF-AND-HALF

COARSE SALT AND FRESHLY GROUND
BLACK PEPPER TO TASTE

1 POUND GOOSE-FOOT SHOOTS
(*CHÉNOPODES*) OR BABY SPINACH

1 LAKE TROUT, 2 TO 2¼ POUNDS,
READY TO COOK

1 LARGE EGG YOLK

1½ TEASPOONS BUTTER

ZEST OF 2 ORANGES, CHOPPED

PINCH OF CONFECTIONERS' SUGAR

SALT AND FRESHLY GROUND BLACK
PEPPER TO TASTE

LAKE TROUT IN A SALT CRUST WITH CHIGNIN BERGERON SAUCE

To make the salt crust, mix the flour and salt, then stir in the water, working it well into the dough. Form into a ball and refrigerate for 1½ hours.

To make the vegetable bouillon, in a stockpot, combine the water, onions, carrots, shallot, garlic, bouquet garni, sugar cubes, and salt. Simmer for 20 minutes, skim, and pour through a fine sieve.

To make the Chignin Bergeron sauce, in a saucepan, cook the shallot in a little butter. Pour in the wine and cook until reduced to one-quarter the original volume. Pour in the vegetable bouillon. Cook until reduced by half. Strain the mixture through a fine sieve, then add the half-and-half. Season with salt and pepper. Keep warm in a water bath.

Rinse the goose-foot shoots in several changes of water. Plunge into boiling salted water for 20 seconds and drain. Refresh in a large bowl of ice water, then drain well.

Preheat the oven to 450°F. Roll out the dough ¼ inch thick, set the fish in the center, and cover it, overlapping the dough by a generous 1 inch. Moisten the seam with a little water to seal it. Trim any excess dough. Place the fish on a baking sheet. Brush with the egg yolk. Bake about 8 minutes.

Melt the butter and stir in the orange zest, sugar, salt, and pepper. Stir into the reserved greens.

To serve, crack the salt crust and remove it. Lift off the fillets from the fish and cut each in half lengthwise. Garnish each plate with a piece of fish and a spoonful of greens. Spoon some of the sauce onto each plate, but don't pour it over the fish.

NOTE: Chef Veyrat makes this dish with a local fish called *la féra du lac,* which is found in Lake Annecy. You can use freshwater trout or other mild freshwater fish.

Don't hesitate to use the blender to emulsify the Chignin Bergeron sauce. Just before serving, check the seasoning one last time, and add 2 or 3 more tablespoons of Chignin Bergeron to add a slight acidity to the sauce.

Preparation: 40 minutes

Cooking time: 20 minutes

Serves 6

—

24 PERCH FILLETS

2 OUNCES FRESH SPINACH

2 OUNCES CHERVIL

2 OUNCES FLAT-LEAF PARSLEY

2 OUNCES WATERCRESS

SALT TO TASTE

2 CUPS MEDIUM-GRAIN SEMOLINA

2 TABLESPOONS OLIVE OIL, PLUS MORE
FOR THE FISH

ABOUT ½ CUP SEYSSEL OR OTHER
LIGHT WHITE WINE (SEE NOTE)

1 TABLESPOON COLD BUTTER

FRESHLY GROUND BLACK PEPPER TO
TASTE

2 CUPS VEAL STOCK

1 TABLESPOON BALSAMIC VINEGAR

1 BUNCH CHERVIL, STEMMED AND
CHOPPED

PERCH FILLETS WITH HERB GNOCCHI IN A WARM HERB-AND-SEYSSEL VINAIGRETTE

Trim the perch fillets and remove all small bones with tweezers. Cut into long strips and set aside in the refrigerator.

Stem and rinse the spinach, 2 ounces chervil, the parsley, and watercress. Bring a pot of unsalted water to a boil and plunge in the herbs and greens. Blanch for 5 minutes, then refresh in ice water. Drain very well and purée until smooth in a food processor. Set aside in the refrigerator.

Bring ⅓ cup water to a boil in a heavy saucepan, salt the water, and stir in the semolina. Cover and set aside for 5 minutes. Add 1 tablespoon of the olive oil, the herb purée, 3 tablespoons of the wine, and the butter. Stir and season with salt and pepper. Keep warm.

Heat the veal stock and ¼ cup wine in a saucepan; whisk in the vinegar and 1 tablespoon olive oil. Season with salt and pepper. Just before serving, add 1 tablespoon wine and the chopped chervil.

Salt and pepper the fish and cook in a large skillet with a little olive oil.

Spoon an oval-shaped mound of the herb gnocchi on the center of each dinner plate. Place the fish around the gnocchi and spoon the hot vinaigrette over the top. Sprinkle with salt and pepper and serve.

NOTE: Seyssel is a delicate, pale white wine from Savoy.

Tommes and Reblochons, honeys and wines—all Savoyard products in a corner of the market.

Preparation: I hour

Cooking time: 40 minutes

Serves 4

—

4 OUNCES WALNUTS IN THE SHELL

1 LARGE FENNEL BULB PLUS 12 BABY
FENNEL BULBS

10 TABLESPOONS UNSALTED BUTTER

SALT AND FRESHLY GROUND BLACK
PEPPER TO TASTE

2 ARCTIC CHAR

1¼ CUPS CRÉPY OR SIMILAR LIGHT
WHITE WINE, PREFERABLY FROM SAVOY

1 SHALLOT, MINCED

PINCH OF CURRY POWDER

1 TABLESPOON HEAVY CREAM

CHAR WITH SAUCE CRÉPY, WALNUTS, AND FENNEL

Shell the walnuts, blanch, and coarsely chop. Set aside to dry. Trim the large fennel, cutting away the tough, stringy outer layer of the bulb. Finely chop the bulb.

Heat 3 tablespoons of the butter in a large saucepan over medium heat, add the chopped fennel, and cook until softened. Season with salt and pepper.

Clean, scale, and fillet the fish. With tweezers, carefully remove all small bones from the fillets. Cut each fillet in half and trim neatly. Set aside in the refrigerator.

Trim the small fennel bulbs and blanch them in boiling salted water. Drain and refresh under cold running water. Set aside until just before serving.

Bring the wine, shallot, and curry to a boil in a saucepan over medium heat. Boil until reduced by two-thirds. Stir in the cream, return to a boil, and quickly whisk in 3 tablespoons of the butter. Season with salt and pepper and set aside in a water bath to keep warm.

In separate pans, heat the walnuts and chopped fennel.

Heat 2 tablespoons of the butter in a large nonstick skillet; salt and pepper the fish and cook. Melt the remaining 2 tablespoons of butter in a medium skillet and sauté the fennel bulbs until tender.

To serve, spoon some chopped fennel and nuts in the center of each dinner plate. Pour some sauce over the top. Set 2 pieces of fish and 3 fennel bulbs on each plate. Garnish with freshly ground black pepper and a little salt. Serve with the remaining sauce.

Preparation: 1½ hours

Cooking time: 1 hour

Serves 4

—

for the filling:

2 OUNCES ASPARAGUS, JULIENNED

1 SMALL ARTICHOKE BOTTOM, TRIMMED
AND JULIENNED

1 SMALL ZUCCHINI, JULIENNED

1 TO 2 TABLESPOONS UNSALTED BUTTER

SALT AND FRESHLY GROUND BLACK
PEPPER TO TASTE

2 CUPS SHELLED FRESH ENGLISH PEAS

for the pasta:

2 CUPS ALL-PURPOSE FLOUR

4 LARGE EGG YOLKS

1 TEASPOON OLIVE OIL

2 TEASPOONS SALT

1 LARGE EGG WHITE, LIGHTLY BEATEN

for the vegetable garnish and sauce (see Note):

8 BABY ONIONS

1¾ TO 2¼ CUPS UNSALTED BUTTER

2 POUNDS GREEN CABBAGE

SALT AND FRESHLY GROUND BLACK
PEPPER TO TASTE

12 BROCCOFLOWER FLORETS

8 RADISHES

1 CUP SHELLED FRESH ENGLISH PEAS

12 ASPARAGUS TIPS, 2 INCHES LONG

5 OUNCES PURPLE FIELD MUSHROOMS
(*MOUSSERONS VIOLETS*)

4 OUNCES CHANTERELLE MUSHROOMS

4 OUNCES HORN-OF-PLENTY
MUSHROOMS (*TROMPETTES-DES-MORTS*)

8 GARLIC CLOVES, UNPEELED

¾ CUP SHEEP'S MILK YOGURT
(SEE NOTE)

½ TO ⅔ CUP CRÈME FRAÎCHE

⅔ CUP APREMONT (SEE NOTE)

DASH OF OLIVE OIL

DASH OF RED WINE VINEGAR

1 BUNCH FRESH HERBS,
PREFERABLY CHIVES AND CHERVIL,
STEMMED AND CHOPPED

MARKET-GARDEN RAVIOLI WITH SHEEP'S MILK YOGURT AND APREMONT SAUCE

To make the filling, in a skillet, cook the asparagus, artichoke, and zucchini separately in a little butter. Salt and pepper to taste. Cook the peas in boiling salted water; work through a fine sieve to purée. Mix all the vegetables.

To make fresh pasta, pour the flour into a bowl and add the egg yolks, olive oil, salt, and few drops of water. Mix and form into a smooth ball. Cover and set aside in a cool place for 1 hour.

Roll out the dough and cut into 4-inch squares. Drop a spoonful of filling onto the center of each square. Brush the edges with beaten egg white and fold to make a triangle. Cook the ravioli in plenty of gently boiling salted water for 1 to 2 minutes. Drain on a clean kitchen towel.

To make the vegetable garnish and sauce, peel the baby onions and cook in salted water with 1 tablespoon of the butter.

Discard the outer leaves and trim the tough cores from the cabbage. Rinse the cabbage and blanch in rapidly boiling salted water. Refresh under cold running water and drain well. Melt 2 tablespoons of the butter in a skillet, add the cabbage leaves, and cook, stirring, until tender but not too soft. Sprinkle with salt and pepper.

Cook the broccoflower florets until tender in boiling salted water. Refresh and drain.

Clean the radishes and cook until tender in a saucepan with 1 tablespoon butter, water to cover, and salt and pepper.

Cook the peas until just tender in boiling salted water and refresh quickly.

Cook the asparagus tips until tender in boiling salted water. Refresh and drain.

Clean and trim all the mushrooms. Sauté in ½ cup butter. Salt and pepper to taste.

Cook the garlic cloves in boiling water until tender. Drain, cool, and peel.

Heat the yogurt and crème fraîche in a saucepan. Stir in the wine, olive oil, and vinegar. Whisk in 6 tablespoons butter, piece by piece. Stir in the chopped herbs and season with salt and pepper.

Reheat all the vegetables separately in 1 to 2 tablespoons butter. Plunge the ravioli into lightly salted simmering water to warm it. Remove with a slotted spoon and place in the center of deep plates. Arrange the vegetables around the sides and spoon the sauce over the top. Sprinkle with salt and pepper.

NOTE: In keeping with the spirit of this dish, the choice of vegetables should vary from season to season.

Yogurt made from sheep's milk is difficult to obtain in the United States. You can substitute crème fraîche or a good-quality cow's milk yogurt. Apremont is a delicate white wine from the Savoy.

Preparation: 1½ hours

Cooking time: 1 hour

Serves 4

—

for the court bouillon:

3 TENDER CARROTS

2 SHALLOTS

2 PARSLEY SPRIGS

1 FRESH THYME SPRIG

2 GARLIC CLOVES

2 BAY LEAVES

1 LEMON, PEELED WITH A SERRATED KNIFE

1 ONION, STUDDED WITH 1 WHOLE CLOVE

25 WHITE PEPPERCORNS, CRACKED

¼ CUP COARSE SEA SALT

4 CUPS *ROUSSETTE DE SAVOY* OR SIMILAR FRESH, CRISP WHITE WINE

2 CUPS WATER

20 CRAYFISH, CLEANED

1½ POUNDS VEAL SWEETBREADS

SALT

12 FRESH MORELS

9 TABLESPOONS UNSALTED BUTTER

for aromatics:

2 CARROTS

1 MEDIUM ONION

2 SHALLOTS

1 SMALL LEEK

1 GARLIC CLOVE

1 FRESH THYME SPRIG

2 BAY LEAVES

1 WHOLE CLOVE

4 CUPS VEAL CONSOMMÉ OR STOCK

20 GARLIC CLOVES, UNPEELED

4 OUNCES FRESH SPINACH

2 TABLESPOONS ALL-PURPOSE FLOUR

LARGE PINCH OF CURRY POWDER

MUSTARD

2 CUPS HEAVY CREAM

PAUPIETTES OF VEAL SWEETBREADS, WITH CRAYFISH, MORELS, AND A WHITE WINE GARLIC SAUCE

To prepare the court bouillon, chop the carrots and shallots and place in a large nonreactive saucepan along with the parsley, thyme, garlic, bay leaves, lemon, and onion. Pour in 3 cups of the wine and the water. Add the peppercorns and salt. Bring to a boil, then simmer for about 30 minutes. Strain through a fine sieve, return to the heat, and bring to a boil. Plunge the crayfish into the boiling court bouillon; return to a boil, and boil 3 minutes. Remove from the heat and let cool. Remove the crayfish and store in the refrigerator.

Pierce the sweetbreads with a larding needle (or knitting needle) and soak in cold water for 1 hour, changing the water once or twice. Blanch for 3 minutes in boiling salted water. Drain, rinse, and trim, discarding the skin.

Stem the morels. Soak for 30 minutes in tepid water. Lift out to drain, and blanch in boiling water.

To prepare the aromatics, peel and chop the vegetables. In a large deep sauté pan, heat 3 tablespoons of the butter and cook the aromatics until softened. Set the sweetbreads on top of the vegetables. Add ¾ cup of the wine and the consommé to cover. Cover and cook gently for 15 minutes. Remove the sweetbreads and keep warm.

Meanwhile, cook the garlic cloves until tender in boiling salted water. Peel and keep warm.

Stem the spinach and blanch the leaves in boiling salted water. Drain.

To make the sauce, strain the sweetbreads cooking liquid into a saucepan. Add the remaining ¼ cup wine and reduce the liquid by half. Stir 1 tablespoon butter and the flour together; whisk it into the sauce along with the curry and mustard. Whisk in the cream and reduce once again to obtain a sauce of a nice consistency.

Peel the crayfish and reheat.

Cut the sweetbreads into 4 serving pieces. Roll up each piece in a spinach leaf to make *paupiettes*; you will need 1 *paupiette* per person. Keep warm. Drain the morels and cook in 2 tablespoons of the butter.

Strain the sauce through a fine sieve into another saucepan. At the last minute, whisk in 3 tablespoons butter bit by bit over medium heat. Cut the *paupiettes* in half and place on plates. Arrange the crayfish and morels around the *paupiettes*. Surround with the sauce and serve.

Preparation: 1½ hours

Cooking time: 3 hours

Serves 8

—

for the meringue:

4 LARGE EGGS WHITES

½ CUP GRANULATED SUGAR

½ CUP CONFECTIONERS' SUGAR

for the lace cookies:

4 CUPS SUGAR

1½ CUPS ALL-PURPOSE FLOUR

GRATED ZEST AND JUICE OF 4 ORANGES

1 CUP UNSALTED BUTTER, MELTED

for the pears:

4 RIPE PEARS

JUICE OF 1 LEMON

¾ CUP HONEY

1 TABLESPOON UNSALTED BUTTER

for the apples:

4 GOLDEN DELICIOUS APPLES

¼ CUP SUGAR

1 TABLESPOON UNSALTED BUTTER

2 TABLESPOONS PASTRY CREAM
(SEE NOTE)

for the sabayon:

4 LARGE EGG YOLKS

¼ CUP CONFECTIONERS' SUGAR

¾ CUP VIN DE RIPAILLE (SEE NOTE)

1 CUP FRESH RASPBERRIES

LACE COOKIES FROM THONON-LES-BAIN WITH PEARS, APPLES, AND RASPBERRIES AND SABAYON SAUCE

To make the meringue, preheat the oven to 200°F. Beat the egg whites until stiff peaks form. With a wooden spoon, lightly fold in the sugars. Form into 16 ovals about 2 inches long on a baking sheet lined with parchment paper. Bake the meringues for about 3 hours. Store in an airtight container.

To make the lace cookies, preheat the oven to 350°F. In a large bowl, combine the sugar, flour, orange juice and zest, and melted butter. Set aside for 1 hour. Using a large spoon, spread three-quarters of the batter onto a buttered baking sheet. Onto a second buttered baking sheet, drop small mounds of the batter and spread into small ovals. Bake for 6 to 7 minutes. Cut the large cookie into long strips about 1 inch wide. Quickly wrap the strips around 16 individual oval molds. When the cookies have hardened, remove from the molds and store in a dry place. Pinch the end of each cookie oval to form a little wing. Store in a dry place.

To cook the pears and apples, peel and core the pears; sprinkle with lemon juice to prevent browning. Cut into cubes. Cook with the honey and butter in a skillet over medium heat until lightly caramelized. Drain and set aside.

Peel and core the apples. Cut into cubes and brown in the sugar and butter in a skillet over medium heat. They should be uniformly golden, but take care that they don't turn to mush. Drain in a colander. Toss in a bowl with the pastry cream.

To make the sabayon, in a small deep skillet, combine the egg yolks, sugar, and wine. Whisk over low heat, then cook, whisking, in a water bath or the top of a double boiler until light and frothy, about 5 minutes. Keep warm in the water bath.

To serve, set 2 lace cookie ovals on each dessert plate. Place a meringue oval in the center of each cookie oval. Fill one oval with pears, the other with apples. Spoon the sabayon over the fruits and onto the plate. Sprinkle with raspberries. Serve immediately.

NOTE: The basic ingredients for the chef's pastry cream are 1 cup milk, 5 tablespoons sugar, 1 tablespoon flour, 1 tablespoon cornstarch, 2 large egg yolks, and 1 vanilla bean. Prepare according to the standard method.

Vin de Ripaille is a dry and fruity wine that comes from the region known as Haute-Savoie—near the Swiss border and close to Thonon-les-Bain.

MÂCON

A LAND OF VINEYARDS AND OF GASTRONOMIC OPULENCE, THE MÂCON IS LOCATED IN THE SOUTH OF BURGUNDY ABOUT SIXTY MILES NORTH OF LYON FROM WHICH IT IS SEPARATED BY BEAUJOLAIS AND THE DOMBES. TWO SCENES, TWO DÉCORS, MAKE UP THIS LAND ON BOTH SIDES OF THE SAÔNE, A WIDE, MAJESTIC, AND TRANQUIL RIVER. ON THE RIGHT, THE HILLS RISE UP IN THREE LEVELS. ON THE LEFT, THE BRESSE PLAIN STRETCHES OUT TO THE EAST UP TO THE WALLS OF THE JURA, WHICH SEPARATE FRANCE FROM SWITZERLAND, AND THE ALPS OF SAVOY.

IT IS HERE THAT "THE MIDI BEGINS TO SING A LITTLE," AS GASTON ROUPNEL, A GREAT BURGUNDIAN, HAS SAID. INDEED, IN THIS REGION THE INFLUENCES OF THE MIDI HAVE ALWAYS CROSSED THOSE OF NORTHERN EUROPE. THIS IS AS APPARENT IN THE ROMAN TILES OF THE ARCHITECTURE AS IN THE LANDSCAPE. THE POET LAMARTINE, BORN IN MÂCON, EVEN CLAIMED THAT HIS HOMETOWN HAD SOMETHING "SPANISH" ABOUT IT. AT NOONDAY, ONE CAN HEAR THE CHIRRING OF THE FIRST CICADAS IN THE THICKETS OF ACACIA.

BRESSE OFFERS A STRONG CONTRAST TO THE HILLS OF THE RIGHT BANK. AN ALLUVIAL PLAIN, IT IS THE FRUIT OF THE DEPOSITS OF THE SAÔNE, THE AIN, AND OF NUMEROUS RIVERS AND STREAMS THAT FEED THESE TWO GREAT TRIBUTARIES OF THE RHÔNE. BRESSE IS WATER, GRASS, RICH PRODUCTIVE EARTH, AND SECRET LANDSCAPES OF WOODS AND RUTTED PATHS THAT OPEN ONTO FIELDS WHERE RICH FARMS AND GREAT FLOCKS PROSPER. FOR CENTURIES, THE AREAS OF LOUHANS AND BOURG HAVE BEEN THE FOOD-PROVIDING LANDS FOR NOT ONLY THE MÂCON BUT ALSO FOR BURGUNDY AND THE LYONNAIS. NOT COUNTING THE WINE, WHICH COMES FROM THE HILLSIDES, ALL THE GIFTS OF AGRICULTURE PARTICIPATE IN BRESSE IN A UNFLAGGING PROSPERITY WHICH EXPRESSES ITSELF, FIRST AND FOREMOST, IN THE CUISINE.

A GLIMPSE AT TRADITION

Old-Fashioned Tripe with White Burgundy

Cut 2½ to 3 pounds cleaned tripe into ¼-inch strips. In a large enameled cast-iron casserole or stainless-steel pot, melt 5 tablespoons unsalted butter. Add 2 chopped onions and 2 minced shallots. Cook over medium-high heat, stirring often, until softened but not browned. Add the tripe, several fresh thyme sprigs, and 1 or 2 fresh bay leaves. Add 1 bottle dry white Burgundy (preferably Mâcon) and enough chicken stock or water to cover. Season with salt, pepper, and a pinch of quatre-épices (a mixture of cinnamon, clove, nutmeg, and pepper, available in some specialty food stores). Cover and cook over medium-low heat for about 3 hours. After 1½ hours cooking, add 4 sliced carrots. When done, adjust the seasoning and stir in some chopped fresh herbs. Sprinkle the top with fresh bread crumbs, drizzle with some melted butter, and run under a broiler until lightly browned.

Bresse is famous not
only for its chickens,
which are controlled like
great wines, but also for
its game and game birds.
To the left, a hare
hunter and his dogs.
ABOVE: The covered
mill at Vonnas on the
Veyle River.

The enigmatic rock at
Solutré and its neighbor
in Vergisson plow
through an ocean of
vines like the bows of
great ships. They domi-
nate the appellations of
Pouilly-Fuissé and Saint-
Véran, where the white
wines of a great finesse
and distinction, which
are famous throughout
the world, are produced.

Georges Blanc, president of the Interprofessional Poultry Committee of Bresse since 1986. He holds in his arms a capon born in April that will compete in December.

OPPOSITE: In Curtafond, Régine and Roger Sibelle, raisers of consistently award-winning poultry. To the left, their "colors of France" capons: blue feet, white feathers, and red crest.

BOTTOM: View from Saint-Laurent: Mâcon and its eleventh-century bridge on the Saône. Still a crossroads of Europe.

Georges Blanc is one of the first great French chefs to have understood the importance of a synergy between his diverse activities. Because of this he is also a wine grower.

Not satisfied with having one of the finest wine cellars in the world (120,000 bottles in more than 2,500 different appellations), Georges Blanc has realized an old dream: that of creating his own vineyard from fallow land. In 1985, he planted 42 acres of Chardonnay in an appellation zone on a site particularly well exposed to Azé, in the Mâcon. Thus was born the domaine of Azenay. Resting on an ultramodern *cuvage*, where the latest in wine technology was set up, the first award-winning vintages of Georges Blanc saw a rapid success both in France and abroad. Under the name of "Cellier d'Azenay," Georges Blanc also opened a prestigious wine shop, which highlights the best wines of French wine growers. A creator permanently on the watch at the summit of the hierarchy, Georges Blanc offers an alliance between tradition and his personal research.

Begin 2 days before

Preparation: 1½ hours

Cooking time: 3 hours

Serves 8

•

2 LEMONS

¾ CUP PLUS 2 TABLESPOONS OLIVE OIL

8 SMALL TOMATOES

SALT AND FRESHLY GROUND BLACK
PEPPER TO TASTE

SUGAR

1 TEASPOON CHOPPED FRESH
THYME LEAVES

2 GARLIC CLOVES, MINCED

10 TO 12 OUNCES ASSORTED WILD
MUSHROOMS, CLEANED

ABOUT 10 TABLESPOONS UNSALTED
BUTTER

24 TINY PEARL ONIONS

24 TINY BABY CARROTS,
WITH FRESH TOPS

4 OUNCES SHELLED FRESH FAVA BEANS

½ GREEN CABBAGE

2 WHOLE GARLIC CLOVES, UNPEELED

4 OUNCES FRESH GREEN PEAS

20 CHICKEN BACKS WITH "OYSTERS"
(SEE NOTE)

2 TABLESPOONS VEGETABLE OIL

for the lemon butter sauce:

4 TABLESPOONS UNSALTED BUTTER, CUT
IN PIECES AND WELL CHILLED

½ CUP WATER

JUICE OF 1 LEMON

¾ CUP DRY WHITE BURGUNDY,
PREFERABLY MÂCON

2 TABLESPOONS CHOPPED FRESH HERBS

SALT AND FRESHLY GROUND BLACK
PEPPER TO TASTE

SEA SALT TO TASTE

WATERCRESS, FOR GARNISH

SPRING STEW OF CHICKEN "OYSTERS" WITH LEMON AND MÂCON WINE

Scrub the lemons well, dry, and cut into thick rounds. Place in a small saucepan and pour over ¾ cup olive oil. Cook over very low heat for 1 hour and cool. Set aside covered. Bring back to heat and cook again for 1 hour every 8 hours for 2 days.

Preheat the oven to 225°F. Peel the tomatoes, halve, and remove the seeds. Season with salt and pepper and sprinkle with sugar. Brush with the remaining 2 tablespoons olive oil. Sprinkle with the thyme leaves and minced garlic. Place on a baking dish lined with parchment and bake for 1½ to 2 hours.

Trim the mushrooms and lightly cook in 2 tablespoons of the butter. Season with salt and pepper. Set aside. Peel the onions and cook in a little salted water with 1 tablespoon of the butter and a pinch of sugar. Cook until the water has evaporated and the onions are glazed but not browned. Peel the carrots and cook the same way as the onions. Set aside. Blanch the fava beans in boiling salted water, peel, and reserve.

Separate the leaves of the cabbage and remove the hard ribs from the center of each leaf. Blanch the trimmed leaves in a large pot of boiling water and drain. Rinse under cold running water and drain again, pressing hard against the strainer to eliminate excess moisture. Cook in 3 tablespoons of the butter until some of the water that the leaves give off has evaporated, being careful to keep the cabbage crisp, not soggy.

Cook the whole garlic cloves in boiling salted water until softened. Rinse under cold running water, peel, and set aside. Cook the green peas in boiling salted water until tender. Rinse under cold running water. Drain and set aside.

Preheat the oven to 400°F. Season the backs with salt and pepper. Place in a large casserole and pour in the vegetable oil. Cook over medium-high heat until lightly browned. Cover and bake for 5 minutes. Remove from the oven, cover, and let sit for 5 minutes. Carefully dislodge the "oysters" from their cavities and discard the backs.

To prepare the lemon butter sauce, cut the butter into small pieces, place on a plate, and chill until very cold. In a small saucepan, combine the water with the lemon juice. Bring to a boil over high heat. Whisking constantly, add the butter bit by bit until well incorporated. Pour the wine into a separate saucepan and boil until almost no liquid remains. Add the butter sauce and 3 tablespoons of the oil used to preserve the lemons. Stir in the herbs and season with salt and pepper. Keep warm.

Reheat the vegetables, separately in 1 tablespoon butter each. Decoratively arrange the vegetables in warmed deep serving plates. Cut the preserved lemons into wide strips and add to the plates. Add the "oysters" and spoon over a small amount of the lemon butter sauce. Grind over some fresh pepper, sprinkle with sea salt, and garnish with watercress.

NOTE: The "oyster" of the chicken is the tender morsel found in the hollow of each of the iliac bones, just above the tail. The French name for this delicacy is *sot-l'y-laisse*, which literally means "the fool leaves it there."

SNAILS WITH WATERCRESS, WHITE BEANS, AND SAINT-VÉRAN

Preparation: 1 1/2 hours

Cooking time: 35 minutes

Serves 6

—

4 DOZEN SNAILS WITH SHELLS

1 1/2 CUPS DRY WHITE BURGUNDY, PREFERABLY SAINT-VÉRAN

3/4 CUP CHICKEN STOCK OR WATER

2 SHALLOTS, MINCED

1/2 CUP FINELY CHOPPED ONION

1/2 CUP FINELY CHOPPED CARROT

1 BOUQUET GARNI

SALT TO TASTE

2 CUPS LOOSELY PACKED WATERCRESS LEAVES

1 CUP LOOSELY PACKED SPINACH LEAVES

1 CUP LOOSELY PACKED FLAT-LEAF PARSLEY LEAVES

3/4 CUP DRIED WHITE BEANS, SOAKED OVERNIGHT IN COLD WATER

1 SMALL ONION, STUDDED WITH 1 WHOLE CLOVE

1 CARROT, PEELED AND COARSELY CHOPPED

2 TABLESPOONS UNSALTED BUTTER

3 TABLESPOONS CRÈME FRAÎCHE

FRESHLY GROUND BLACK PEPPER TO TASTE

1 TABLESPOON WINE VINEGAR

1 TABLESPOON OLIVE OIL

Place the snails (without the shells) in a large saucepan. Add half the wine, all the chicken stock, half the shallots, the chopped onion, carrot, and bouquet garni. Season with salt and cook over very low heat for about 2 hours. Remove from the heat and let the snails cool in the liquid.

Meanwhile, bring a large pot of (unsalted) water to a boil. Add the watercress, spinach, and parsley. Boil for 5 minutes and drain, reserving the cooking liquid. Plunge the blanched greens into a bowl of ice water to refresh. Drain well, transfer to a food processor, and process until smooth. Add a small amount of the cooking liquid as needed to obtain a thin purée. Set aside.

Drain the beans and place in a small saucepan. Add the studded onion and the coarsely chopped carrot. Pour in enough cold water to cover. Simmer until the beans are tender. Season with salt at the end of the cooking. Set the beans aside in their own cooking liquid.

Cut the snails lengthwise in half. Melt the butter over medium-high heat. Add the remaining shallot and the snails. Cook over medium-low heat, stirring often, until the shallots are slightly softened, 2 to 3 minutes. Add the remaining 3/4 cup wine and boil until the liquid has reduced by half. Stir in the crème fraîche and increase the heat to high. Add the green purée and the beans. Season with salt and pepper. Add the vinegar and olive oil. Spoon the snails into their shells with a small amount of the sauce. Place on large shallow serving plates and spoon over the remaining sauce and beans.

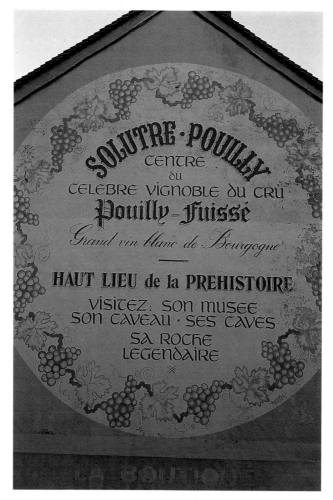

Preparation: 1½ hours

Cooking time: 35 minutes

Serves 6

—

4 WHOLE SOLE, 1½ TO 2 POUNDS EACH

12 OUNCES THIN GREEN BEANS
(*HARICOTS VERTS*)

1½ CUPS UNSALTED BUTTER

4 OUNCES SHALLOTS, THINLY SLICED

1½ CUPS DRY WHITE BURGUNDY,
PREFERABLY POUILLY-FUISSÉ

2 TABLESPOONS CRÈME FRAÎCHE

SALT AND FRESHLY GROUND BLACK
PEPPER TO TASTE

JUICE OF 1 LEMON

SEA SALT TO TASTE

FRESH CHIVES, FOR GARNISH

SOLE COOKED ON THE BONE WITH GREEN BEAN PURÉE AND POUILLY-FUISSÉ SAUCE

Skin, eviscerate, and trim the soles, removing the heads. Cut each fish into 3 equal pieces, without removing the bones. Keep refrigerated until ready to cook.

Trim the ends of the green beans and soak in cold water for 1 hour. Drain and plunge into a large pot of boiling salted water. Cook until tender, then drain and refresh under cold running water. Work the beans through a grinder fitted with the medium blade. Transfer to a saucepan and warm gently over medium heat with 2 tablespoons of the butter.

In a large skillet, heat 7 tablespoons of the butter. Season the sole with salt and pepper and add to the skillet. Cook over low heat, turning carefully, until firm to the touch but not browned. Watch carefully and remove the fish from the skillet when just done. (The small pieces closer to the tail of the sole are thinner and cook more quickly than the thicker parts.) Carefully remove the fish from the bones and gently trim into 24 same-sized rectangular pieces.

In a small heavy saucepan, heat 3 tablespoons of the butter. Add the shallots and cook, stirring often, over medium-low heat until softened but not browned, 3 to 5 minutes. Reserve 2 tablespoons of the wine and pour the rest into the saucepan. Bring to a boil and cook until the amount of liquid has reduced to 1 tablespoon. Whisk in the crème fraîche. Working on and off the heat, incorporate the remaining ¾ cup butter bit by bit. Season with salt and pepper. Add the reserved 2 tablespoons wine. Stir the lemon juice into the green beans.

Decoratively arrange 4 rectangles of fish on each of 6 warmed serving plates. Add the green bean purée and spoon over some of the sauce with the shallots. Season with several grinds of pepper and sea salt. Garnish with chives and serve at once.

In the Place aux Herbes market in Mâcon, tulips announce spring.

Preparation: 45 minutes

Cooking time: 2 hours

Serves 4

—

12 SMALL TOMATOES

SALT TO TASTE

2 TEASPOONS SUGAR

FRESHLY GROUND BLACK PEPPER TO
TASTE

OLIVE OIL

1 TEASPOON FRESH FLOWERING THYME
LEAVES, CHOPPED

1 GARLIC CLOVE, MINCED

1 LARGE FREE-RANGE CHICKEN,
4½ TO 5 POUNDS (SEE NOTE)

13 TABLESPOONS UNSALTED BUTTER

1 CARROT, COARSELY CHOPPED

1 ONION, COARSELY CHOPPED

1 CELERY RIB, THICKLY SLICED

1 GARLIC CLOVE, UNPEELED

1 BOUQUET GARNI

1 TABLESPOON ALL-PURPOSE FLOUR

2 CUPS DRY WHITE WINE,
PREFERABLY CHARDONNAY

ABOUT 2 CUPS CHICKEN STOCK

1 TABLESPOON CHOPPED FRESH TOMATO

8 OUNCES WILD MUSHROOMS,
PREFERABLY CHANTERELLES

5 OUNCES PEARL ONIONS, PEELED

1 SHALLOT, MINCED

4 OUNCES SLAB BACON, CUT INTO
1 × ¼-INCH STRIPS

COARSE SEA SALT TO TASTE

SEVERAL FRESH THYME SPRIGS,
FOR GARNISH

FRICASSEE OF FREE-RANGE CHICKEN WITH ROASTED TOMATOES AND WILD MUSHROOMS

Preheat the oven to 250° F. Peel the tomatoes, halve, and remove the seeds. Season with salt and sprinkle with the sugar. Season the interior of each half with pepper. Brush with olive oil and sprinkle with the thyme leaves and minced garlic. Place the tomatoes on a large baking sheet lined with parchment and cook until very soft, 1½ to 2 hours. Reserve.

Remove the legs of the chicken and cut each in half at the joint. Remove the breast and cut in half, leaving the breast on the bone. In a large skillet, heat 5 tablespoons of the butter. Add the chicken pieces and cook over medium-high heat, turning often, until browned on all sides. Season with salt and pepper. Add the carrot, onion, celery, garlic, and bouquet garni. Stir well and sprinkle in the flour. Cook for a few minutes longer, until the flour is lightly browned. Pour in the wine and enough of the chicken stock to cover. Add the chopped tomato, cover, and simmer gently for 25 to 30 minutes.

Trim, clean, and blanch the mushrooms. Pat dry with clean kitchen towels and sauté with 2 tablespoons of the butter in a large skillet over high heat until the water that they give off has evaporated. Season with salt and pepper.

Brown the pearl onions, shallot, and bacon in 3 tablespoons of the butter. Add a little of the cooking liquid from the chicken and simmer until tender.

When the chicken is done, transfer the pieces to a large plate or platter. Remove the breast meat from the bone. Strain the cooking liquid through a fine sieve over the pearl onion mixture. Cook until slightly reduced and stir in the remaining 3 table-spoons butter. Season with salt and pepper.

To serve, arrange the mushrooms decoratively on 4 warmed serving plates. Garnish the plate with the oven-cooked tomatoes and the pearl onions. Add the pieces of chicken and spoon over the sauce. Season with several grinds of pepper and sea salt. Decorate with sprigs of fresh thyme and serve at once.

NOTE: The original recipe calls for a *poulet de Bresse,* the finest chickens available in France. To be certified, the bird must come from the Bressane breed and be raised near Bresse, a village in Burgundy. The birds must be "free-range" and be fed according to certain high standards. These are not available in the United States, but a good-quality free-range chicken will work just fine for this recipe.

The Ferme de l'Ile in Vonnas, a building from the eleventh century. Marcelle and Jeanette Lacombe are like flowers.

—

1 LARGE FREE-RANGE CHICKEN,
ABOUT 5 POUNDS

for the marinade and the cooking:

4 CUPS DRY WHITE WINE,
PREFERABLY CHARDONNAY

2 QUARTS STRONG RED WINE

4 CUPS CHICKEN STOCK

1½ CUPS RUBY PORT

1 CUP COGNAC

1 CUP WINE VINEGAR

12 OUNCES SALT PORK, DICED AND
BLANCHED IN BOILING WATER FOR
5 MINUTES

12 OUNCES BONELESS, SKINLESS
CHICKEN BREAST, DICED

4 OUNCES PEELED CARROTS, COARSELY
CHOPPED

4 OUNCES ONIONS, QUARTERED

1 LARGE LEEK, TRIMMED AND THICKLY
SLICED

4 GARLIC CLOVES

1 BOUQUET GARNI

for the stuffing:

4 OUNCES CHOPPED BLACK TRUFFLES

6 OUNCES COOKED FOIE GRAS

1 SHALLOT, MINCED AND COOKED

½ CUP CRÈME FRAÎCHE

¼ CUP TRUFFLE JUICE

2 LARGE EGGS

2 LARGE EGG YOLKS

SALT AND FRESHLY GROUND BLACK
PEPPER TO TASTE

4 OUNCES CAUL FAT

30 WHITE MUSHROOMS

2 CUPS CHICKEN STOCK

for the sauce:

½ CUP BLOOD (SEE NOTE)

3 TABLESPOONS UNSALTED BUTTER

1 OUNCE PURÉED FOIE GRAS

SALT AND FRESHLY GROUND BLACK
PEPPER TO TASTE

CHICKEN BALLOTINE À LA ROYALE

Completely bone the chicken, reserving the wings, neck, and liver for another use. (This can be done by a butcher.) Crack the trimmed bones and place in a very large bowl. Add all of the marinade ingredients. Season the boned chicken with salt and pepper. Place the chicken in the marinade, cover, and refrigerate for 24 hours. Drain the chicken and separate the marinade, the bones, the vegetables, and the dices of salt pork and chicken. Set aside.

To prepare the stuffing, chop the dices of salt pork and chicken breast and place in a large bowl. Add all of the stuffing ingredients and mix well. Place the chicken skin side down on a large work surface. Fill with the stuffing and gently form into the original shape of the chicken. Use kitchen string and a trussing needle to sew all of the openings and secure the stuffing. Wrap well in the caul fat and place in the center of a damp large kitchen towel. Roll the chicken in the towel to form a cylinder in the shape of a classic ballotine. Tie with kitchen string and refrigerate for 12 hours.

To cook the ballotine, combine half of the liquid marinade and the 2 cups chicken stock in a straight-sided pot large enough to hold the stuffed chicken snugly. Add the chicken, cover, cook over very low heat (not more than 150°F) for 6 hours. (This step is essential to conserve the creamy moist texture of the dish.)

Meanwhile, flute the mushrooms for garnish: Hold the blade of a very sharp paring knife at a slight angle to the center of the mushroom. Cut a thin curved strip from the center to the edge of the cap. Continue cutting strips, turning the mushroom at the same time as the knife but in the opposite direction. Trim away the stem. (The mushrooms can be served without fluting, if desired. Simply cut away the stem and leave the caps whole.)

To prepare the sauce, brown the reserved bones from the marinade in a large skillet. Add the vegetables from the marinade, cook a few minutes longer, and pour in the remaining half of the liquid marinade. Cook slowly over low heat for 2½ hours. Remove from the heat and add the blood. (Do not boil once you have thickened the sauce with blood.) Strain this mixture through a fine sieve into a small saucepan. Working over low heat, whisk in the butter and puréed foie gras. Do not boil. Season with salt and pepper.

Carefully slice the ballotine and arrange on individual serving plates. Surround with the sauce and garnish with the fluted mushrooms. Serve with a side dish of your choice or by itself. The dish is rich enough to stand on its own.

NOTE: In Europe, fresh blood is often sold with game animals. Pig's blood is often substituted and is perfect for this recipe. It is available in the United States from specialty butchers but might need to be ordered in advance. Finely chopped raw liver can be substituted with excellent results.

An armful of *mousseron* mushrooms from the fields, my favorite mushrooms.

4 RIPE TOMATOES

SALT TO TASTE

1 TEASPOON SUGAR

FRESHLY GROUND BLACK PEPPER TO
TASTE

OLIVE OIL

1 TEASPOON FRESH FLOWERING THYME
LEAVES, CHOPPED

1 GARLIC CLOVE, MINCED

3 TO 3⅓ POUNDS FROG'S LEGS

ABOUT 10 TABLESPOONS UNSALTED
BUTTER

1½ CUPS DRY WHITE WINE,
PREFERABLY MÂCON BLANC

24 SPRING ONIONS, TRIMMED

2 LEEKS, WHITE PART ONLY

2 SHALLOTS, MINCED

½ TEASPOON MILD CURRY POWDER

1 TABLESPOON ALL-PURPOSE FLOUR

1¼ CUPS CRÈME FRAÎCHE

COARSE SEA SALT TO TASTE

FRESH CHERVIL SPRIGS, FOR GARNISH

CIRCLES OF FROG'S LEGS WITH TOMATOES AND CURRY SAUCE

Preheat the oven to 250° F. Peel the tomatoes, halve, and remove the seeds. Season with salt and sprinkle with the sugar. Season the interior of each half with pepper. Brush with olive oil and sprinkle with the thyme and minced garlic. Place the tomatoes on a large baking sheet lined with parchment and cook until very soft, 1½ to 2 hours. Reserve.

In a saucepan, combine the frog's legs with 6 tablespoons of the butter and half the wine. Cook over low heat until the flesh has turned white and is firm to the touch. Remove from the heat and drain, reserving the cooking liquid. Debone the legs, being careful to not tear the flesh. Set aside, covered, with the strained cooking liquid.

Bring a large pot of salted water to a boil. Add the spring onions and bring back to a boil. Simmer until tender. Drain, cool under cold running water, and set aside.

Cut the leeks into thin julienne strips and cook in 2 to 3 tablespoons of the butter over low heat until softened. Season with salt and pepper. Set aside.

In a small heavy saucepan, combine the remaining ¾ cup wine with the shallots. Bring to a boil over high heat and reduce by half. Add 1 cup of the frog's leg cooking liquid and the curry powder. Stir together 1 tablespoon of the butter and the flour and whisk it into the pan. Divide the sauce between 2 small saucepans. Add the crème fraîche to one saucepan. Cook both over medium-high heat until thick and smooth.

Place a 2-inch metal flan ring, at least 1½ inches tall, in the center of each of 4 serving plates. Place one of the cooked tomato halves in the bottom of each ring. Mix the frog's legs with the sauce without cream in a small bowl. Stir to coat and season with salt and pepper. Spoon a layer of the coated frog's legs over the tomato. Add a spoonful of the cooked leeks. Top with another layer of frog's legs and season with pepper. Place another tomato half on top of the frog's legs and brush the tomato with a little olive oil. Surround the rings with a little of the creamy sauce and place the remaining frog's legs and cooked leeks decoratively around the edges of the plates. Garnish with the spring onions and several sprigs of chervil. Carefully remove the rings and serve at once.

Preparation: 1 1/2 hours

Cooking time: 30 minutes

Serves 4

for the cookie crisps:
1/2 CUP SUGAR

1/4 CUP ALL-PURPOSE FLOUR

1 TEASPOON GRATED ORANGE ZEST

JUICE OF 1/2 ORANGE

2 TABLESPOONS UNSALTED BUTTER, MELTED

for the pears:
4 CUPS SUGAR

2 CUPS WATER

1 VANILLA BEAN

4 FIRM PEARS, PEELED, HALVED, AND CORED

1/2 CUP HONEY

for the pistachio custard sauce:
1 CUP MILK

1 VANILLA BEAN

2 LARGE EGG YOLKS

1/3 CUP SUGAR

1 TO 2 OUNCES PISTACHIO PASTE, AVAILABLE FROM MAIL-ORDER PASTRY SUPPLIERS

for the spoom:
1 1/4 CUPS SUGAR

JUICE OF 1/2 LEMON

JUICE OF 1/2 ORANGE

1/2 CUP PLUS 2 TABLESPOONS WATER

1 CUP SPARKLING WINE, PREFERABLY CRÉMANT DE BOURGOGNE

2 LARGE EGG WHITES

FRESH MINT LEAVES, FOR GARNISH

HONEY-ROASTED PEARS WITH PISTACHIO CUSTARD SAUCE AND SPARKLING WINE SPOOM

To prepare the cookie crisps, mix the sugar with the flour in a large bowl. Add the orange zest and the orange juice, little by little, to form a smooth batter. Gently stir in the melted butter. Set aside to rest for 1 hour.

Preheat the oven to 325°F and butter a large baking sheet. Use the back of a spoon to spread the batter in one thin layer on the baking sheet. Cook for 6 to 7 minutes. While it is hot, cut into 1 1/4-inch-wide strips. Use the warm strips to line small oval molds, pressing them against the sides. Let cool and unmold. Keep in a cool dry spot until ready to assemble the dish.

To prepare the pears, combine the sugar and the water in a large saucepan. Add the vanilla bean and bring to a boil over high heat. Boil the syrup for 5 minutes, then add the pears. Reduce the heat and gently poach until softened but still slightly firm. Cool completely. Reserve the vanilla bean to use for garnish.

To make the custard sauce, scald the milk with the vanilla bean in a small saucepan. In a heatproof bowl, whisk the egg yolks with the sugar until light. Add the hot milk and stir until the sugar is dissolved. Return the mixture to the saucepan and cook over medium-low heat, stirring constantly, until slightly thickened. Remove the pan from the heat, add the pistachio paste, and blend well. Set aside to cool. Remove the vanilla bean and refrigerate until ready to serve.

To prepare the spoom, combine half the sugar, the lemon and orange juices, and 1/2 cup water in a large saucepan. Bring to a boil over high heat, remove from the heat, and stir in the sparkling wine. Mix well and freeze. Twenty minutes before serving, combine the remaining sugar with 2 tablespoons water in a large saucepan. Bring to a boil and boil to just below the soft-ball stage, about 230°F on a candy thermometer. Beat the egg whites until stiff, and with the beaters in motion, slowly pour in the boiling syrup. Beat until the meringue is cool. Remove the sorbet from the freezer and slightly soften. Using a rubber spatula, delicately fold the meringue into the sorbet. (Do not stir or the mixture will liquefy.) Return to the freezer.

To assemble the dish, cut each pear half into 4 slices. Place the honey in a large skillet and heat until it starts to caramelize. Add the pear pieces to the honey and cook over medium heat, turning often, until golden. Drain on a rack and set 24 of the nicest slices aside. Finely dice the remaining pear pieces. Finely cut the reserved vanilla bean lengthwise into thin "antennae." Place one cookie crisp in the center of each of 4 individual serving plates. Fill the centers with equal amounts of the diced pears. On each side of the crisps, decoratively arrange 3 pear slices. Garnish with the vanilla bean "antennae" and two teardrop-shaped spoonfuls of the pistachio sauce. Top the pears in the crisps with a scoop of the spoom and decorate with a mint sprig. Serve at once.

The Bresse rooster at the corner of the restaurant, bathed in the light of early morning.

Preparation: 1½ hours

Cooking time: 1 hour 10 minutes

Serves 4

—

2 GRAPEFRUIT

2 ORANGES

CONFECTIONERS' SUGAR

4 OUNCES RASPBERRIES

8 OUNCES STRAWBERRIES,
HULLED AND HALVED

4 OUNCES WILD STRAWBERRIES
(*FRAISES DES BOIS*)

1½ CUPS SPARKLING WINE,
PREFERABLY BRUT D'AZENAY
(CRÉMANT DE BOURGOGNE)

JUICE OF 2 ORANGES

1 TO 2 TABLESPOONS FRESH LEMON
JUICE

1 TABLESPOON SUGAR

RED FRUIT, CITRUS FRUIT, AND CANDIED ZESTS WITH SPARKLING WINE

With a large serrated knife, cut a slice from the top and bottom of the grapefruit. Working from the top to the bottom, cut away the zest, pith, and skin following the curve of the fruit. Cut down through the flesh on either side of the membrane to remove whole sections. Keep the sections covered in the refrigerator until ready to assemble the dish.

Trim the grapefruit peel into long pieces about the size of a thick French fry. Bring a large pot of water to a boil and add the peels. Boil for 5 minutes, then refresh under cold running water. Repeat this procedure 5 times. After they have been blanched, transfer to a scale and weigh. In a large saucepan, add an equal weight of sugar, the peels, and a couple spoonfuls of water. Start cooking over medium-low heat and gradually increase the heat until the mixture boils. Reduce the heat to low and simmer until the peels are transparent, about 50 minutes. Using a slotted spoon, transfer the candied peels to drain on wire racks.

Repeat this step with the oranges.

Arrange 3 grapefruit sections and 3 orange sections decoratively on individual serving plates. Form triangles of raspberries on one end of the plate and place the strawberries on top of the sectioned fruit. Arrange the wild strawberries on the opposite end of the raspberries and cover the plates well. Chill thoroughly.

In a small bowl, combine the sparkling wine, orange juice, lemon juice, and sugar. Whisk well to blend, then chill.

Just before serving, decoratively arrange the candied peels around the plates of fruit. Spoon on the wine mixture and serve at once.

BEAUJOLAIS - LYONNAIS

Today, as in the past, Lyon is a crossroads of business and other highly important influences. Through this place pass travelers and goods going to or coming from the countries of the Mediterranean and the Alps toward northwestern France and northern Europe. Before the invention of the railroad or the airplane, it was here that one left the Rhône for the Saône and for the other founding river of France: the Loire. All arrived at the wharves of Roanne by the great roads of the Lyonnais and Beaujolais. The gastronomy of the Lyonnais and the importance of the wines of Beaujolais were born of the necessity of satisfying the demands of such a large number of people in transit as well as feeding the local population. The cuisine and the wines naturally show the diversity of tastes and refinements. The tastes of the sturdy carters, those of the traveler and of the canvasser, those of the merchant and the banker, those of the noblewoman and the powerful lord—all found appropriate dishes here. To the local dishes of fish, innards, and charcuterie, complemented by waves of the "third river" (Beaujolais), are added those that are only possible by close alliance with neighboring lands: *primeurs*, game from the Dombes, the riches of Bresse and Bugey, meats from Forez, the Vivarais, from Viennois and the Dauphiné, fruits of all seasons from the Rhône Valley, truffles from the Valentinois, cheeses from nearby mountains often eaten in their first youth. Yet the Lyonnais element asserts itself over all. It gives its own interpretation, adding to it that element that makes it a cuisine. Lyon is the cradle of the creative stove. Beaujolais, a solid unassuming wine, suitable for loosening tongues and relationships, deserves a place of honor in this good trade.

A GLIMPSE AT TRADITION

Hot Sausages Cooked in Wine Branch Ashes

—

Dig a hole in soil and build a fire using grapevine trimmings. Burn down to a gray ash. In a large piece of aluminum foil, combine fresh sausages with red wine and wine sediments. (Sediments, lie-de-vin, are found in the bottom of the barrels used to store wine. Composed primarily of tannins and yeasts, these residues are scraped out of barrels and used for cooking in some wine regions.) Seal the packets as tightly as possible and place on top of the ashes. Cook slowly for 1 hour. Remove from the heat and open carefully. Cut the sausages into thick slices and serve with fresh butter, good crusty bread, and hot potatoes. Serve with a light, fresh Beaujolais wine.

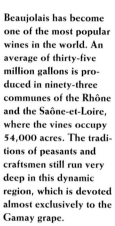

Beaujolais has become one of the most popular wines in the world. An average of thirty-five million gallons is produced in ninety-three communes of the Rhône and the Saône-et-Loire, where the vines occupy 54,000 acres. The traditions of peasants and craftsmen still run very deep in this dynamic region, which is devoted almost exclusively to the Gamay grape.

At the north of the appellation, ten famous *crus* produce great wines, which may be aged for a long time: Brouilly and Côte de Brouilly, Régnié, Morgon, Chiroubles, Fleurie, Moulin-à-Vent, Chénas, Juliénas, and Saint-Amour.

The first rule in this profession is never to cheat. Georges Duboeuf has given this commercial principle a universal value.

The Beaujolais region is at the crossroads of three climates; while this may put the harvests at risk, it can also produce miracles. On the whole, the vineyards receive good sun and autumn is warm. The flowering takes place in the first two weeks of June; the harvests, in the last half of September. As is the wine that will come from them, these harvests are very popular in this land of sharecroppers.

In a mere thirty years, Georges Duboeuf has garnered all titles. It has been said that he is the king, the pope, the poet of Beaujolais. He could well be, in addition, the father of modern Beaujolais, which has become, perhaps, the best-known wine in the world. With his perfect knowledge of wine growing and the ten *crus* that together make Beaujolais, Georges Duboeuf has succeeded in creating a style: a Beaujolais that is honest and easy drinking, free of the diluting of the past, a pure Gamay, "mischievous and talkative" that animates the cooking of amateurs as well as that of chefs. If the legend of this son of Crêches-sur-Saône has taken hold, it is because of his professional obstinacy in remaining true to the principle that Paul Blanc impressed on him at the start of his career: "Never cheat." Duboeuf has maintained his idea: to respect the personality of Beaujolais while selling only those wines that he likes.

MICHAEL TROISGROS

Restaurant Troisgros
Roanne
Loire

———

Preparation: 40 minutes

Cooking time: 1½ hours

Serves 4

●

4 PERCH, ABOUT 12 OUNCES EACH

SALT AND FRESHLY GROUND BLACK
PEPPER TO TASTE

½ CUP (4 OUNCES) IMPORTED FRENCH
LENTILS, PREFERABLY *LENTILLES DE PUY*

1 GARLIC CLOVE, MINCED

1 TO 2 OUNCES SLAB BACON,
DICED AND COOKED CRISP

2 SHALLOTS, MINCED

10 TABLESPOONS UNSALTED BUTTER

1 TEASPOON TOMATO PASTE

¾ CUP LIGHT RED BURGUNDY,
PREFERABLY GAMAY DE LA CÔTE
ROANNAISE

3 TO 4 OUNCES SMOKED BEEF MARROW,
CUT INTO ¼-INCH-THICK SLICES

ALL-PURPOSE FLOUR

SNIPPED FRESH CHIVES

COARSE SEA SALT

CRACKED PEPPERCORNS

PERCH FILLETS À LA ROANNAISE WITH SMOKED MARROW

Eviscerate and scale the fish. Remove the fillets and make 3 small parallel incisions in the skin of each fillet to score. Season with salt and pepper.

Rinse the lentils and place in a large saucepan (see Note). Cover with cold water, bring to a boil, and cook until tender. Drain well, season with salt, pepper, half of the minced garlic, and the bacon.

To prepare the sauce, cook the shallots in 2 tablespoons of the butter over medium-high heat until softened but not browned. Stir in the tomato paste and add the wine. Cook until reduced by three-quarters. Strain through a fine sieve and whisk in 4 tablespoons of the butter. Season with salt and pepper.

Poach the marrow in gently simmering salted water until tender, about 2 minutes. Do not boil or the marrow will fall apart.

Preheat the oven to 400°F. Dust the fish fillets with a little flour and shake off the excess. Melt the remaining 4 tablespoons butter in a large skillet. Add the fish, skin side down, and cook over medium-high heat until the skin is crisp. Transfer to an oiled baking sheet and finish cooking the fillets in the oven, about 2 minutes.

To assemble the dish, spread a small amount of the lentils in the center of individual serving plates. Top with the perch fillets, skin side up. Roll the marrow in the snipped chives, the remaining minced garlic, sea salt, and peppercorns and place on top of the fish. Drizzle the sauce on the side and serve at once.

NOTE: You can add a tiny dice (*brunoise*) of carrots to the lentils when you cook them.

**Burning the branches
after pruning.**

Begin the day before

Preparation: 1½ hours

Cooking time: 8½ hours

Serves 12

——

5 WHOLE OXTAILS

1 POUND BEEF BLADE OR CHUCK ROAST

8 OUNCES BEEF SHORT RIBS

2 LARGE MARROW BONES

3 CALVES' FEET

3 CARROTS, PEELED

3 ONIONS, EACH STUDDED WITH
1 CLOVE

1 SMALL CELERY ROOT (CELERIAC),
PEELED AND QUARTERED

2 BOUQUETS GARNIS

2 WHITE TURNIPS, PEELED AND TRIMMED

2 LEEKS, TRIMMED

3 JUNIPER BERRIES

COARSE SALT

WHOLE BLACK PEPPERCORNS

4½ TO 5 POUNDS SHALLOTS

8 OUNCES GOOSE FAT
(SEE NOTE, PAGE 96)

2 TEASPOONS SUGAR

1 BOTTLE HEARTY RED WINE, PREFERABLY
BANYULS

3 BOTTLES BEAUJOLAIS WINE

ABOUT 1 CUP UNSALTED BUTTER

SALT TO TASTE

40 SMALL FIRM-FLESHED POTATOES

2 LOBES FRESH DUCK FOIE GRAS

FRESHLY GROUND BLACK PEPPER TO
TASTE

SEA SALT TO TASTE

OXTAIL COMPOTE WITH FOIE GRAS *JULIÉNAS*

The day before serving, prepare a pot-au-feu. Trim one of the oxtails of all fat and cut between the vertebrae into thick slices. Place in a large stockpot and add the beef roast, short ribs, marrow bones, and 1 of the calves' feet. Pour in enough cold water to cover and bring to a boil over high heat. Skim frequently to remove all the impurities that rise to the top. Set aside 2 of the carrots, 1 of the onions, ¼ of the celery root, and 1 bouquet garni. Add the remaining carrot, onions, celery root, 1 bouquet garni, the turnips, leeks, juniper berries, coarse salt, and black peppercorns to the pot with the meat. Reduce the heat to low and simmer, skimming often, for 4 hours.

Meanwhile, trim the remaining oxtails and cut each into thick slices. Refrigerate. Set 36 of the shallots aside. Peel the others and set aside.

When the pot-au-feu is done, remove the meats. Strain the cooking liquid, pressing down on the vegetables and seasonings to extract as much flavor as possible. Reserve the vegetables and all meats for another use. (They make an excellent meal in themselves.) Keep the strained liquid refrigerated until ready to use.

The next day, heat about two-thirds of the goose fat in a large pot. Add the remaining oxtails and cook over medium-high heat, turning often, until uniformly browned.

Meanwhile, cut the peeled shallots in half and place in a large saucepan with the remaining goose fat and the sugar. Cook over medium-high heat, stirring often, until golden brown.

Skim off the fat from the pot with the oxtails. Pour in the hearty red wine and increase the heat to high. Boil until almost all of the liquid has evaporated. Pour in the Beaujolais and boil again until almost all of the liquid has evaporated.

Preheat the oven to 300°F. Degrease the cooking liquid from the pot-au-feu and pour it into the pot with the oxtails; bring back to a boil, skimming frequently to remove any impurities that rise to the top. Add the reserved carrots, onion, celery root, and the second bouquet garni. Add the remaining 2 calves' feet and the browned shallots. Season lightly with salt, cover, and transfer to the oven. Bake, stirring from time to time, until the meat falls easily off the bones, about 4 hours.

Remove the meat from the oxtails and calves' feet. Place the meat in a bowl and ladle over enough of the cooking liquid to cover. Set aside.

Strain the cooking liquid through a fine sieve, pressing hard on the solids to extract as much flavor as possible. Pour the strained liquid into a large saucepan and bring to a boil over high heat. Boil, skimming often, until the liquid has reduced by half. Set aside.

While the oxtails are cooking, prepare the whole shallots and the potatoes. Butter a roasting pan and add the unpeeled shallots. Season with salt and bake in the oven with the oxtails, stirring often, until very tender. Peel and cover to keep warm. Peel the potatoes and shape each into a small oval about the size of a large olive. Sauté in 2 tablespoons of the butter in a large ovenproof skillet until lightly browned, about 5 minutes. Cover, add 4 more tablespoons of the butter, and place in the oven with the shallots. Bake until tender. When done, remove from the oven, add a small amount of the beef cooking liquid, and set aside.

Cut the foie gras into thick slices. Season with salt and pepper and keep cool.

Warm the oxtail compote. Heat the reduced beef cooking liquid and whisk in 8 tablespoons of the butter, cut into pieces. Season with salt and pepper.

Place a large nonstick skillet over high heat. When very hot, add the foie gras slices and cook each side until golden brown.

On each plate, place 2 spoonfuls of the oxtail compote in the center. Add one of the foie gras slices and surround with 3 of the whole shallots and 3 ovals of potato. Ladle over some of the beef sauce, season with some ground pepper, and sprinkle with sea salt. Serve at once.

Preparation: 1½ hours

**Cooking time: 2 hours
10 minutes**

Serves 6

for the beans:

1 CUP DRIED WHITE BEANS

1 BOUQUET GARNI

1 GARLIC CLOVE

1 CARROT, PEELED AND DICED

1 WHOLE ONION,
STUDDED WITH A CLOVE

SALT TO TASTE

1 ONION, FINELY CHOPPED

2 TABLESPOONS UNSALTED BUTTER

for the sauce:

10 TABLESPOONS UNSALTED BUTTER

1 TO 1½ POUNDS ASSORTED CHICKEN
PARTS, COARSELY CHOPPED

1 CUP FINELY CHOPPED CARROTS

1 CUP FINELY CHOPPED ONIONS

1 LEEK, TRIMMED AND THINLY SLICED

1 CELERY RIB, THINLY SLICED

3 GARLIC CLOVES

1 FRESH THYME SPRIG

2 FRESH BAY LEAVES

1 WHOLE CLOVE

2 TABLESPOONS ALL-PURPOSE FLOUR

2 BOTTLES BEAUJOLAIS WINE

2 CUPS VEAL STOCK

SALT AND PEPPER TO TASTE

for the herb cakes:

1 MEDIUM ALL-PURPOSE POTATO

1 LEEK, THICKLY SLICED

1 GARLIC CLOVE, PEELED

1 BUNCH FRESH FLAT-LEAF PARSLEY

1 BUNCH FRESH CHERVIL

12 OUNCES FRESH SPINACH LEAVES

1 BUNCH WATERCRESS

2 HEADS BOSTON LETTUCE

4 LARGE EGGS

3 TO 4 TABLESPOONS CRÈME FRAÎCHE

FRESHLY GRATED NUTMEG, TO TASTE

SALT AND PEPPER TO TASTE

for the chicken thighs and "oysters":

4 LARGE CHICKEN THIGHS

6 TABLESPOONS UNSALTED BUTTER

15 CHICKEN BACKS WITH "OYSTERS"
(SEE NOTE, PAGE 130)

4 TABLESPOONS UNSALTED BUTTER

FRESHLY PARSLEY LEAVES, FOR GARNISH

SEA SALT TO TASTE

ROLLED CHICKEN THIGHS AND CHICKEN "OYSTERS" IN BEAUJOLAIS WITH HERB CAKES AND WHITE BEANS

To prepare the beans, soak the beans in cold water for at least 2 hours. Drain and transfer to a large saucepan. Pour in enough cold water to cover and bring to a boil over high heat, skimming to remove any impurities that rise to the top. Add the bouquet garni, garlic, carrot, and whole onion. Cover and reduce the heat to low. Cook until tender, 1½ to 2 hours, depending on the moisture content of the dried beans. Season with salt at the end of cooking.

To make the sauce, melt 6 tablespoons of the butter in a stockpot or soup kettle. Add the chicken parts and cook over medium-high heat, stirring, until lightly colored. Add the carrots, onions, leek, celery, garlic, thyme, bay leaves, and clove. Sprinkle in the flour and stir to coat. Add the wine, bring to a boil, and flame. Add the veal stock, season with salt and pepper, reduce the heat to medium-low, and simmer for 1 hour. Strain through a fine sieve and reserve.

To make the cakes, bring a large pot of salted water to a boil and preheat the oven to 325° F. Peel and dice the potato. Starting with the longest-cooking vegetables like the potatoes, leek, and garlic, boil each separately until tender. End with the most delicate vegetables like the spinach and lettuce. Drain well, rinse under cold running water, and squeeze out excess moisture. Transfer to a food processor and process until smooth. Add the eggs and crème fraîche. Season with nutmeg, salt, and pepper. Carefully butter 6 small individual molds. Fill the molds with the vegetable mixture. Place the molds in a large roasting pan and pour in enough boiling water to come halfway up the sides. Transfer to the oven and cook until a knife inserted in the center comes out clean, 30 to 40 minutes. Keep warm.

Bone the chicken thighs and season with salt and pepper. Form into thick "sausages" and sew the ends closed. Melt 4 tablespoons of the butter in a large skillet. Add the thighs and cook over medium-high heat until browned on all sides. Remove from the heat and wrap each in parchment paper. Finish cooking in a steamer, about 15 minutes. Keep warm until just before serving.

Preheat the oven to 400° F. Melt 2 tablespoons butter in a large casserole. Add the chicken backs and cook over medium-high heat until lightly browned. Transfer to the oven and finish cooking, 4 to 5 minutes. Remove from the oven, cover loosely with foil, and let rest for 15 minutes. Carefully dislodge the "oysters" from their cavities and discard the backs. Keep warm.

To finish the beans, cook the chopped onion in the butter over medium-high heat until softened. Add the beans and cook for about 6 minutes, covered. Keep warm.

To assemble the dish, heat the sauce over medium-high heat and whisk in 4 tablespoons butter. Ladle a small amount of the sauce over the bottom of 6 warmed serving plates. Place a spoonful of the beans at the top of each plate. Set one of the herb cakes in the center and garnished with a leaf of parsley, if desired. Arrange the "oysters" decoratively between the beans and the cake. Cut the thigh rolls into thin slices and arrange around the other side of the cake. Grind over some fresh pepper and season with sea salt just before serving.

Preparation: 1½ hours

Cooking time: 2 hours

Serves 4

—

for the ravioli:

1 WHOLE LARGE GARLIC HEAD,
SEPARATED INTO CLOVES
BUT NOT PEELED

4 OUNCES SHELLED GREEN PEAS

8 6-INCH SQUARES FRESH PASTA

1 LARGE EGG YOLK, LIGHTLY BEATEN

for the wild mushroom and pea garnish:

8 OUNCES WILD MUSHROOMS,
PREFERABLY *MOUSSERONS* (SEE NOTE)

4 TABLESPOONS UNSALTED BUTTER

SALT AND FRESHLY GROUND BLACK
PEPPER TO TASTE

4 OUNCES SHELLED GREEN PEAS

16 GARLIC CLOVES, UNPEELED

for the squabs:

½ CUP UNSALTED BUTTER

8 OUNCES ASSORTED CHICKEN (OR
POULTRY) NECKS, WINGS, AND BACKS,
COARSELY CHOPPED

SALT AND FRESHLY GROUND BLACK
PEPPER TO TASTE

1 ONION, QUARTERED

6 TO 8 WHITE MUSHROOMS,
QUARTERED

2 GARLIC CLOVES, UNPEELED

1 BOUQUET GARNI

2½ CUPS DRY WHITE WINE,
PREFERABLY WHITE BEAUJOLAIS

2 CUPS CRÈME FRAÎCHE

4 SMALL SQUABS

½ CARROT, FINELY CHOPPED

½ ONION, FINELY CHOPPED

2 FRESH THYME SPRIGS

1 BAY LEAF

¼ CUP WATER

2 OUNCES COOKED FOIE GRAS, PURÉED

SEA SALT TO TASTE

SQUAB WITH GARLIC AND PEA-FILLED RAVIOLI AND WHITE BEAUJOLAIS

To make the ravioli, bring a pot of salted water to a boil. Add the garlic and bring back to a boil. Cook until tender, drain, and peel. Cook the peas in boiling salted water until tender and drain. Combine the garlic and the peas in a food processor and purée until smooth. Work through a fine sieve to obtain a smooth purée. Transfer to the refrigerator and chill thoroughly.

Arrange the pasta sheets on a large work surface. Place a spoonful of the pea mixture about the size of a walnut in the center of each sheet. Paint the edges of the pasta with the egg yolk and fold the sheets diagonally to form large triangles. Make sure there are no trapped air bubbles, then crimp the edges to tightly seal. Poach briefly in boiling salted water. Refresh in cold water and drain flat on clean kitchen towels.

To prepare the mushroom and pea garnish, rinse the mushrooms several times in cold water to remove grit. Drain well and sauté briefly in 1 tablespoon of the butter. Season well and reserve. Cook the peas in boiling salted water until tender. Drain and reserve.

Bring a small pot of salted water to a boil. Add the 16 garlic cloves and bring back to a boil. Drain, peel, and reserve.

To prepare the squabs, heat 6 tablespoons of the butter in a large saucepan. Add the chopped chicken parts and cook over medium-high heat until lightly browned. Season with salt and pepper. Add the onion, mushrooms, garlic, and bouquet garni. Cook a few minutes to release the flavors, then pour in 2 cups of the wine. Boil until reduced to just a couple of tablespoons, then stir in the crème fraîche. Cook, uncovered, for 30 minutes. Press through a fine sieve. Set the sauce aside.

Preheat the oven to 400°F. Season the squabs with salt and pepper. In a large casserole, heat the remaining 2 tablespoons butter. Add the squabs, carrot, onion, thyme, and bay leaf. Cook over medium-high heat, turning often, until the squabs are golden brown. Pour in the water, cover, and bake for 15 minutes, basting often.

Remove the squabs to a large plate or platter and cover to keep warm. Pour off any fat in the casserole and pour in the remaining ½ cup wine. Cook over high heat, stirring often, until the wine has evaporated. Pour in the strained creamed sauce and bring back to a boil. Strain into a large saucepan and whisk in the puréed foie gras. Season with salt and pepper, then transfer to a food processor. Process the sauce until smooth. Keep warm. Reheat the ravioli for 30 seconds in boiling water. Reheat the mushrooms, peas, and garlic separately in 1 tablespoon butter each.

Remove the legs from the squabs and carefully separate the breast from the carcass. Trim the pieces well. On 4 warmed serving plates, arrange 2 ravioli and 2 spoonfuls of the peas. Place 2 legs and 2 breasts of squab in between the ravioli. Garnish with the mushrooms and the cooked whole garlic cloves. Spoon over some of the foie gras sauce. Season with sea salt and a grind of black pepper. Serve at once.

NOTE: The original recipe calls for a variety of mushrooms (*mousserons* or meadow mushrooms) that are difficult to find. Any flavorful wild mushroom can be substituted.

In Saint-Amour, in Beaujolais, vineyards are pruned by families.

Begin the day before

Preparation: 2 hours

Cooking time: 7½ hours

Serves 10

—

for the marinade:

8 OUNCES BONED WILD DUCK LEGS

1½ POUNDS WILD DUCK BREAST FILLETS

2 OUNCES PORK, PREFERABLY FROM THE SHOULDER, DICED

2 OUNCES VEAL FILLET, DICED

1 POUND FRESH LARD, DICED

1½ CUPS TRUFFLE JUICE

3 CUPS RUBY PORT

1¾ CUPS COGNAC

1¾ CUPS DRY WHITE WINE, PREFERABLY WHITE BEAUJOLAIS

for the sauce:

BONES AND SCRAPS OF WILD DUCK

1 BOTTLE WHITE BEAUJOLAIS

2 BOTTLES RED BEAUJOLAIS, PREFERABLY MOULIN À VENT

2 TABLESPOONS UNSALTED BUTTER

1 TABLESPOON VEGETABLE OIL

1½ CUPS FINELY CHOPPED CARROTS

1 CUP FINELY CHOPPED ONIONS

½ CUP FINELY CHOPPED CELERY

3 TABLESPOONS ALL-PURPOSE FLOUR

3 CUPS CHICKEN STOCK

1 BOUQUET GARNI

10 BLACK PEPPERCORNS

for the tourtes:

2 LARGE EGGS

2 LARGE EGG YOLKS

½ CUP FRESH BLOOD (SEE NOTE, PAGE 138)

SALT AND FRESHLY GROUND BLACK PEPPER TO TASTE

2 POUNDS PUFF PASTRY

1 TABLESPOON UNSALTED BUTTER

2 SHALLOTS, MINCED

¾ CUP COGNAC

¼ CUP RUBY PORT

1 TEASPOON RED CURRANT JELLY

1¾ CUPS CRÈME FRAÎCHE

WILD DUCK TOURTE WITH MOULIN À VENT

To make the marinade, thinly slice the boned duck legs and 1 pound of the duck breast fillets. Place in a large shallow bowl and add the pork, veal, and lard. Add the truffle juice, port, Cognac, and wine. Add the remaining ½ pound whole breast fillets to the marinade. Cover and refrigerate overnight. The next day, drain and reserve the liquid and the solids separately.

To make the sauce, place the bones and scraps of duck in a bowl. Add enough of the white and red wines to cover (one-third white and two-thirds red). Marinate overnight.

The next day, drain and reserve the liquid and solids separately. Heat the butter and vegetable oil in a large skillet. Add the marinated bones and scraps to the skillet. Cook over medium-high heat, stirring, until lightly browned. Add the carrots, onions, and celery. Cook a few minutes longer to soften, then sprinkle with the flour. Cook 2 to 3 minutes longer. Add the liquids from both of the marinades, the chicken stock, bouquet garni, and peppercorns. Bring to a boil, reduce the heat to medium-low, and simmer for 4 to 5 hours. Strain the liquid. Discard the solids.

To make the tourtes, cut the marinated whole duck breasts fillets into large dice and set aside. Combine the marinated sliced duck, pork, veal, and lard and put through a meat grinder fitted with a medium blade. Stir in one of the eggs, the egg yolks, and blood. Add the diced duck breasts and mix well. Season well with salt and pepper (1 teaspoon salt and ½ teaspoon pepper per pound of stuffing). Transfer the stuffing to a large piece of parchment paper and, using the paper, form a roll about 2 inches in diameter. Twist the ends of the paper closed to seal. Transfer to a covered pot large enough to hold the roll flat. Add about 1 cup of the strained liquid to the bottom of the dish. Cover and cook the roll over low heat (no hotter than 175°F) for about 1½ hours. Remove the roll and cut into 10 thick slices.

Preheat the oven to 500°F. Roll half the puff pastry out thin and cut ten 4-inch circles. Place one of the duck roll slices on the center of each pastry circle. Beat the remaining egg and, using a pastry brush, wet the pastry edges well. Roll the remaining puff pastry out thin and cut 10 more circles slightly larger than the first ones. Place on top of the smaller circles and crimp the edges to seal. Brush the tops with the beaten egg and place on large baking sheets. Bake for 5 minutes. Reduce the oven heat to 375°F and bake until golden, 20 to 25 minutes.

Heat 1 tablespoon butter in a small saucepan. Add the shallot and cook over medium-high heat, stirring, until softened. Pour in the Cognac and the port, increase the heat to high, and bring to a boil. Boil until the liquid has almost evaporated. Add the currant jelly and the crème fraîche. Boil until slightly thickened. Add the remaining strained liquid and boil until thick and reduced. Strain into another saucepan and keep warm.

Cut a small wedge out of each tourte and arrange on individual serving plates with the wedge off to one side. Add a spoonful of the sauce and serve the remaining sauce on the side. Serve with a green salad or seasonal vegetable.

The Moulin à Vent, lord of the *crus* of Beaujolais and the most ancient of appellations.

Preparation: 1½ hours

Cooking time: 10 minutes

Serves 4

●

for the cornucopia:

¾ CUP SUGAR

7 TABLESPOONS ALL-PURPOSE FLOUR

¼ CUP GROUND RED PRALINE
(SEE NOTE)

6 TABLESPOONS BUTTER, MELTED

JUICE OF 1 ORANGE

1 TEASPOON GRATED ORANGE ZEST

for the red wine granité:

¾ CUP LIGHT RED WINE

¾ CUP SUGAR

1½ TEASPOONS GRATED ORANGE ZEST

JUICE OF 1 LEMON

1 CUP GRAPE JUICE

for the citronella syrup:

1½ CUPS WATER • 2 CUPS SUGAR

1 TEASPOON CITRONELLA INFUSION
(SEE NOTE)

for the fruit:

24 TRIMMED PINEAPPLE "STICKS"

24 GRAPEFRUIT SECTIONS

24 ORANGE SECTIONS

4 KIWIS • 1 PEACH • 4 FIGS

8 SMALL CLUSTERS RED CURRANTS

4 OUNCES RASPBERRIES

4 OUNCES STRAWBERRIES

1 BANANA, THICKLY SLICED

½ CUP PURÉED GREEN APPLE PULP

½ CUP PURÉED, SWEETENED, AND
STRAINED RASPBERRY PULP

CORNUCOPIA OF FRESH FRUIT WITH RED WINE GRANITÉ

To make the cornucopia, in a large bowl, combine the sugar, flour, ground praline, butter, and orange juice and zest. Mix well and set aside to rest for 1 hour. Preheat the oven to 325°F. Butter a large baking sheet. With the back of a large spoon, spread the batter thinly over the buttered sheet. Bake for 6 to 7 minutes. Cut into long 1-inch-wide strips. Wrap the strips, overlapping, around stainless-steel cornucopia molds that measure about 6 inches long and about 2 inches in diameter at the widest end. Let cool a few minutes and carefully remove.

To make the granité, pour the wine into a large nonreactive saucepan. Add the sugar and the orange zest. Bring to a boil, then remove from the heat and cool. Stir in the lemon juice and grape juice. Pour the mixture into a large shallow metal pan and freeze, stirring with a fork every 15 minutes to break up the crystals. Cover and keep frozen until ready to serve.

To make the citronella syrup, combine the water and sugar in a large saucepan. Bring to a boil over high heat, stirring to dissolve the sugar. Remove from the heat and add the infusion. Cool and chill thoroughly. Peel and quarter the kiwis and peach. Quarter the figs.

To assemble the dessert, arrange the fruit decoratively on serving plates. Spoon over a small amount of the citronella syrup. Place a scoop of the granité on top of the citrus fruits, then add one of the cornucopia. Add a spoonful of the green apple purée and a spoonful of the raspberry purée on either side of the plate. Serve at once.

NOTE: The recipe calls for ground red pralines, a candied almond not available in the United States. The chef suggests substituting ground, toasted hazelnuts and adding a few drops of red food coloring for similar results.

To make the citronella infusion, place a handful of fresh citronella leaves in a small bowl. Pour in just enough warm water to cover. Let sit overnight, then strain. Discard the leaves and taste. If not sufficiently strong in flavor, start over using the weakly infused liquid.

Preparation: 30 minutes

Cooking time: 20 minutes

Serves 4

●

½ BOTTLE BEAUJOLAIS,
PREFERABLY FLEURIE

½ LITER BOTTLE MINERAL WATER

ZEST OF 3 ORANGES

ZEST OF 2 LEMONS

½ CUP SUGAR

SEVERAL BLACK PEPPERCORNS

GROUND CINNAMON TO TASTE

1 POUND FRESH BLACK CURRANTS,
STEMMED

12 RIPE GREEN FIGS

JUICE OF 1 LEMON OR TO TASTE

GREEN FIG COMPOTE WITH FLEURIE

In a large nonreactive saucepan, combine the wine, mineral water, orange zest, lemon zest, sugar, peppercorns, and cinnamon. Bring to a boil over high heat and boil for 15 minutes. Remove from the heat, add the black currants, cover, and infuse for 5 minutes. Transfer to a fine sieve and strain, pushing hard on the solids to extract as much flavor as possible.

Meanwhile, carefully peel the figs and place them in a large bowl. Pour over the strained wine mixture while the mixture is still warm. Cool, cover, and refrigerate.

Just before serving, gently cut the figs into quarters and place in shallow serving bowls or dessert dishes. Taste the syrup and adjust the tartness with sugar or lemon juice as desired. Ladle the syrup over the figs and *refrigerate.* The figs should be served very cold.

THE RHÔNE VALLEY IS A PREEMINENT PLACE OF PASSAGE. LESS THAN 186 MILES LONG, IT JOINS TOGETHER SEVERAL ANCIENT CULTURES: THE LYONNAIS WITH THE PROVENÇAL, THE BURGUNDIAN WITH THE ANGEVIN, THE SAVOYARD WITH THE ARLÉSIEN, THE PAPAL WITH THE ROMAN CULTURE OF NÎMES. THIS, WITHOUT FORGETTING THE GREEK AS A SUBSTRATUM, NOR JUDAISM, WHICH CAME EVEN BEFORE CHRISTIANITY IN THESE LOCALES. THE WHOLE RIVER, FROM VIENNE ON, BEARS THE MARK OF THE ROMANS. BUT ITS BANKS SAW AN EVEN EARLIER CIVILIZATION, FOR THE NAME RHÔNE IS A REFERENCE TO THE VERY FIRST MERCHANTS—FROM RHODES— WHO USED ITS PATH IN THE DAYS OF TRADE IN AMBER, BRONZE, AND WINE. BY NATURE, THERE IS NO UNITY IN GASTRONOMY. SUPERIMPOSED ON ANCIENT INFLUENCES ARE MORE RECENT ONES FROM THE OPULENCE OF LYON, THE POOR LANDS OF THE ARDÈCHE, AND FROM THE DAUPHINÉ, DIVIDED BETWEEN RICH FARMS AND PASTURES AND THE HARSHNESS OF THE ALMOST SOUTHERN MOUNTAINS. INFLUENCES OF THE COMTÉ AND PROVENCE COME UP THE RIVER. "RICH" AND "POOR" CUISINES REFLECT THE MULTIPLE GIFTS OF NATURE: POULTRY, GAME, WHITE AND RED MEATS, DAIRY PRODUCTS, HIGHLY FLAVORED FRUITS AND VEGETABLES, HONEYS, ALMONDS AND WALNUTS, TRUFFLES, FISH FROM THE RHÔNE AND ITS TRIBUTARY STREAMS, OILS AND OLIVES, CHEESES, CHESTNUTS. THE CULTURAL PRECEDENCE AND POWER OF CONVICTION OF THE RHÔNE VALLEY ARE PERHAPS MOST MANIFEST IN ITS WINES, WHICH INCLUDE SEVERAL THAT ARE UNIVERSALLY RECOGNIZED AS THE BEST IN THE WORLD. CÔTE-RÔTIE AND HERMITAGE, FOR EXAMPLE, WERE ALREADY SEDUCING THE ROMANS BEFORE THEIR CONQUEST. RED AND WHITE, FROM AMPUIS TO CHÂTEAUNEUF-DU-PAPE, THEY DEMAND RESPECT AND GIVE BIRTH TO SOME SUMPTUOUS HARMONIES.

A GLIMPSE AT TRADITION

Chicken with Crayfish

Cut a large free-range chicken into serving pieces. Clean and rinse 16 crayfish. In a large skillet, heat 2 tablespoons vegetable oil and 2 tablespoons unsalted butter. Add the chicken and season with salt and pepper. Cook over medium-high heat, turning often, until browned, about 15 minutes. Remove the chicken to a plate or platter and keep warm. Add the crayfish to the skillet, cover, and cook, stirring or tossing often, until bright red, about 3 minutes. Remove the crayfish from the skillet and set aside. Add 2 minced shallots, 2 finely chopped carrots, and 1 finely chopped celery rib to the hot skillet. Cook a few minutes, until lightly colored. Return the chicken to the skillet. Add 1½ cups dry white wine, preferably Condrieu, and increase the heat to high. Boil until the liquid has reduced by three-quarters. Pour in 1½ cups chicken stock and bring to a boil. Cook about 10 minutes. Remove the chicken to a warmed ovenproof platter and keep warm, covered, in a very slow oven. Strain the liquid from the skillet into a large saucepan. Peel the crayfish tails and add the shells to the strained liquid. Boil until reduced by half. Add the juice of 1 lemon and strain through a fine sieve. Whisk in 2 tablespoons unsalted butter. Add 1 peeled, seeded, and diced tomato. Season the sauce to taste with salt and freshly ground black pepper. Arrange the crayfish around the chicken. Spoon the sauce over the chicken and sprinkle with finely chopped fresh tarragon. Serve at once.

From north to south, the unity of Rhône wines comes from the river. The northern vineyards, from Vienne to Valence, are undoubtedly the oldest in France and occupy the dizzying slopes of the hills where Syrah for the red wines and Viognier, Roussanne, and Marsanne for the whites triumph in a half-dozen heroic appellations including the legendary Côte-Rôtie and Hermitage. The southern vineyards extend over almost 125,000 acres, divided among the Ardèche, the southern Drôme, the Gard, and the Vaucluse where Châteauneuf-du-Pape is located.

RHÔNE VALLEY

On the right bank of the Rhône, at the foot of the famous Dentelles de Montmirail, the vineyard of Beaumes de Venise produces a great, naturally sweet wine.

The Rhône Valley has always been equally famous for its orchards. On the terraces of the hills of the Dauphiné, cherries, peaches, and apricots precede pears and apples. As Jacques Pic said so well, the Valence region is a land of convergences: from the north comes the cooking of the Lyonnais *mères*, from the east truffles, from the west chestnuts and game, and from the south vegetables and herbs.

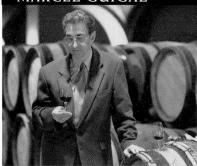

The fine history of the Guigal family reflects the continuing glory of the wines of the Côte-Rôtie. Three generations on land twenty-four centuries old.

The vineyards of Côte-Rôtie spread out over 373 acres. A great part lies in the commune of Ampuis opposite Vienne, which once gave the wine its name. It has been twenty-four hundred years since the Syrah vines climbed the slopes and produced a sumptuous red wine. Étienne Guigal founded the company in 1946. Marcel, his son, took the reins in 1961. Philippe, the grandson, is heir to a house that is emblematic of the appellations of the southern Côtes du Rhône. The Guigals are proprietors in the Côte Brune and the Côte Blonde, notably of the vineyards of La Mouline, La Landonne, and La Turque. They recently acquired two vineyards in Condrieu, the appellation of white wines from the Viognier grape. In 1984, they purchased the Vidal-Fleury company and, in 1995, the Château d'Ampuis on the Rhône. Together, they choose, grow, and sell the greatest *crus* of the Rhône Valley.

A Friend's Recipe

ALAIN PIC

Valence
Drôme

Begin the day before

Preparation: 1 hour

Cooking time: 50 minutes

Serves 4

—

14 OUNCES DUCK FOIE GRAS

SALT AND FRESHLY GROUND PEPPER

1¼ POUNDS BEEF FILLET, WELL TRIMMED

20 BABY CARROTS

16 MINIATURE FENNEL BULBS

12 BABY LEEKS

6 OUNCES FRESH BABY GREEN PEAS

9 TABLESPOONS PLUS 4 TEASPOONS
UNSALTED BUTTER

2 CARROTS, FINELY CHOPPED

1 ONION, FINELY CHOPPED

1 CELERY RIB, THINLY SLICED

1 LEEK, HALVED AND THINLY SLICED

1 SHALLOT, MINCED

1 GARLIC CLOVE, MINCED

1 BOUQUET GARNI

1½ CUPS RHÔNE VALLEY RED WINE,
PREFERABLY CORNAS

LAYERED BEEF WITH CORNAS SAUCE

Cut the foie gras into thin slices. Season well with salt and pepper. Heat a large non-stick skillet and add the slices. Cook over high heat until well browned. Drain on paper towels.

Cut the beef fillet lengthwise into 3 long slices. Flatten each lightly and season with salt and pepper. Place one of the slices flat on a large work surface. Arrange slices of foie gras on top and add another slice of beef. Top with the remaining foie gras and then the last slice of beef. Tie securely with kitchen string and wrap tightly in plastic wrap. Refrigerate overnight.

Peel and trim the baby carrots, fennel bulbs, and leeks. Blanch each separately in boiling salted water. Blanch the peas in boiling salted water. Set aside.

Preheat the oven to 425°F. Melt 3 tablespoons of the butter in a large ovenproof skillet. Remove the plastic wrap from the beef and place the beef in the skillet. Sauté over medium-high heat, turning often, until browned on all sides. Transfer to the oven and cook for about 5 minutes. Remove the beef and cover with foil to keep warm.

Pour off the fat in the skillet. Add the chopped carrots, onion, celery, leek, shallot, garlic, and bouquet garni. Pour in the wine. Cook over medium heat for 15 to 20 minutes. Transfer the contents of the skillet to a food processor and process until smooth. Strain through a fine sieve into a small saucepan. Working on and off the heat, whisk in 6 tablespoons butter bit by bit. Season with salt and pepper.

Heat the baby carrots, fennel bulbs, leeks, and peas separately over high heat in a teaspoon of butter each. Remove the strings from the beef fillet and cut into slices. Arrange on hot plates and surround with the heated vegetables. Spoon on the sauce and serve at once.

A hundred-year-old in the Rhône Valley.

Begin the day before

Preparation: 2 hours

Cooking time: 4 hours

Serves 10 to 12

—

1¼ POUNDS BONED CHICKEN

12 OUNCES BONELESS PORK SHOULDER

2 CUPS COGNAC

2 CUPS RUBY PORT

2 CUPS DRY VERMOUTH

2 QUARTS CÔTE RÔTIE

4 CUPS WHITE RHÔNE WINE

1½ POUNDS CALF'S SWEETBREADS

2 ONIONS, THINLY SLICED

2 CARROTS, THINLY SLICED

SALT AND FRESHLY GROUND BLACK
PEPPER TO TASTE

2 BOUQUETS GARNIS

1 CUP BEEF CONSOMMÉ

5 POUNDS ASSORTED CHICKEN BACKS,
NECKS, AND WINGS,
WELL TRIMMED OF FAT

4 TABLESPOONS UNSALTED BUTTER

½ CELERY RIB, FINELY CHOPPED

2 GARLIC CLOVES, MINCED

2 CUPS VEAL STOCK

2 LARGE EGGS

2 LARGE EGG YOLKS

1½ OUNCES CHOPPED TRUFFLE

2 TABLESPOONS FRESH BLOOD
(SEE NOTE, PAGE 138)

2 TABLESPOONS HEAVY CREAM

2 TABLESPOONS MINCED SHALLOTS,
COOKED

4 OUNCES COOKED DUCK FOIE GRAS,
CUBED

2 TO 2½ POUNDS PUFF PASTRY DOUGH

1 HEAD GREEN CABBAGE

2 OUNCES PURÉED FOIE GRAS

SWEETBREAD TOURTE WITH CÔTE RÔTIE

Place the boned chicken and pork in a large bowl. Add the Cognac, port, vermouth, red wine, and white wine. Cover and marinate overnight in the refrigerator.

Preheat the oven to 400°F. Place the sweetbreads in a large bowl and rinse under cold running water until there are no traces of pink. Place in a saucepan and pour in enough cold water to cover. Bring to a boil over high heat and boil for 5 minutes. Drain well and trim. Butter a large ovenproof skillet, add the sweetbreads, and surround with 1 of the onions and 1 of the carrots. Season with salt and pepper. Add 1 bouquet garni and bring to a simmer over low heat on top of the stove. Pour in the consommé, cover, and transfer to the oven. Bake 25 to 30 minutes, then cool. Keep refrigerated until ready to assemble the dish.

In a large soup kettle or stockpot, cook the chicken carcasses over medium-high heat in 2 tablespoons of the butter until browned. Add the remaining 1 onion, 1 carrot, and 1 bouquet garni. Add the celery and garlic. Cook until the vegetables are slightly softened. Pour in the marinade from the chicken and pork and increase the heat to high. Boil rapidly until reduced by three-quarters. Add the veal stock and bring to a boil, skimming to remove any impurities that rise to the top. Reduce the heat to very low (150°F) and keep at this temperature to poach the stuffing.

Grind the chicken and pork in a meat grinder with the coarsest blade. Place in a large bowl and add the eggs, 1 of the egg yolks, the truffle, blood, cream, shallots, salt, and pepper. Mix well, then fold in the cubes of foie gras.

Peel the cooked sweetbreads and cut into 1½-inch cubes. Place a piece of plastic wrap flat on a large work surface. Make a layer of some of the ground meat mixture around 2½ inches wide in the center. Arrange the sweetbreads along the center and top with another layer of the ground meat mixture. Roll into a cylinder that measures about 2½ inches in diameter. Repeat with the remaining meat mixture and sweetbreads. Tie a knot on each end of the cylinders to seal. Poach in the simmering liquid for 3 hours. Remove from the heat and cool. Reserve the liquid. Cut each cylinder into 1½-inch-thick slices, cover, and chill.

Preheat the oven to 400°F. Roll the puff pastry out about ⅛ inch thick and cut out 4½-inch circles for the bottoms and 6-inch circles for the tops. Refrigerate.

Separate the cabbage leaves and rinse well. Blanch the leaves in a large pot of salted water and drain. Cut out the thick rib in the center of each leaf. Wrap each slice of the meat stuffing in a cabbage leaf. Place 1 stuffed leaf on the center of a smaller pastry circle. Brush the edges with the remaining egg yolk and top with the larger circles. Crimp the edges to seal. Bake on a baking sheet for 20 minutes.

Strain the liquid that the cylinders simmered in and place in a large saucepan. Whisk in the puréed foie gras and bring to a boil. Season with salt and pepper. Stir in the remaining 2 tablespoons butter just before serving.

Cut a small wedge out of each tourte and place on individual serving plates with the wedge off to one side. Spoon over a small amount of the sauce and serve the remaining sauce on the side. Serve with a green salad and seasonal vegetables.

Begin the day before

Preparation: 2 hours

Cooking time: 4 hours

Serves 4

—

1 PIKE PERCH, ABOUT 3½ POUNDS

2 BOTTLES SAINT JOSEPH WINE

10 JUNIPER BERRIES • 1 SPRIG THYME

1 BAY LEAF

4 GARLIC CLOVES, UNPEELED

2 TABLESPOONS EACH BUTTER AND OIL

1 POUND TRIMMED LEAN FISH BONES

2 CARROTS • 1 ONION •1 LEEK,

½ CELERY RIB

1½ TEASPOONS TOMATO PASTE

2 TO 3 TABLESPOONS FLOUR

for the stuffed mushrooms:

8 LARGE WHITE MUSHROOMS

5 TABLESPOONS BUTTER

JUICE OF 1 LEMON • SALT

2 OUNCES SMALL WHITE MUSHROOMS

1 SHALLOT AND 1 GARLIC CLOVE, MINCED

2 TABLESPOONS HEAVY CREAM

¼ CUP TOASTED FRESH BREAD CRUMBS

NUTMEG • CURRY POWDER

1 LARGE EGG YOLK

for the stuffed onions:

4 SMALL SPRING ONIONS

2 TABLESPOONS BUTTER

½ CUP FINELY CHOPPED MUSHROOMS

PINCH OF CHOPPED FRESH PARSLEY

¾ CUP VEGETABLE BOUILLON

2 TABLESPOONS MEDIUM SEMOLINA

4 FRESH SAVORY SPRIGS

for the stuffed potatoes:

4 MEDIUM FIRM-FLESHED POTATOES

PINCH OF SAFFRON THREADS

1 TABLESPOON BUTTER, SOFTENED

½ CUP DRIED BEANS, SOAKED

1 CARROT • 1 ONION • ½ CELERY RIB

1 FRESH PARSLEY SPRIG

2 OUNCES TINY GREEN BEANS

2 TABLESPOONS HEAVY CREAM

½ CUP PREPARED BÉCHAMEL SAUCE

1 LARGE EGG YOLK

CHOPPED PARSLEY • CHOPPED CHERVIL

1 TO 2 CUPS VEGETABLE BOUILLON

to finish the dish:

2 SHALLOTS, MINCED

9 TABLESPOONS BUTTER

¾ CUP VEAL STOCK

SAINT JOSEPH–MARINATED PIKE PERCH FILLETS WITH STUFFED VEGETABLES

Scale, eviscerate, and fillet the fish. Trim the fillets well, remove all the bones with tweezers, and place the fillets in a large, shallow bowl. Pour in 1 bottle Saint Joseph, add the juniper berries, thyme, bay leaf, and garlic. Cover and marinate for 12 hours.

In a large saucepan, melt the butter with the vegetable oil. Add the fish bones and cook over medium-high heat, stirring often, for about 2 minutes. Chop the carrots, onion, leek greens, celery, and add with the tomato paste. Stir well and sprinkle in the flour. Pour in the remaining bottle of wine. Bring to a boil over medium-high heat, stirring often and skimming off any impurities that rise to the top. Reduce the heat to medium-low and simmer for 30 minutes. Pass through a fine sieve and set aside.

To prepare the stuffed mushrooms, carefully clean the caps and discard the stems of the large mushrooms. Place 4 in a skillet and pour in 1 cup water, 2 tablespoons of the butter, and half the lemon juice; season with salt. Flute the remaining 4 caps (see page 138) and add to the skillet. Cook over high heat for 3 minutes. Drain, reserving the cooking liquid. Butter a baking dish and set the unturned mushrooms inside (these are the ones to be filled). Finely chop the small mushrooms. Heat 2 more tablespoons of the butter in a small skillet. Add the chopped mushrooms, the shallot, and garlic. Cook over medium-high heat until softened, about 2 minutes. Add the cream, bread crumbs, pinch each of nutmeg and curry, egg yolk, and parsley. Fill the large mushroom caps with this mixture and top with the fluted mushroom caps. Squeeze over the remaining lemon juice and drizzle with 1 tablespoon melted butter. Set aside.

For the stuffed onions, preheat the oven to 425° F. Cut a small slice off the top of each onion. Reserve the small slice and carefully scoop out the centers of the onions, leaving a 2-layer-thick shell. Blanch the shells in boiling salted water for 3 minutes and drain. Finely chop the scooped-out parts of the onion. Heat the butter in a large skillet. Add the chopped onion and mushrooms. Cook over medium-high heat until softened, about 5 minutes. Bring the vegetable bouillon to a boil and stir in the semolina. Cook for 3 to 4 minutes, until the liquid has been absorbed. Add to the onion and mushroom mixture. Season with salt and pepper. Filled the scooped-out onion shells with the stuffing and set in a buttered baking dish. Place the reserved small slices on top, moisten the dish with a bit of vegetable bouillon, and bake for 30 minutes, basting from time to time. Garnish with the savory just before serving.

To prepare the potatoes, peel them and cut a small slice off the top of each. Scoop out the centers of the bottoms to make a thick shell. Bring a large pot of salted water to a boil and add the saffron. Cook the potato shells in the boiling water until yellow and slightly softened. Drain well and place in a large saucepan spread with the softened butter. Cook until tender.

Drain the dried beans and place in a medium saucepan. Add the carrot, onion, celery, and parsley. Add enough cold water to cover and bring to a boil. Reduce the heat to medium and cook until the beans are softened, 30 to 45 minutes. Drain. Blanch the green beans in a large amount of salted water until tender, about 5 minutes. Drain and dice.

Preheat the oven to 425° F. Reduce the cream in a large saucepan until thickened. Add the dried and green beans to the reduced cream. Stir well to coat, then add the béchamel sauce, egg yolk, and pinch each parsley and chervil. Season well with salt and pepper. Fill the scooped-out potato bottoms with this mixture and place the potato slices on top. Arrange in a casserole and add enough vegetable bouillon to cover the potatoes. Cover and bring to a boil on top of the stove. Transfer to the oven and bake, basting often, until crispy on the bottom. Brush with melted butter just before serving.

To finish the dish, drain the fish fillets and cut each one in half. Reserve the marinade.

Preheat the oven to 375° F. In a medium saucepan, cook the shallots in 1 tablespoon of the butter until softened. Add the marinade, bring to a boil, and boil until reduced by half. Add the veal stock and again reduce by half. Strain through a fine sieve and into a large saucepan. Rewarm over low heat just before serving and whisk in 4 tablespoons of the butter bit by bit.

Season the fish with salt and pepper. Cook the fish in a large skillet with the remaining 4 tablespoons butter. Meanwhile, bake the mushrooms for 5 to 8 minutes.

To serve, place the stuffed vegetables on one side of warmed plates. Ladle a small amount of the sauce on the plate and top with the fish. Season with salt and fresh pepper. Serve at once.

Begin 2 days before

Preparation: 1 hour

Cooking time: 1 hour 40 minutes

Serves 10

●

2 LARGE FREE-RANGE CHICKENS,
4 TO 5 POUNDS EACH

1½ TO 2 CUPS WHITE RHÔNE WINE

½ ONION

2 BOUQUETS GARNIS

12 OUNCES THINLY SLICED PROSCUITTO

4 OUNCES WILD MUSHROOMS, COOKED
AND THINLY SLICED

4 OUNCES COOKED DUCK FOIE GRAS

SALT AND FRESHLY GROUND BLACK
PEPPER TO TASTE

1 CUP LENTILS, PREFERABLY
LENTILLES DE PUY

2 ONIONS, FINELY CHOPPED

1 CARROT, DICED

1 CELERY RIB, DICED

2 TABLESPOONS UNSALTED BUTTER

1 BOTTLE RED RHÔNE WINE,
PREFERABLY SYRAH

10 OUNCES MÂCHE

VINAIGRETTE TO TASTE

CHICKEN TERRINE WITH LENTILS IN SYRAH

Skin and bone the chickens. Cut the flesh into thin strips and marinate overnight in the white wine, ½ onion, and 1 bouquet garni.

Preheat the oven to 250°F. Line a terrine mold with the proscuitto. Fill the terrine halfway with alternate layers of the marinated chicken and the mushrooms. Place a layer of the foie gras in the center and top with more alternating layers, ending with a layer of chicken. Season with salt and pepper throughout the process. Fold the ends of the prosciutto over the top and cover. Bake in a water bath for 1½ hours. Remove from the oven, cool, weight, and refrigerate for twenty-four hours.

Pick over the lentils and soak for 1 to 2 hours in cold water. Combine the remaining onion, the carrot, and celery in a large saucepan. Add the butter and cook over medium-high heat, stirring often, until softened. Drain the lentils and add to the saucepan. Mix well and pour in the red wine. Bring to a boil over high heat, skimming to remove any impurities. Add the remaining bouquet garni and season with salt and pepper. Reduce the heat to medium and cook until the lentils are tender but not mushy. Drain and cool.

Carefully clean the lettuce and spin dry. Season with vinaigrette. Place a small bunch on one side of a large serving plate. Season the lentils with vinaigrette, salt, and pepper to taste. Place a nice slice of the chicken terrine in the center of the plate and a spoonful of the lentils on the side. Serve at once.

176

RHÔNE VALLEY

1 GUINEA HEN, WITH NECK

2 TABLESPOONS GRAPESEED OIL

1 TABLESPOON FINELY CHOPPED CHIVES

2 TABLESPOONS FINELY CHOPPED ONION

1 OUNCE CURED HAM, FINELY DICED

1 TABLESPOON FINELY DICED FRESH
GINGER

1 OUNCE WILD MUSHROOMS,
PREFERABLY *TROMPETTES DES MORTS*,
DICED

1 CUP PLUS 1 TABLESPOON DRY WHITE
RHÔNE WINE

SOY SAUCE TO TASTE

DRY SHERRY TO TASTE

1 TABLESPOON CORNSTARCH DISSOLVED
IN 2 TABLESPOONS COLD WATER

SALT AND FRESHLY GROUND BLACK
PEPPER TO TASTE

½ CUP UNSALTED BUTTER

1 CARROT, FINELY CHOPPED

1 ONION, FINELY CHOPPED

1 SMALL LEEK, GREENS ONLY,
FINELY CHOPPED

1 CELERY RIB, FINELY CHOPPED

1 BOUQUET GARNI

1½ CUPS RED RHÔNE WINE, PREFERABLY
HERMITAGE

1 CUP CHICKEN STOCK

24 4-INCH FRESH PASTA SQUARES

1 LARGE EGG YOLK

20 BABY LEEKS

1 TABLESPOON VEGETABLE OIL

½ CUP WATER

COARSE SEA SALT TO TASTE

GUINEA HEN WITH RAVIOLI AND HERMITAGE

Trim the guinea hen and remove the wings. Reserve the wings, neck, and any scraps. Remove the legs and thighs but leave the breasts on the carcass. Bone the legs and thighs, then finely chop the flesh using a large sharp knife. (Do not use a food processor for this step. It will turn the mixture into a smooth pâté rather than a rough-textured filling more suitable for the ravioli.) Keep the carcass with the breasts refrigerated.

Heat the grapeseed oil in a small skillet. Add the chopped chives and onion. Cook over medium-high heat, stirring, until softened. Add the chopped guinea hen meat and cook rapidly for 1 minute. Add the ham, ginger, and mushrooms; cook for 1 minute longer. Add 1 tablespoon white wine and season with soy sauce and sherry. Stir in the cornstarch paste and mix well. (This entire procedure should not take more than 3 minutes.) Season the mixture with salt and pepper. Cover and chill.

Heat 2 tablespoons of the butter in a large skillet. Add the guinea wings, neck, and scraps. Cook over medium-high heat until browned. Add half of the chopped carrot, half of the chopped onion, leek, and celery and the bouqiet garni. Cook about 5 minutes longer. Pour in all but a dash of the red wine and cook, uncovered, until almost all of the liquid has evaporated. Pour in the chicken stock, reduce the heat to medium-low, and cook, covered, for 2 hours.

Once the filling for the ravioli is completely chilled, place the pasta squares flat on a large work surface. Divide the filling between half the squares. Use a pastry brush to paint the edges of the squares with egg yolk and top with the remaining squares. Press the edges to seal. With a scallop-edged cookie cutter that measures about 3 inches in diameter, cut the ravioli into rounds. Poach in simmering salted water for 3 minutes. Transfer to a bowl of ice water to refresh, drain, and transfer to a clean kitchen towel.

Trim and cook the baby leeks in boiling salted water. Cool under cold running water and set aside.

Preheat the oven to 450°F. Heat 2 tablespoons of the butter with the vegetable oil in a large ovenproof skillet. Add the guinea hen carcass with the breasts still attached to the skillet and brown on all sides over medium-high heat. Transfer to the oven and bake for about 35 minutes. After 20 minutes, add the remaining carrot, onion, leek green, and celery to the skillet. Cook for 8 minutes, then pour in the remaining 1 cup white Rhône wine. Baste the carcass and turn often throughout the process.

At the end of the cooking, remove the guinea and cover with foil to keep warm. Skim off any fat in the skillet. Pour in the ½ cup water and stir to dislodge the solids on the bottom. Stir in the chicken stock reduction. Strain through a fine sieve into a large saucepan. Whisk in the remaining 3 tablespoons butter, season with salt and pepper, and keep warm.

Just before serving, add the remaining dash of red wine to the sauce. Remove the breast fillets from the carcass and cut into thick slices. Reheat the ravioli in simmering water. Drain well. Arrange 3 slices of the guinea hen breast, alternating with the ravioli, on warmed serving plates. Place the leeks decoratively on the plate. Spoon the sauce over and season with pepper and coarse salt. Serve at once.

Preparation: 25 minutes

Cooking time: 25 minutes

Serves 4

●

6 RIPE LARGE WHITE PEACHES

½ CUP SUGAR

¾ CUP WATER

1 BUNCH FRESH MINT

1 CUP BEAUMES DE VENISE

MINT-INFUSED WHITE PEACHES WITH BEAUMES DE VENISE

Bring a large pot of water to a boil. Add the peaches and leave in the water for just a few seconds. Remove and refresh under cold running water. Carefully peel the peaches and place in a stainless-steel saucepan. In a separate saucepan, combine the sugar and the water. Bring to a boil and add three-quarters of the mint. Pour this syrup over the peaches and simmer the peaches for about 5 minutes. Cool in the syrup.

Remove the peaches and bring the syrup to a boil. Boil until reduced by three-quarters. Cool. Remove the mint, add the Beaumes de Venise, and chill.

Cut the peaches into 6 to 8 wedges each. Arrange the wedges decoratively in shallow serving bowls. Pour the chilled syrup over and refrigerate for 1 hour. Garnish with the remaining mint and serve very cold.

for the filling:
¾ CUP SUGAR

3 LARGE EGGS

JUICE OF 2 ORANGES

4 TABLESPOONS (½ STICK) UNSALTED
BUTTER

1 CUP HEAVY CREAM, WHIPPED STIFF

for the cake:
¾ CUP UNSALTED BUTTER, SLIGHTLY
SOFTENED

¾ CUP SUGAR

JUICE OF 2 ORANGES

GRATED ZEST OF 2 ORANGES

2 LARGE EGGS

1 TEASPOON BAKING POWDER

1 CUP ALL-PURPOSE FLOUR

or the sabayon:
4 LARGE EGG YOLKS

½ CUP SUGAR

¾ CUP CLAIRETTE DE DIE (SEE NOTE)

CANDIED ORANGE ZEST, FOR GARNISH

ORANGE CAKE ROLL WITH
SABAYON CLAIRETTE DE DIE

To make the filling, combine the sugar, eggs, and orange juice in the top of a double boiler. Mix well with a whisk and cook over simmering water, stirring often, until thick and lemon colored, about 25 minutes. Remove from the heat, strain, stir in the butter, and cool to room temperature. Cover and refrigerate until well chilled. Fold in the whipped cream and refrigerate.

To make the sponge cake, preheat the oven to 350°F and butter a jelly-roll pan. Line the pan with waxed paper, butter the paper, and dust with flour. With an electric mixer, cream the butter and sugar. Add half the orange juice and all the orange zest. On low speed, add the eggs and mix well. Gradually add the baking powder and flour. Mix just until the batter is thick and smooth. Pour into the pan and spread evenly. Bake until lightly browned around the edges and set in the center, 18 to 20 minutes.

Remove the cake from the oven and sprinkle over some of the remaining orange juice. Immediately spread the cream filling over the surface of the cake and roll into a cylinder. Trim the ends on a diagonal and sprinkle over the remaining juice. Refrigerate until ready to serve.

To make the sabayon, combine the egg yolks, sugar, and ½ cup of the Clairette de Die in a large heavy saucepan. Whisk over very low heat until thick and foamy, about 5 minutes. (Do not boil.) Whisk in the remaining ¼ cup of Clairette de Die.

Slice the cake roll and arrange 2 slices on 4 serving plates. Spoon over a small amount of the sabayon, garnish with the candied orange zest, and serve any remaining sabayon on the side.

NOTE: Clairette de Die is a sweet sparkling wine from the eastern part of the Rhône Valley, made with a blend of Muscat and Clairette grapes. Any light, sweet wine can be used as a substitute.

PROVENCE - CÔTE D'AZUR

Since the time of Emperor Napoleon III, who received the Comté of Nice from the kings of Sardinia, winters in Provence-Côte d'Azur have been gentler than in heaven and the summers more golden. As everyone has verified, the azure on this part of the coast has rarely been lacking. It has even become a meteorological model. From Menton to Cannes, the rococo palaces of the Belle Époque and the modern façades of glass crowd almost without a break against the yellowed walls of ancient Christian fortresses. Farther west, the rocks of the Estérel and Les Maures protect a coastline where gardens and vineyards plunge down to the beach. Even though they have been transformed into major tourist spots, the villages of sailors and fishermen have kept their original colors. Mountain and sea are found in a gastronomy that is made up of their two cuisines. They join together with and complement the generous wines, be they red, white, or rosé. The cuisine of the back country is that of the sun, coarse yet rich in aromas and subtle flavors obtained from products of a grand simplicity. Veal, beef, lamb, and game are the meats. Long-simmering dishes, prepared with great skill and taste, triumph here. The basis of the cuisine is in the native fruits and vegetables that express the power of the earth in their flesh and juices. The other cuisine, that of the sea, is one of the most varied and lively there is. To a long and strong tradition is added a quickness to adapt, from one day to the next, to what the fishermen's nets and lines bring in. It has also been from the sea that outside influences have entered; spices, dyes, and innovations have never been lacking. Faraway lands have always made themselves known through great ports.

A GLIMPSE AT TRADITION

Duckling with Bitter Orange

Clean and trim a duckling, reserving the neck and wings. Truss and set aside in the refrigerator. Remove the zest of 1 bitter orange and ½ lemon; cut the zest into long, thin julienne strips. Cut away the pith from the orange and remove the sections whole. Set aside.

Sauté the duckling and reserved parts in 2 tablespoons unsalted butter in a skillet until browned and slightly rare in the center, about 30 minutes. Remove from the skillet, drain, remove the trussing strings, and transfer to a serving platter. Cover loosely and keep warm.

In a small saucepan, combine 2 sugar cubes and 1 tablespoon water. Boil over high heat until the mixture forms a dark caramel. Add 1 tablespoon vinegar and remove from the heat. Deglaze the skillet used to cook the duckling with ¾ cup dry white wine. Add a little veal stock and the caramel. Bring to a boil and cook rapidly for several seconds. Add the juice of 1 bitter orange and the juice of ½ lemon. Boil to reduce the mixture, strain, and add 5 strips each of the orange and lemon julienne. Whisk 2 tablespoons unsalted butter into the sauce and spoon over the duckling. Garnish with the orange sections and serve at once.

Provence begins on the limestone of the Alpilles, a hint of the landscape of the nearby Alps, and stretches out along the Rhône in the Comté of Nice. If the cities are still well marked by the Roman world, the countryside expresses a harmony of design and vegetation that makes one think more of Greece. This feeling of an eternal springtime of the world, which a northerner will always cherish, undoubtedly comes from this.

The olive tree is the symbol of ancient Mediterranean civilizations. Olive oil is the source of a culinary richness and inspiration that is equal to that of bread, wine, and salt.

The vineyards of Provence die off only to be reborn. A survey of its land is extremely complicated, like that of all ancient civilized lands. In the Var, vineyards today occupy more than half of all agricultural land. Despite being very cut up, the vineyards are regrouped under four large regional appellations, and there are four superb local communal AOC appellations: Palette, Cassis, Bandol, and Bellet (near Nice).

Provence, and especially the Var, annually produce an average of 105 million gallons of rosé, white, and red wines.

For tourists, the palm tree is the symbol of the Côte d'Azur. The first palm tree was planted in the last century by the writer Alphonse Karr.

DOMAINES OTT

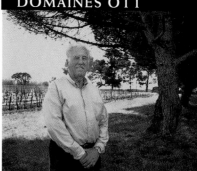

Marcel Ott, the founder of a great line of wine growers, chose from the beginning to respect nature and to make authentic wines.

With the Ott family, the guiding principle has always been that there are no great wines without great grapes. And great grapes, carefully selected at harvest time, only come from clean and healthy vines. In the three vineyards that make up their holdings, Château de Selle, Clos Mireille, and Château Romassan, the search for quality begins with the keenest respect for the soil. Whether in Côte de Provence or in Bandol, the range of wines of the domaine Ott is the exact expression of the soils: the barren grounds of the Château de Selle; schist, clay, and sea spray for the Clos Mireille near Fort de Brégançon; the gentle slopes of Château Romasson, Bandol appellation. To this respect for the soil are added growing methods that favor mechanical working of the earth, natural products, manual harvesting, and the selection of grapes in order to save only fruits in perfect condition.

ALAIN DUCASSE

Le Louis XV
Monaco

Begin 6 hours ahead

Preparation: 50 minutes

Cooking time: 35 minutes

Serves 4

●

6 SMALL PEARS (SEE NOTE)

6 BARTLETT PEARS

3 CUPS HEARTY RED WINE, PREFERABLY
BELLET ROUGE

1 CUP SUGAR

2 VANILLA BEANS

1 SMALL PIECE CINNAMON STICK

ZEST OF 1 LEMON

ZEST OF 1 ORANGE

3 CLOVES

POACHED PEARS WITH RED WINE GRANITÉ

Peel the small pears, halve lengthwise, and remove the cores. Peel, halve, core, and thinly slice the Bartlett pears.

In a large nonreactive saucepan, combine the wine, sugar, vanilla beans, cinnamon stick, lemon zest, orange zest, and cloves. Bring to a boil over high heat. Add the small pear halves and bring back to a boil. Remove from the heat. Carefully place the thin pear slices in a strainer that can be lowered into the saucepan. Set the slices in the hot poaching liquid to cook until cooked through but not mushy. When done, remove the pears and strain the poaching liquid. Let cool completely.

To make the granité, pour half the poaching liquid into a bowl. Freeze, stirring frequently with a fork, for at least 6 hours.

Pour the remaining half of the poaching liquid into a large nonreactive saucepan. Boil until the mixture has reduced to a thick syrup.

On each of 4 serving plates, arrange the thin pear slices in a fanned circle over the bottoms. Use a pastry brush to "paint" the slices with the reduced poaching liquid.

Arrange 3 of the poached pear halves on top of the thin slices on each plate. Cut the bottoms on a slight diagonal so that the halves sit upright at an angle. Delicately place a scoop of the granité in the center. Serve at once.

NOTE: The original recipe calls for Martin-Sec pears, which are almost impossible to find outside the Rhône Valley. Seckel or Fiorello pears are good substitutes.

A flowering vault of peach trees in a Provençal orchard.

━

24 BABY ARTICHOKES

2 GLOBE ARTICHOKES

1 LARGE LEMON, HALVED

2 CUPS PLUS 3 TABLESPOONS OLIVE OIL

3 CUPS DRY WHITE WINE,
PREFERABLY FROM PROVENCE

1 CUP WATER

1 GARLIC CLOVE, UNPEELED

1 FRESH THYME SPRIG

1 BAY LEAF

SEVERAL WHOLE CORIANDER SEEDS

COARSE SEA SALT TO TASTE

FRESHLY GROUND BLACK PEPPER TO
TASTE

8 PRAWNS (JUMBO SHRIMP)

½ CARROT, DICED

½ ONION, DICED

½ LEEK, GREENS ONLY, THINLY SLICED

½ CELERY RIB, THINLY SLICED

1 SMALL BOUQUET GARNI

1 GARLIC CLOVE, MINCED

2 TEASPOONS TOMATO PASTE

2 TOMATOES, QUARTERED

ABOUT 4 CUPS CRÈME FRAÎCHE

2 TABLESPOONS BALSAMIC VINEGAR

FRESH BASIL LEAVES, FOR GARNISH

ARTICHOKES STUFFED WITH PRAWNS

Remove the tough outer leaves of all the artichokes but do not break off the stalks. With a sharp paring knife, cut off the smaller inner leaves around the heart to expose the bottoms. Cut away all but about ⅜ inch of the stems and trim the ends into a point. Scoop out the chokes with a small spoon. Rub the cut surfaces with the lemon halves. Place the bottoms in a large saucepan with 2 cups olive oil, 1½ cups wine, the water, garlic clove, thyme, bay leaf, coriander seeds, salt, and pepper. Cook over low heat until the artichokes are tender. Set the baby artichokes aside and cut the bottoms of the large artichokes into ⅜-inch dice.

Peel the prawns and refrigerate. Crush the shells. Pour 3 tablespoons oil into a large saucepan and heat over high heat until very hot. Add the shells and cook, stirring, until lightly browned. Add the carrot, onion, leek greens, celery, bouquet garni, and minced garlic. Stir in the tomato paste and the tomatoes. Reduce the heat to medium and cook, stirring constantly, for 2 minutes. Pour in the remaining 1½ cups wine, increase the heat to high, and boil until reduced to 1 to 2 tablespoons. Add enough of the crème fraîche to cover and bring to a boil. Reduce the heat to medium and cook, skimming often, for 30 minutes. Strain into a separate saucepan and reserve.

Lightly oil a large nonstick skillet. Heat until very hot, add the prawns, and cook over high heat, turning often, until firm and bright pink. Add the vinegar, stir well, and remove from the heat.

Cut 4 of the prawns into ⅜-inch dice and add to the diced artichokes. Add a little of the sauce, set aside, and keep warm.

Set aside 12 of the prettiest artichoke bottoms. Cut the stems off the remaining bottoms to form a stable base. Place 3 of these on each of 4 individual serving plates. Fill with the diced artichokes and prawns. Place one of the artichokes with a stem on top of each filled artichoke and spoon over a small amount of the sauce.

Cut the remaining prawns lengthwise in half. Arrange attractively around the artichoke bottoms. Season with coarse salt and freshly ground black pepper. Garnish with basil and serve at once.

Preparation: 40 minutes

Cooking time: 15 minutes

Serves 4

—•—

2 DOZEN FRESH SMALL OYSTERS

4 TABLESPOONS UNSALTED BUTTER

10 OUNCES WILD MUSHROOMS,
TRIMMED AND THINLY SLICED

1 SHALLOT, MINCED

¾ CUP DRY WHITE WINE,
PREFERABLY CASSIS

¾ CUP CRÈME FRAÎCHE

JUICE OF 1 LEMON

SALT AND FRESHLY GROUND BLACK
PEPPER TO TASTE

1 TABLESPOON SNIPPED FRESH CHIVES

SEVERAL LEAVES FRESH CHERVIL,
FOR GARNISH

WILD MUSHROOM SOUP WITH OYSTERS AND WHITE WINE

Working over a small bowl, shuck the oysters and reserve all the liquid. Place the oysters in a sauté pan. Filter the liquid to remove any sand and pour over the oysters. Set aside.

Melt half the butter in a medium skillet. Add the mushrooms and cook over medium-high heat, stirring often, until softened. Add the shallot and cook a minute or two longer. Pour in the wine, increase the heat to high, and boil until reduced by half. Add the crème fraîche and boil until slightly reduced.

Just before serving, gently warm the oysters. Add a spoonful of the cooking liquid from warming the oysters to the mushroom soup. Stir in lemon juice to taste. Add the remaining 2 tablespoons butter and season with salt and pepper. Stir in the chives.

Pour into warmed shallow bowls and add the drained oysters. Garnish with the chervil and serve at once.

Preparation: 1½ hours

Cooking time: 2 hours

Serves 4

—•—

8 RIPE TOMATOES

ABOUT 1 TEASPOON SUGAR

SALT AND FRESHLY GROUND BLACK
PEPPER TO TASTE

ABOUT ½ CUP OLIVE OIL

1 FRESH THYME SPRIG

1 GARLIC CLOVE, MINCED

2 FENNEL BULBS

7 TABLESPOONS UNSALTED BUTTER

1 CARROT

1 ONION

1½ TO 2 OUNCES CURED HAM

2 ARTICHOKES

1 LEMON, HALVED

3 DOZEN LARGE SNAILS, PREFERABLY
FROM BURGUNDY

¾ CUP DRY WHITE WINE, PREFERABLY
CÔTEAUX D'AIX

1 SHALLOT, MINCED

2 TABLESPOONS CRÈME FRAÎCHE

1 TEASPOON DIJON MUSTARD

VINEGAR TO TASTE

½ CUP COURT BOUILLON MADE WITH
WHITE WINE, WARMED

SNIPPED CHIVES, FOR GARNISH

OVEN-COOKED TOMATOES WITH FENNEL AND SNAILS

Preheat the oven to 225°F. Peel the tomatoes and cut a ⅜-inch-thick slice off the top. Squeeze gently to remove the seeds. Sprinkle with a little sugar and salt. Season the interiors of the tomatoes with pepper. Brush lightly with olive oil and sprinkle over the thyme and garlic. Place the tomatoes in a baking dish and cook for 1½ to 2 hours.

Trim the fennel bulbs and carefully cut into small cubes. Blanch the cubes in boiling salted water. Drain well and cook in 1 tablespoon butter in a skillet until tender.

Peel the carrot and finely dice. Peel the onion and thinly slice. Finely dice the ham. Set aside.

Bend back the stems of the artichokes until they break off. Remove the tough outer leaves. Trim the bottoms of the artichokes and use a small spoon to scoop out the choke. Rub well with the lemon halves. Cut the bottoms into cubes and cook in 2 tablespoons oil in a skillet until tender. Season with salt and pepper and set aside.

Cut 10 of the snails lengthwise in half and set aside. Finely dice the remaining 26 snails and set aside.

Melt 2 tablespoons butter in a small saucepan. Add the carrot and onion. Cook over medium-high heat until slightly softened. Pour in ¼ cup of the wine and add the fennel. Cook a few minutes longer, then add the ham and the diced snails. Add another tablespoon butter, season with salt and pepper, and keep warm.

In a separate nonreactive saucepan, combine the shallot with the remaining ½ cup wine. Bring to a boil over high heat and cook rapidly until reduced by two-thirds. Add the crème fraîche, bring to a boil, and whisk in 2 more tablespoons butter. Season with salt and pepper.

Prepare a tepid vinaigrette sauce using the mustard, ¼ cup oil, vinegar to taste, and the warm court bouillon. Season with salt and pepper and keep warm.

Gently warm the halved snails in 1 tablespoon butter.

Place a stainless-steel flan ring that measures about 2 inches in diameter and 1½ inches high in the center of 4 serving plates. Place 1 tomato (rewarm, if necessary) in each ring and cover with a spoonful of the fennel mixture. Top with another tomato and lightly brush with oil.

Surround the tomatoes with the diced artichokes and the halved snails. Remove the ring, spoon over a small amount of the vinaigrette sauce, and garnish with chives. Serve at once.

Preparation: 1¼ hours

Cooking time: 35 minutes

Serves 4

➖

6 BABY ARTICHOKES

JUICE OF ½ LEMON

1 CUP PLUS 3 TABLESPOONS OLIVE OIL

1 CUP DRY WHITE WINE, PREFERABLY PALETTE BLANC

SALT AND FRESHLY GROUND BLACK PEPPER TO TASTE

½ CUP WATER

1 GARLIC CLOVE, UNPEELED

1 FRESH THYME SPRIG, PLUS MORE FOR GARNISH

1 FRESH BAY LEAF

SEVERAL CORIANDER SEEDS

7 TABLESPOONS UNSALTED BUTTER

3 ONIONS, VERY THINLY SLICED

PINCH OF SUGAR

6 RED MULLET OR *ROUGETS DE ROCHE*, 14 TO 16 OUNCES EACH

4 OUNCES FRESH ANCHOVIES

1 GARLIC CLOVE, BOILED UNTIL TENDER

2 TABLESPOONS RED WINE VINEGAR

1 ANCHOVY FILLET PACKED IN OIL, DRAINED

2 SHALLOTS, MINCED

2 TABLESPOONS CRÈME FRAÎCHE

4 SLICES FIRM FRESH WHITE BREAD FOR CROUTONS

½ TEASPOON DIJON MUSTARD

2 TABLESPOONS CHOPPED FRESH PARSLEY, CHIVES, OR CHERVIL

RED MULLET À L'ANCHOYADE WITH ARTICHOKES AND WHITE WINE

Cut the stems from the artichokes, slice the bottoms flat, and trim the leaves. Thinly slice the artichokes and place in a large saucepan. Add the lemon juice, ½ cup olive oil, ¾ cup wine, and the water. Season with salt and pepper, add the unpeeled garlic, a thyme sprig, bay leaf, and coriander seeds. Cook over medium heat until the artichokes are tender. Keep warm.

Melt 3 tablespoons butter in a large skillet. Add the onions, sprinkle with the sugar, and season with salt and pepper. Cook over medium-high heat, stirring often, until the onions are very soft and lightly caramelized. Set aside.

Scale and eviscerate the fish. Reserve the livers. Fillet the fish and use tweezers to remove any small bones. Keep the fillets cold until ready to prepare.

Fillet the fresh anchovies, remove all bones, and trim well. Cook in a small skillet with the fish livers and a drop of olive oil. Transfer to a food processor and add the cooked garlic, ½ cup olive oil, 1 tablespoon vinegar, the cooked onions, and the canned anchovy fillet. Process until smooth, then work through a fine sieve.

In a small saucepan, combine the shallots and the remaining ¼ cup wine. Boil over high heat until almost all of the liquid has evaporated. Add the crème fraîche and bring back to a boil. Whisk in 4 tablespoons, season with salt and pepper, and strain through a sieve.

Cut the bread into triangles and cook in 2 tablespoons olive oil in a skillet until browned on both sides. Cool, then spread the anchovy mixture on top, mounding it decoratively.

In a small saucepan, combine the mustard with the remaining 1 tablespoon vinegar and a little of the artichoke cooking liquid. Stir in the strained butter sauce, season with salt and pepper, and keep warm.

Season the fish fillets with salt and pepper. Place a large skillet over high heat and add 1 tablespoon olive oil. When the skillet is very hot, add the fish and cook until firm to the touch and lightly browned.

To assemble the plates, quickly warm the croutons in a hot oven and place on one side of large serving plates. Place 2 fish fillets in the center of the plate and surround with the artichokes. Add the parsley to the sauce and spoon a small amount over the plate. Garnish with sprigs of fresh thyme and serve any remaining sauce on the side.

Small rock fish in Provence.

━

2 RACKS OF LAMB, TRIMMED

1 CUP OLIVE OIL, PLUS MORE FOR
BRUSHING

7 GARLIC CLOVES

SEVERAL FRESH THYME SPRIGS

4 RIPE TOMATOES

SUGAR

SALT AND FRESHLY GROUND BLACK
PEPPER TO TASTE

6 SMALL CARROTS

ABOUT ½ CUP UNSALTED BUTTER

6 SMALL WHITE TURNIPS

12 SMALL RED RADISHES

1½ POUNDS GREEN PEAS IN PODS

1 POUND FRESH SPINACH

12 FRESH MOREL MUSHROOMS

4 OUNCES BLACK OLIVES, PITTED

1 SMALL CAN (2 OUNCES) ANCHOVIES,
DRAINED

½ TEASPOON DRAINED CAPERS

1 TEASPOON RED WINE VINEGAR,
OR TO TASTE

3 SHALLOTS, MINCED

½ CUP BLACK CURRANT SYRUP
(CRÈME DE CASSIS)

4 CUPS HEARTY RED WINE,
PREFERABLY BANDOL

1 CUP VEAL STOCK

½ CUP WATER

FRESH BASIL LEAVES, FOR GARNISH

MARINATED LAMB FILLETS IN TAPENADE WITH BANDOL SAUCE

Remove the bones from the racks (or ask the butcher to do so), separating the fillets. In a dish large enough to hold the fillets snugly, combine ¾ cup olive oil, 1 garlic clove, and a sprig or two of thyme. Cover and refrigerate overnight.

Preheat the oven to 225°F. Peel the tomatoes and cut a ⅜-inch thick slice off the top. Squeeze gently to remove the seeds. Sprinkle with a little sugar and salt. Season the interiors of the tomatoes with pepper. Brush lightly with olive oil and sprinkle over with thyme leaves and 1 minced garlic clove. Place the tomatoes in a baking dish and cook for 1½ to 2 hours.

Peel the carrots and cut into 2 or 3 pieces, depending on their size. Trim each piece into an oval. Place the trimmed carrots in a small saucepan and pour in enough water to cover. Season with salt, add a pinch of sugar, and 1 teaspoon butter. Bring to a boil over high heat, reduce the heat to medium-low, and cook until all of the water has evaporated.

Peel the turnips and prepare them as you did the carrots.

Score the radishes with a fork and trim the stems to about ⅜ inch. Cook in boiling water until tender. Cook 5 of the garlic cloves in boiling salted water until tender. Drain under cold running water, peel, and set aside.

Shell the peas and cook in salted water until tender. Drain under cold running water.

Trim the spinach of large stems and rinse well. Plunge the leaves into a large pot of boiling salted water and blanch. Drain well and reserve.

Trim and rinse the morels in a large amount of tepid water. Blanch in boiling water for 5 minutes. Drain well and set aside.

Using a mortar and pestle, crush the olives with half of a cooked garlic clove. Add the anchovy fillets and capers. Pound the mixture into a coarse paste and gradually add the remaining ¼ cup olive oil. Season with the vinegar, salt, and pepper. Set aside.

In a nonreactive saucepan, heat 1 tablespoon butter. Add the shallots and cook over medium heat, stirring often, until tender. Add the black currant syrup and wine. Increase the heat to high and boil until reduced by half. Add the veal stock, bring back to a boil, and reduce until thickened. Remove from the heat and swirl in 2 tablespoons butter bit by bit. Cover to keep warm.

Remove the lamb fillets from the marinade. Preheat the oven to 100°F. Set a lightly oiled skillet over medium-high heat. Season the lamb with salt and pepper and add to the skillet. Cook until lightly browned on one side, about 2 minutes. Turn and cook 2 to 3 minutes longer. Transfer to a serving platter and warm in the oven for 10 minutes.

Pour off the fat from the skillet and add the water. Bring to a boil over high heat, whisking to pick up any cooked bits left on the bottom. Cook until thickened and reduced. Stir into the wine sauce.

Just before serving, reheat all the vegetables (including the cooked garlic) separately in butter to taste and arrange decoratively on large serving plates. Cut the lamb into 12 thick medallions. Lightly brush one side of each medallion with a small amount of the olive mixture and arrange on the plates. Ladle a small amount of the sauce over the bottom of the plates. Garnish with basil leaves and serve at once.

48 KUMQUATS, RINSED AND DRIED

SUGAR

¾ CUP PLUS 3 TABLESPOONS DRY WHITE
WINE, PREFERABLY CÔTE DE VAROISE

30 CLEMENTINES

2 ENVELOPES UNFLAVORED GELATIN

4 LARGE EGG WHITES

1 CUP CRÈME FRAÎCHE, WHIPPED

FRESH MINT LEAVES

CLEMENTINE AND KUMQUAT MOLD WITH VAROISE WINE

Weigh 24 of the kumquats and place in a large saucepan with a little water. Add the equivalent of their weight in sugar. Bring to a boil, reduce the heat, and simmer for about 2 hours.

In a separate saucepan, combine the remaining kumquats with ¾ cup wine and ½ cup sugar. Cook until tender. Transfer these kumquats with the cooking liquid to a food processor and process until smooth. Set aside.

Peel the clementines and separate into segments. Remove the white pith from the peels. Blanch the peels in a large amount of boiling water and drain. Repeat this process 3 times. Place the blanched peels in a saucepan and add their weight in sugar. Bring to a boil, reduce the heat, and simmer for about 2½ hours. Drain and cut into small diamond shapes to use for garnish.

Using a juice extractor, juice a quarter of the clementine segments. Keep the remaining segments refrigerated. Heat a small amount of the clementine juice in a medium saucepan and sprinkle 1 envelope gelatin. Remove the pan from the heat and let sit for 5 to 10 minutes to soften. Cut the candied kumquats into thin rounds. Stir in the remaining clementine juice, 3 tablespoons wine, and the candied kumquats.

Line the bottoms and sides of round molds that measure about 2 inches in diameter and 1¾ inches high with the rounds of kumquats. Add a teaspoonful of the jellied clementine juice to the bottom of each mold. Refrigerate.

Beat the egg whites until stiff. Soften the remaining envelope of gelatin in 2 tablespoons cold water. Heat 1½ cups sugar with a little water in a small saucepan. Bring to a boil and boil until it reaches the hard-ball stage, 248°F. With the beaters in motion, pour the hot syrup onto the egg whites. Add the softened gelatin and beat until cool. Fold in the puréed kumquat mixture, the remaining clementine gelatin with any remaining rounds of kumquats. Fold in the whipped crème fraîche. Fill the kumquat-lined molds with the mixture, being careful to keep the rounds in place. Refrigerate overnight.

Unmold the dessert in the center of individual serving plates. Surround with the clementine segments and garnish with the diamond-shaped candied clementine peels. Decorate with mint leaves and serve at once.

OVER TIME, LANGUEDOC AND ROUSSILLON HAVE BEEN FORMED BY WIND AND LIGHT. THE SEA HERE CLOSES OFF THE WEST OF THE MEDITERRANEAN AND CARRIES WITH IT THE INFLUENCE OF THE EAST. THE HISTORY OF MAN IN ROUSSILLON IS MUCH OLDER THAN IN LANGUEDOC. IN TAUTAVEL IN PYRÉNÉES-ORIENTALES, MAN'S PRESENCE IS ESTIMATED AT FOUR HUNDRED THOUSAND YEARS. THE GODS, INEVITABLY GREEK, HAVE EYES PAINTED BLUE, THE SIGN OF A GREAT AND ANCIENT CIVILIZATION.

SHELTERED BY THE CÉVENNES, THE MINERVOIS, THE CORBIÈRES, AND THE ALBÈRES, WHEAT, OLIVE TREES, AND VINEYARDS HAVE ABUNDANTLY FURNISHED THE THREE BASICS OF HUMAN NOURISHMENT—BREAD, WINE, AND OIL—FROM THE BEGINNING OF TIME. TEN COOL RIVERS COME FROM THE CLOUDS TO IRRIGATE THE TIERS OF THE LANDSCAPE WHERE, ON TERRACES BETWEEN THE FIELDS AND SHADED BY PLANE TREES, MAN TAKES TIME IN SUMMER TO REMEMBER THE ICE OF WINTER. WHILE OTHER LANDS MAY FAVOR BOILING, THE ART OF LANGUEDOC-ROUSSILLON IS IN ROASTING, THE QUICK MOVEMENT OVER COALS, THE FIRE THAT PURIFIES MEAT AND FISH AND GIVES ITS POWER TO CONDIMENTS AND TO ELABORATE SAUCES, QUINTESSENCE OF AN ACCOMPLISHED CUISINE. RED, ROSÉ, OR WHITE, THE WINES GO MARVELOUSLY WITH DISHES FRESH FROM THE FIRE, WITH STEWS, MOLLUSKS, AND CRUSTACEANS, SHELLFISH AND SNAILS, BEEF AND LAMB, LOTTE, AND TUNA, WITH REDUCTIONS OF EVERYTHING ESSENTIAL, WITH CARAMELIZED DISHES. AT THE END OF AN ARC OF GRAVELLY LAND AND PONDS, ROUSSILLON IS A KIND OF GARDEN PERCHED OVER THE SEA. ITS PEOPLE ARE SAGES OF TASTE AND MANNERS. MAILLOL LIVED THERE FOR DECADES. IT IS NOT BY CHANCE THAT IN THIS LAND, IN THE SECRET OF SHADOWS, THE OLDEST WINE ON EARTH IS MADE: BANYULS, A MONUMENT TO REFINED CIVILIZATION.

A GLIMPSE AT TRADITION

Fish Stew Sétoise

—

Peel 4 garlic cloves and cut lengthwise in half. Remove any green sprouts in the center. With a mortar and pestle, pound the garlic with 1 egg yolk to form a rough paste. Season with salt and pepper. Gradually add olive oil, pounding constantly, until the mixture is thick and emulsified. Set aside. (A spoonful of boiled potatoes can be incorporated into the aïoli, if desired.)

Cut monkfish fillets into thick slices and place in a large pot. Thinly slice the white part of a leek, 2 onions, and 2 carrots and add to the pot. Add 2 crushed garlic cloves, 1 bouquet garni, and 1 strip dried orange peel. Pour in a little dry white wine and 4 cups water. Bring to a boil, skim off any impurities that rise to the top, reduce the heat slightly, and cook for 20 minutes.

Place a thick slice of stale bread in the center of shallow serving bowls. Arrange pieces of the cooked fish on top. Sprinkle lightly with saffron. Strain the cooking liquid into a large pan and boil until reduced by half. Remove from the heat and whisk in the aïoli. Ladle the sauce over the fish and serve at once.

In Languedoc-Roussillon, the vines climb the hills to occupy small valleys between ridges encroached on by wastelands. Alluvium and pebbles make excellent soil.

The sea, the rounded hills of the Pyrénées-Orientales, and one upright yew tree express everything about this soil where the great sculptor Maillol experienced his first artistic feelings. Wine, here, precedes the Phoenicians, the first navigators seen on the horizon. BELOW: A much sought-after tree, the cork oak.

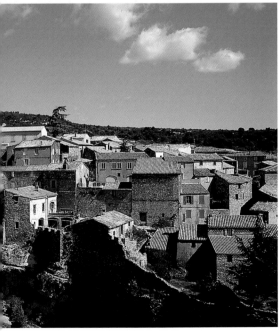

A lacework of walls and flat roofs under the blue black light of day: all the rawness of this sun-drenched land.

The modern renewal of taste for natural sweet wines has come from this Catalan doctor and wine grower in Banyuls and Collioure.

From Carcassonne, between Minervois and Corbières, to Collioure (BELOW), the port of the Albères, are vineyards where more than forty percent of French wines are still produced. Much separates the millions of gallons of good table wine (often from Aramon) from the sumptuous Maury, Banyuls, and Rivesaltes made by *mutage* from Grenache grapes and aged for months in barrels with jealous care.

Banyuls is a wine that is over a thousand years old. Books and memory led Doctor Parcé to the sources of the often mistreated wine of his region. At the Mas Blanc, property of the Parcé family since 1635, the wine growers go about their business as in the seventeenth century. On the named places of the domaine, varietals of large harvest grapes (Carignan) have been banished in favor of the old vines of Syrah or Mourvèdre (certain ones are seventy years old), to which are blended Grenache and Counoise. Harvests are totally by hand, and the grapes undergo two sortings (at harvest and reception). They macerate in *cuves à pigeage* (where the grapes are pressed by foot), and the pressings are done under light pressure. The Collioure and Banyuls from the domaine sometimes take five years, avoiding to the utmost oxidation in the barrels. The great "Parcés" continue their slow aging in bottles.

THE POURCEL BROTHERS

Restaurant "Le Jardin des Sens"
Montpellier
Hérault

Preparation: 1 hour

Cooking time: 55 minutes

Serves 6

●

6 SMALL ANGLER FISH TAILS
(OR SMALL MONKFISH FILLETS),
12 TO 14 OUNCES EACH

1 POUND BREAD DOUGH

3 OR 4 SMALL ONIONS
(ABOUT 8 OUNCES)

3 TO 4 TABLESPOONS OLIVE OIL

2 TO 3 OUNCES PITTED BLACK OLIVES,
THINLY SLICED

4 OR 5 ANCHOVY FILLETS (ABOUT
1 OUNCE) PACKED IN OIL, DRAINED

SALT AND FRESHLY GROUND BLACK
PEPPER

COARSE SEA SALT,
PREFERABLY *SEL DE GUÉRANDE*

8 RIPE MEDIUM TOMATOES,
THINLY SLICED

10 FRESH THYME SPRIGS

6 TABLESPOONS UNSALTED BUTTER

3 SHALLOTS, MINCED

2 GARLIC CLOVES, MINCED

1½ CUPS DRY WHITE WINE, PREFERABLY
CHARDONNAY FROM LANGUEDOC

¾ CUP FISH STOCK

3 RIPE MEDIUM TOMATOES, PEELED,
SEEDED, AND DICED

12 GARLIC CLOVES

1 SMALL BUNCH FRESH CHIVES

JUICE OF ½ LEMON

ROASTED ANGLER FISH WITH TOMATO AND ONION TART, CHARDONNAY SAUCE, AND FRESH THYME

Peel the angler fish tails and leave whole on the bone. Trim well and keep refrigerated until ready to prepare.

Preheat the oven to 350°F. Roll out the bread dough about ⅜ inch thick. Cut out 6 rounds that measure about 5 inches in diameter. Place on baking sheets and set aside.

Peel and thinly slice the onions. Cook in a small amount of olive oil in a skillet until softened but not browned. Add the olives and anchovies. Cook over low heat until the mixture is soft and thickened. Season with salt and pepper. Spread thinly over the dough rounds. Top with the tomato slices, overlapping as for a tart. Sprinkle with coarse salt, pepper, and fresh thyme leaves stripped from 1 of the sprigs. Drizzle with a little olive oil and bake until golden and crisp, 30 to 40 minutes.

Heat 2 tablespoons butter in a large saucepan. Add the shallots and minced garlic. Cook over medium-high heat until softened. Add the wine, increase the heat to high, and boil until reduced by half. Add the fish stock, the diced tomatoes, and 3 thyme sprigs. Boil again until reduced by half. Remove from the heat and whisk in the remaining 4 tablespoons butter. Season with salt and pepper.

Meanwhile, heat 1 tablespoon olive oil in a large nonstick skillet. Add the fish and the whole garlic cloves. Cook over high heat, turning the fish often, until browned, about 8 minutes. Drain the fish on paper towels and cut lengthwise along the bone to remove the fillets.

Place a tart in the center of each of 6 serving plates. Arrange 2 fillets of the fish on top and garnish with the bone ends, the whole cooked garlic, and the remaining thyme sprig. Add a little olive oil, a few snipped chives, and the lemon juice to the sauce. Serve the sauce on the side.

Preparation: I hour 20 minutes

Cooking time: I hour

Serves 4

●

1 TO 2 LARGE ONIONS (ABOUT 8
OUNCES)

¾ CUP OLIVE OIL

1 CUP PLUS 2 TABLESPOONS DRY WHITE
WINE, PREFERABLY
COTEAUX DU LANGUEDOC

JUICE OF 2½ LEMONS

6 BOUQUETS GARNIS

CORIANDER SEEDS

WHOLE PEPPERCORNS

SALT

12 OUNCES BUTTON MUSHROOMS

8 TINY FENNEL BULBS

8 OUNCES CARROTS

12 BABY ARTICHOKES

32 SMALL RADISHES

24 SMALL SHALLOTS, UNPEELED

1½ TO 2 POUNDS FRESH COD FILLETS

7 TABLESPOONS UNSALTED BUTTER

FRESHLY GROUND BLACK PEPPER TO
TASTE

COARSE SEA SALT TO TASTE

YOUNG VEGETABLES À LA GRECQUE WITH COD AND WHITE WINE

Peel and finely chop the onions. In a large saucepan, cook the onions in the olive oil over medium heat, stirring often, until softened but not browned, 4 to 5 minutes. Add 1 cup wine and the juice of 2 lemons. Divide the onions and liquid between 6 separate small saucepans. Add 1 bouquet garni, 10 coriander seeds, and 5 peppercorns to each saucepan. Season with salt.

Quickly rinse the mushrooms; cut in half if large. Place the mushrooms in one of the saucepans. Cover and cook over high heat for 10 minutes. Set aside.

Trim the fennel bulbs and place in one of the saucepans cook over medium-high heat for 15 minutes.

Peel the carrots and cut into ⅛-inch-thick slices. Place in one of the saucepans, and cook over medium heat for 15 minutes.

Remove the stems of the artichokes, cut the bases flat, and pull off the leaves. Trim the bottoms and scoop out the chokes with a small spoon. Rub with a little lemon juice and place in one of the saucepans. Cover and cook over medium heat for 20 minutes.

Score the radishes with a fork and trim the stems to about ⅜ inch. Place in one of the saucepans, cover, and cook over low heat for about 10 minutes.

Place the shallots in a small skillet; cover with cold water, season with salt, and bring to a boil. Reduce the heat slightly, and cook 10 to 15 minutes, depending on the size. Peel the shallots and transfer to the last of the saucepans, and cook over medium heat for 10 minutes.

Keep all of the vegetables separate.

Trim and carefully bone the cod. Cut into 4 uniform pieces and set aside.

Place the remaining 2 tablespoons wine in a saucepan and cook over high heat until almost evaporated. Add the liquid from the saucepans of cooked vegetables and whisk in 4 tablespoons butter. Season with salt and pepper. Keep warm.

Season the fish with salt and pepper. Cook in 3 tablespoons butter in a large skillet over medium-high heat until slightly browned and firm to the touch.

Gently warm all of the vegetables and place decoratively on serving plates. Spoon over a small amount of the sauce, place a piece of the fish in the center, and season with coarse salt and ground pepper. Serve at once.

Preparation: 1½ hours

Cooking time: 45 minutes

Serves 4

—

for the shellfish:

8 OUNCES PERIWINKLES

20 COCKLES (SEE NOTE)

12 SMALL CLAMS (SEE NOTE)

8 OUNCES MUSSELS, DEBEARDED

2 TABLESPOONS CHOPPED FRESH PARSLEY

4 SHALLOTS, MINCED

3 SMALL FRESH THYME SPRIGS

1 BAY LEAF

1¼ CUPS DRY WHITE WINE, PREFERABLY
FROM CORBIÈRES

2 TABLESPOONS VINEGAR

4 TABLESPOONS UNSALTED BUTTER

for the garnish and sauce:

ABOUT 1½ CUPS OLIVE OIL

2 MEDIUM ONIONS, FINELY CHOPPED

8 MEDIUM TOMATOES, PEELED, SEEDED,
AND DICED

1 GARLIC CLOVE, PEELED AND CRUSHED

1 BOUQUET GARNI

SALT AND FRESHLY GROUND BLACK
PEPPER TO TASTE

2 TABLESPOONS CHOPPED FRESH HERBS

2 MEDIUM EGGPLANTS, TRIMMED AND
THINLY SLICED

4 CÈPES OR PORCINI MUSHROOMS
(*BOLETUS EDULIS*)

6 TABLESPOONS UNSALTED BUTTER

2 TABLESPOONS CRÈME FRAÎCHE

4 LARGE EGGS

COARSE SEA SALT TO TASTE

POACHED EGGS WITH MUSSELS, COCKLES, CLAMS, AND WHITE WINE

To prepare the shellfish, scrub the periwinkles, cockles, and clams well. Rinse the mussels in plenty of cold water. In a large pan, combine 1 tablespoon parsley, half of the minced shallots, 1 thyme sprig, half of the bay leaf, ¾ cup wine, 1 tablespoon vinegar, and 2 tablespoons butter cut into small pieces. Add the mussels and cook over high heat, stirring often, until they open. Drain well and strain the liquid through a sieve lined with dampened cheesecloth. Remove the mussels from their shells. Set aside, covered with a little of the strained cooking liquid.

Cook the periwinkles in salted water for 5 minutes. Drain well and use a needle or pin to pull the flesh from the shells. Set aside, covered with a small amount of their cooking liquid.

Cook the cockles as you did the mussels, using ½ tablespoon chopped parsley, 1 shallot, 1 thyme sprig, ¼ of the bay leaf, ¼ cup wine, ½ tablespoon vinegar, and 1 tablespoon butter. Remove the cooked cockles from their shells, strain the liquid, and set aside, covered with some of the strained liquid.

Cook the clams as you did the cockles, using the remaining parsley, shallot, thyme, bay leaf, wine, vinegar, and butter. Shell and keep covered with the strained cooking liquid.

To make the garnish and sauce, heat ¾ cup olive oil in a large heavy saucepan. Add the onions and cook over medium-high heat until slightly softened. Add the tomatoes, garlic, and bouquet garni. Season with salt and pepper and cook, stirring often, until the tomatoes are very soft. Season again with salt and pepper, then work through a sieve, pushing hard on the solids. Add 1 tablespoon of the chopped herbs and set aside, covered, to keep warm.

Sprinkle the eggplant slices with salt and set aside for 15 to 20 minutes to draw out the bitter liquid. Pat dry with paper towels. Heat ½ cup olive oil in a large skillet. Add the eggplant and cook over medium-high heat, turning often, until lightly browned. Set aside, covered, to keep warm.

Clean the mushrooms and blanch quickly in boiling salted water. Drain and thickly slice. Heat ¼ cup olive oil in a large skillet. Add the mushrooms slices, season with salt and pepper, and cook until they start to give off liquid. Drain well. Melt 2 tablespoons of the butter in a large skillet. Add the mushroom slices and cook over high heat until browned. Set aside on paper towels to drain.

To assemble the dish, boil the mussels cooking liquid in a large heavy saucepan until reduced by half. Stir in the crème fraîche, then whisk in the remaining 4 tablespoons butter. Season with salt and pepper. Stir in ½ tablespoon of the chopped herbs.

Break one of the eggs into a small saucer without breaking the yolk. Place a sufficient quantity of the cooking liquid from the shellfish in a large saucepan and bring to a boil. Reduce the heat to a simmer and slip in one of the eggs. Cook 3 to 5 minutes. Use a slotted spoon to transfer the egg to a kitchen towel to drain. Repeat with the remaining 3 eggs.

Divide the tomato mixture between 4 shallow serving bowls. Arrange the eggplant slices, overlapping, in the shape of a flower in each one. Place the mussels, periwinkles, cockles, and clams decoratively around the eggplant and the mushroom slices between them. Place an egg in the center and spoon over some of the sauce. Season with sea salt, pepper, and garnish with the remaining ½ tablespoon chopped herbs. Serve at once.

NOTE: Cockles are a common edible European bivalve. Hard-shell clams are perfect substitutes. Cockles must be purged in salted water for 24 hours before using.

The original recipe called for a specific mollusk, *amandes,* rather than small clams. These are difficult to find outside Europe. Steamer clams or cherrystones can be used instead.

LANGUEDOC - ROUSSILLON

for the chicken:

28 LARGE CHICKEN WINGS

2 CUPS FRESH BREAD CRUMBS

1¼ CUPS MILK

SALT AND FRESHLY GROUND BLACK
PEPPER TO TASTE

½ BUNCH FRESH CHERVIL,
FINELY CHOPPED

½ BUNCH FRESH CHIVES,
FINELY CHOPPED

½ BUNCH FRESH PARSLEY,
FINELY CHOPPED

for the custards:

1 POUND PEELED FRESH PUMPKIN,
CUT INTO CUBES

1 SMALL ALL-PURPOSE POTATO,
PEELED AND DICED

3 GARLIC CLOVES, PEELED

1 LARGE EGG

⅔ CUP CRÈME FRAÎCHE

SALT AND FRESHLY GROUND BLACK
PEPPER TO TASTE

FRESHLY GRATED NUTMEG TO TASTE

for cooking the wings:

12 TABLESPOONS UNSALTED BUTTER

SALT AND FRESHLY GROUND BLACK
PEPPER TO TASTE

½ CARROT, DICED

½ ONION, FINELY CHOPPED

½ LEEK, GREENS ONLY, FINELY CHOPPED

1 CELERY RIB, THINLY SLICED

¾ CUP PLUS 1 TABLESPOON HEARTY RED
WINE, PREFERABLY MAURY

¾ CUP CHICKEN STOCK

HERB-STUFFED CHICKEN WINGS BRAISED IN RED WINE WITH PUMPKIN GARLIC CUSTARD

To prepare the chicken, remove and discard the tips of the wings. Cut between the joints to separate the two pieces. Reserve the flat halves for making stock. Bone the "drumettes" and keep refrigerated.

Place the bread crumbs in a large saucepan. Bring the milk to a boil and pour over the bread crumbs. When the milk has been absorbed, season with salt and pepper. Cook, stirring, over medium heat until the mixture starts to pull away from the side of the pan. Turn out into a buttered dish and cool. Stir in the herbs. Stuff the boned "drumettes" with this filling and sew the ends closed. Refrigerate for 1 hour.

To make the custards, preheat the oven to 300°F and prepare a water bath. Cook the pumpkin and potato in salted water until tender. Drain well and pass through a food mill into a large saucepan. Cook over medium-high heat, stirring constantly, until any excess moisture has evaporated.

Cook the garlic cloves in boiling salted water until tender. Transfer to a food processor. Add the egg and crème fraîche. Process until smooth. Stir into the pumpkin mixture and season with salt, pepper, and nutmeg. Pour into individual molds and cook in the water bath until firm, about 20 minutes.

To cook the wings, melt 4 tablespoons butter in a large skillet. Add the "drumettes" and cook over medium-high heat, turning often, until brown on all sides, about 5 minutes. Season well with salt and pepper. Add the carrot, onion, leek, and celery and cook until slightly softened. Increase the heat to high and pour in ¾ cup wine. Cook, stirring to loosen any browned bits in the bottom of the skillet, until reduced by half. Add the stock, reduce the heat to medium, and cook, covered, for about 15 minutes.

Unmold the pumpkin custards onto the centers of individual serving plates. Remove the strings from the wings and arrange around the custards. Boil the pan juices remaining in the skillet until reduced and thickened. Whisk in 8 tablespoons butter bit by bit and the remaining 1 tablespoon wine. Spoon this sauce over the wings, give a grind fresh pepper, and serve at once.

At Mas Amiel, Maury wines age in demijohns under the hot sun of the Midi.

Preparation: I hour

Cooking time: 2¹/₂ hours

Serves 4

—

4 PARTRIDGES, PREFERABLY WILD

2 TABLESPOONS UNSALTED BUTTER,
SOFTENED

SALT AND FRESHLY GROUND BLACK
PEPPER TO TASTE

1 SMALL SAVOY OR GREEN CABBAGE

5 TO 10 RINDS OF SLAB BACON,
DEPENDING ON SIZE

3 CARROTS, PEELED AND DICED

2 ONIONS, DICED

1 BOUQUET GARNI

10 TABLESPOONS UNSALTED BUTTER

¹/₂ SPLIT CALF'S FOOT

1¹/₄ CUPS HEARTY RED WINE, PREFERABLY
COLLIOURE

³/₄ CUP PLUS 1 TABLESPOON FORTIFIED
DESSERT WINE, PREFERABLY RIVESALTES
RANCIO

2 TABLESPOONS VEGETABLE OIL

PARTRIDGE WITH BRAISED CABBAGE AND RED WINE

Clean and eviscerate the birds. Pat dry with paper towels and truss. Rub with the softened butter and season well with salt and pepper. Keep refrigerated.

Preheat the oven to 300° F. Separate the cabbage leaves and trim away the tough center ribs. Line the bottom of a large enameled cast-iron casserole with a layer of bacon rinds. Top with the carrots and then the onions. Sprinkle with salt and pepper and add the bouquet garni. Heat 6 tablespoons butter until lightly browned and pour into the casserole. Add a thick layer of the cabbage leaves. Place the halved calf's foot on top of the cabbage and pour in the red wine. Boil on top of the stove to reduce the amount of liquid by three-quarters. Add ¾ cup sweet wine and cover. Transfer to the oven and bake for 2 hours.

After the cabbage has cooked for 1¼ hours, melt 2 tablespoons butter with the vegetable oil in a large skillet. Add the birds and cook over medium-high heat, turning often, until browned on all sides. Remove the calf's foot from the casserole and save for another use. Place the browned birds on top of the cabbage, cover, and cook until the juices run clear when the thigh is pierced with a skewer, about 30 minutes. Do not overcook. Pour the cooking juices from the casserole into a large saucepan. Remove the trussing strings from the birds. Lift off the breasts and cut away the thighs. (Save the carcasses for another use.) Carefully remove the bone from each thigh, leaving the drumstick intact. Return the breasts and legs to the casserole and cover to keep warm.

Skim off the fat from the cooking juices and boil over high heat until reduced by half. Whisk in the remaining 2 tablespoons butter, season with salt and pepper, and add the remaining 1 tablespoon sweet wine. Pour over the partridges and cabbage.

Preparation: 30 minutes

Serves 4

━

2 RIPE, FRAGRANT MELONS

¼ CUP SUGAR

½ BOTTLE SWEET MUSCAT WINE,
PREFERABLY FROM RIVESALTES

4 OUNCES WILD STRAWBERRIES
(*FRAISES DES BOIS*)

FRESH MINT LEAVES, FOR GARNISH

MELON AND WILD STRAWBERRIES IN SWEET WINE

Using a stainless-steel knife, halve the melons. Remove the seeds and all stringy fibers. Using two different melon ballers, cut out large and small balls from the melons. Place in a large bowl and sprinkle with the sugar. Add the wine and macerate in the refrigerator for 2 hours.

Attractively arrange the melon balls in small serving bowls and top with the strawberries. Decorate with mint leaves and serve at once.

For a more elaborate presentation, the fruit can be served in a scooped-out melon shell with edges cut into a zigzag pattern to form a garnish called wolves' teeth.

Preparation: 1 hour

Cooking time: 25 minutes

Serves 6

━

¾ CUP RAISINS, CHOPPED

1 CUP CANDIED CHERRIES, COARSELY
CHOPPED

½ CUP DICED CANDIED ORANGE PEEL

¾ CUP CHOPPED ASSORTED CANDIED
FRUITS

1 BOTTLE SWEET MUSCAT WINE,
PREFERABLY MUSCAT DE LUNEL

¾ CUP GRANULATED SUGAR

2 CUPS HONEY

½ CUP LIGHT CORN SYRUP

1 CUP MINERAL WATER

8 LARGE EGG WHITES

4 CUPS HEAVY CREAM

1½ CUPS WALNUT HALVES

1 CUP SLICED ALMONDS, TOASTED

1½ CUPS CONFECTIONERS' SUGAR

1½ POUNDS FRESH RASPBERRIES

JUICE OF 1 LEMON

FROZEN NOUGAT WITH RASPBERRIES AND SWEET WINE

In a large bowl, combine the raisins, cherries, orange peel, and candied fruits. Reserve 1 tablespoon of the wine and pour the rest over the fruit. Set aside to macerate.

In a large nonreactive saucepan, combine the granulated sugar, honey, corn syrup, and mineral water. Bring to a boil and cook until the mixture reaches the hard-ball stage, 248°F on a candy thermometer. Beat the egg whites until stiff and, with the beaters in motion, pour in the hot syrup. Continue beating until cool. Add the cream. Lightly drain the macerated fruit and fold it into the egg white mixture along with the walnuts and almonds. Pour into a large rectangular terrine mold and freeze.

Sprinkle the confectioners' sugar over 1 pound of the raspberries. Work the mixture through a stainless-steel seive, pressing to extract the juices. Pour in a little water if necessary to ease the process. Flavor with the lemon juice and the reserved 1 tablespoon wine. Chill.

Dip the bottom of the nougat terrine in cold water and unmold it. Cut into slices and serve on individual plates. Surround with some of the raspberry sauce and decorate with the remaining whole raspberries. Serve very cold.

QUERCY · GASCONY

Between the Massif Central and the Pyrénées, the "Pays Basque" spreads out and Vascons became Gascons. On both sides of the Garonne River, however, one must distinguish between what belongs to Guyenne, the Agenais, the Landes, Armagnac, or Béarn. Sharp souls will be able to discern more than subtle nuances between that which comes from the north of the river and that which comes from the south. The Agenais, Quercy, or Chalosse are so many different entities even if they do have a certain family likeness, a certain "accent." Napoleon III and Empress Eugénie, Henri IV and the English of the Black Prince, the bishops of Auch and Cahors, the hardy seamen of Bayonne and Saint-Jean-de-Luz—each in their century left a mark. An undeniable parcelling out of territories and influences remains, which reflects the dispersion of two dozen notable vineyards, of which Cahors is not the least. The vineyards of Irouléguy, Jurançon, Madiran, among others, adorn Béarn and Gascony; those of Bergerac, the Agenais, and Gaillac are the crown of the southwest. Gastronomy here was born of proverbial frugality. It grew more on an alchemy of powerful tastes than from quantity. The things that truly count are the authenticity and robust character of the products, an economy of tastes, and a respect for preparations such as confit or foie gras. Poultry is queen, especially the goose. Along with game and various pork dishes, there are the simple but wisely prepared compositions to accompany superb and substantial vegetables. From the Pyrénées and Causse come great dairy products and admirable beef and lamb. The sea and the *gaves*, or mountain streams, provide fish. It is to the sea as much as to alchemy that is owed the extraction of a great brandy: Armagnac.

A GLIMPSE AT TRADITION

Wood Pigeon Stew

Cut a mature wood pigeon into small pieces. Peel an onion, 3 shallots, and 2 carrots and cut each into fine dice. Melt 2 tablespoons unsalted butter in a large skillet. Add the pigeon and vegetables. Cook over medium-high heat, stirring often, until tender, 7 to 8 minutes. Add 1 minced garlic clove and a little flour. Cook for 3 to 4 minutes longer. Sprinkle in 1 tablespoon Armagnac and flame. Pour in 2 cups Cahors wine (reserving 2 tablespoons), 1 tablespoon strained tomatoes, and 1 bouquet garni. Season with salt and pepper. Reduce the heat to medium, cover, and simmer for 1 hour.

When the hour is up, remove the hearts and livers of 4 small wood pigeons. Skewer and roast over a spit or in a hot oven to sear the birds; they should remain very rare. Meanwhile, strain the contents of the skillet through a fine sieve into a wide sauté pan, pressing hard on the solids to extract as much flavor as possible. Keep this sauce warm over medium-low heat. Skim off any fat from the pan beneath the spit or the roasting pan. Add the hearts and livers to the pan, sprinkle in 1 tablespoon Armagnac, and flame. Pour in the reserved 2 tablespoons Cahors and bring to a boil.

Cut the roasted pigeons in half on a cutting board, catching the juices and reserving them. Place the birds in the pan with the simmering sauce and cook 4 to 5 minutes. Transfer the birds to a warmed serving platter and keep covered loosely with foil. Add the accumulated juices from cutting the birds, the hearts and livers with pan juices, and 4 tablespoons unsalted butter to the sauce and heat through. Pour the sauce over the birds and serve at once with fried croutons.

Beginning with those of the chubby-cheeked Bacchus, who still presides here and there over the fate of the vineyards, all the gifts of nature come together in the opulent southwest, the lands of the Garonne River from Quercy to the Pyrénées. Pious pilgrims heading for Saint-Jacques-de-Compostelle stopped in Cahors, where one sees (ABOVE AT LEFT) the Pont Valantré over the Lot River. The people of Cahors have always been businessmen and were among the first bankers.

An art of living which is unequalled elsewhere flourished here. The Château Lagrezette, at the heart of a well-known vineyard, derives its glory from the often celebrated harmony between its great wine and food prepared by artisans specializing in the transformation of local products.

In the midst of a great renaissance, the vineyards of Cahors are one of the eighteen AOC areas of the southwest. They cover today almost 8,600 acres thickly planted with Auxerrois, Tannat, and Merlot.

A.D. PERRIN (CHÂTEAU LAGREZETTE)

In about fifteen years, Alain Dominique Perrin has given new importance to one of the greatest wines of the southwest: Cahors.

The wines of Cahors, which in the Middle Ages were willingly compared to the most prestigious wine of that era, have once again found expression in the Château Lagrezette, produced by Alain Dominique Perrin. On a sîte that is more than five hundred years old, the domaine of the Château Lagrezette comprises about 125 acres planted with Auxerrois (70 percent), Merlot (26 percent), and Tannat (4 percent). Blending in proportions that vary with the vintage, they make what was once called "black wine" when Guyenne was ruled by the English. The wine of Château Lagrezette is made from grapes that have been handpicked and sorted before pressing. These chosen fruits undergo a long maceration. The blending and aging in new barrels takes place in an unusual cave dug out of the calcareous soil. The Cahors of Lagrezette is a long-keeping wine.

Preparation: 50 minutes

Cooking time: 45 minutes

Serves 4

●

48 CHICKEN WINGS

2 LARGE CUCUMBERS, PEELED, HALVED
LENGTHWISE, AND SEEDED

4 TABLESPOONS UNSALTED BUTTER

SALT AND FRESHLY GROUND BLACK
PEPPER TO TASTE

4 OUNCES MUSHROOMS,
TRIMMED AND DICED

½ SMALL SHALLOT, MINCED

¼ CUP DRY WHITE VERMOUTH

¾ CUP DRY WHITE WINE,
PREFERABLY TURSAN

1 CUP HEAVY CREAM

2 TABLESPOONS CHOPPED FRESH
TOMATO

½ TEASPOON CHOPPED FRESH
TARRAGON

2 TEASPOONS CHOPPED FRESH CHERVIL

PINCH OF SUGAR

CHICKEN WINGS IN WHITE WINE WITH CUCUMBER

Remove the tips of the wings and discard. Separate the remaining wing parts at the joint. Reserve the "drumettes" for another use. Plunge the flat joints into boiling water for 2 to 3 minutes. With a slotted spoon, transfer to drain on clean kitchen towels. Pat dry with paper towels. When cool enough to handle, bone the flat joints by pushing hard on one end with your thumb and pulling away the bones from the opposite end, like removing a knife from a sheath. Discard the bones.

Cut the cucumbers into 2-inch pieces and trim the pieces into ovals. Blanch for 3 minutes in boiling salted water. Drain well and set aside.

Melt 2 tablespoons butter in a large heavy skillet. Add the boned wings and season with salt and pepper. Cook over medium heat, turning often, until lightly browned, about 10 minutes. Remove with a slotted spoon to drain on paper towels. Add the mushrooms and shallot to the skillet. Cook until lightly colored, about 3 minutes. Pour off the fat from the skillet and add the vermouth and white wine. Increase the heat to high and boil until the amount of liquid has reduced by three-quarters. Add the cream, tomato, tarragon, and half of the chervil. Boil again to reduce by half. Season with salt and pepper, reduce the heat to low, and add the boned wings. Keep the wings warm in the sauce but do not boil.

Melt the remaining 2 tablespoons butter in a small skillet. Add the blanched cucumbers and the sugar. Cook over high heat, stirring often, until lightly browned, about 2 minutes. Season with salt and pepper.

Arrange the chicken wings on a large serving platter and spoon over the sauce. Surround with the cucumbers and sprinkle with the remaining 1 teaspoon chervil. Serve at once.

Begin 2 days before

Preparation: 50 minutes

Cooking time: 35 minutes

Serves 4

●

1 LEMON

¾ CUP PLUS 6 TABLESPOONS OLIVE OIL

½ BOTTLE PLUS 1 TABLESPOON DRY WHITE WINE, PREFERABLY FROM GAILLAC

8 CORIANDER SEEDS, CRUSHED

2 LARGE TOMATOES, PEELED, SEEDED, AND DICED

1 TEASPOON CHOPPED FRESH BASIL

1 TEASPOON CHOPPED FRESH TARRAGON

¼ CUP WATER

JUICE OF ½ LEMON

5 TABLESPOONS UNSALTED BUTTER, CUT INTO SMALL PIECES AND CHILLED

SALT AND FRESHLY GROUND BLACK PEPPER TO TASTE

1 TEASPOON SNIPPED FRESH CHIVES

16 SMALL SPRING ONIONS, WHITE PART ONLY

20 SMALL SEA SCALLOPS

LEMON SCALLOPS WITH WHITE WINE AND TOMATO

Scrub the lemon, cut into ⅜-inch-thick slices, and remove the seeds. Pour ¾ cup olive oil into a small saucepan. Bring to a simmer over medium-high heat. Add the lemon slices and reduce the heat to medium-low. Cook for 1 hour. Remove from the heat and cool. Repeat the cooking procedure every 8 hours for 2 days. Drain well and finely dice.

Pour the half bottle of wine in a large nonreactive saucepan and bring to a boil. Boil until reduced by three-quarters. Meanwhile, combine 6 tablespoons olive oil, the coriander seeds, diced tomatoes, basil, tarragon, and diced lemon in a small saucepan. Set aside at room temperature to macerate for 1 hour.

In a separate saucepan, combine the water and lemon juice. Bring to a boil. Working on and off the heat, gradually whisk in the pieces of butter until thick and emulsified. Remove from the heat and season with salt and pepper. Add the chives, reduced wine, and butter sauce to the tomato mixture. Season again with salt and pepper. Blanch the spring onions in boiling salted water for 10 minutes. Drain and refresh in cold water. Drain again.

Preheat the oven to 500°F. Place the scallops on a nonstick baking sheet. Bake until the scallops start to brown, 3 to 4 minutes. Remove from the oven and season with salt and pepper. Carefully dislodge the scallops from the baking sheet with a spatula and season again with salt and pepper.

Add the remaining 1 tablespoon wine to the sauce and gently warm over low heat. Spoon a small amount of the sauce over the bottoms of individual serving bowls. Top with the scallops and garnish with the spring onions. Serve at once.

Begin the night before

Preparation: 30 minutes

Cooking time: 40 minutes

Serves 8

—●—

8 OUNCES DRIED WHITE BEANS

1 CARROT

1 ONION STUDDED WITH 1 WHOLE
CLOVE

COARSE SEA SALT

1 CUP HEARTY RED WINE, PREFERABLY
MADIRAN

⅓ CUP TRUFFLE JUICE

1 CUP CRÈME FRAÎCHE

5 TABLESPOONS UNSALTED BUTTER

SALT AND FRESHLY GROUND BLACK
PEPPER TO TASTE

1½ TO 3 OUNCES BLACK TRUFFLES,
THINLY SLICED

½ CUP WATER

WHITE BEAN SOUP WITH RED WINE AND TRUFFLES

Soak the beans overnight in cold water. Drain well and place in a large pot or kettle. Add the carrot and onion. Bring to a boil over high heat, reduce the heat to medium-low, and simmer, until the beans are tender. Remove from the heat, discard the carrot and onion, and season with coarse salt.

Place ½ cup cooked beans with some of their cooking liquid in a small saucepan. Work the remaining beans with their cooking liquid first through a food mill, then through a fine sieve into a large saucepan. Gently heat, stirring often, until warmed through.

Bring the wine to a boil in a large nonreactive saucepan. Boil until reduced to about 1 tablespoon. Add this reduction to the soup. Stir in the truffle juice and the crème fraîche. Warm over low heat and stir in 3 tablespoons butter. Season with salt and pepper.

Melt the remaining 2 tablespoons butter in a small skillet over medium-high heat. Add the truffles and warm through. Remove with a slotted spoon and set aside. Pour the water into the skillet and bring to a boil over high heat. Boil, stirring to pick up any cooked bits on the bottom of the skillet, until the liquid has reduced and thickened. Pour into the soup. Transfer the soup to a food processor and process briefly.

Gently reheat the reserved beans with their liquid. Place a spoonful of beans in the bottom of warmed shallow bowls. Ladle the hot soup into the bowls. Float the slices of truffles on top. Serve at once, sprinkled lightly with freshly ground pepper.

Preserved in a glass jar at L'Ami Pebeyre in Cahors, this ten-pound truffle was purchased by M. Baudouin in the marketplace of Carpentras— in 1847!

1 LARGE GUINEA HEN,
CLEANED AND TRIMMED

2 TABLESPOONS VEGETABLE OIL

1 SMALL CARROT, DICED

1 SMALL ONION, DICED

½ LEEK, GREENS ONLY, SLICED

¼ CELERY RIB, DICED

1 GARLIC CLOVE, CRUSHED

¾ CUP DRY WHITE WINE, PREFERABLY
BERGERAC

2 CUPS RED WINE, PREFERABLY BUZET

1 BOUQUET GARNI

2 TRUFFLES, ABOUT 1 OUNCE EACH

SALT AND FRESHLY GROUND BLACK
PEPPER TO TASTE

1¾ CUPS CRÈME FRAÎCHE

1 LARGE PIECE CAUL FAT,
CUT INTO 4 PIECES

12 PEARL ONIONS

14 TABLESPOONS UNSALTED BUTTER

PINCH OF SUGAR

8 BABY OR NEW CARROTS

4 BABY WHITE TURNIPS

4 LARGE ASPARAGUS SPEARS, TRIMMED

1 POUND WILD MUSHROOMS,
PREFERABLY *TROMPETTES DES MORTS*,
CLEANED AND TRIMMED

2 CUPS CHICKEN STOCK

ROLLED BREAST AND WRAPPED THIGHS OF GUINEA HEN WITH TRUFFLES AND RED WINE

Cut the guinea hen into pieces, reserving the thighs and breast. Chop the carcass into small pieces and place in a large saucepan. Add the vegetable oil and cook, stirring often, over medium-high heat until well browned. Add the carrot, onion, leek greens, celery, and garlic. Reduce the heat to medium-low and cook until the vegetables are lightly browned, about 10 minutes. Pour off any accumulated fat and add the white wine. Increase the heat to medium-high and cook until almost all the liquid has evaporated. Add the red wine and cook again until almost dry. Pour in enough cold water to cover the contents of the pan and increase the heat to high. Bring to a boil, skimming the surface often. Add the bouquet garni, reduce the heat to medium-low, and simmer, covered, for 2 hours. Strain through a fine sieve and reserve.

Trim and peel the truffles. Cut one into small matchsticks and mince the other.

Spread a large piece of plastic wrap on a work surface. Remove the skin from the guinea hen breast and cut the breast in half. Arrange the two parts lengthwise, touching, in a row down the center of the plastic. Place the matchstick truffle pieces along the top of the breast halves and season with salt and pepper. Tightly roll to form a sort of guinea hen "sausage" with a truffle center. Wrap tightly with the plastic wrap and secure the ends with kitchen string. Keep refrigerated.

Bone the thighs of the guinea hen and remove any tough nerves. Cut the thighs into long, thin slices. Finely chop half of these slices and place in a large bowl. Place this bowl over a larger bowl containing ice and cold water. Incorporate the crème fraîche, beating constantly with a wooden spoon. Add half of the minced truffles and season with salt and pepper.

Spread the squares of caul fat on a work surface. Top one square with one of the thigh slices and spread over a spoonful of the crème fraîche mixture. Cover with another thigh slice and roll tightly in the caul fat. Continue with the remaining ingredients. Keep refrigerated.

Peel the pearl onions and place in a small saucepan. Add 1 tablespoon butter, a pinch of sugar, and salt. Pour in just enough cold water to cover and bring to a boil over medium-high heat. Cook, stirring, until the water has evaporated and the onions are tender and glazed. Cook the carrots and turnips separately in the same manner.

Cook the asparagus spears in boiling salted water until tender, about 5 minutes. Refresh under cold running water. Cook the mushrooms in 2 tablespoons butter and reserve.

Pour the chicken stock into a large wide saucepan and bring to a simmer over medium heat. Add the guinea hen "sausage" and gently poach for 10 minutes. Melt 5 tablespoons butter in a large skillet and add the thighs wrapped in caul fat. Cook over medium-high heat, turning often, until well browned.

Remove the "sausage" from the stock and cover with foil to keep warm. Boil the stock until reduced by one-third. Add the remaining minced truffle, whisk in 4 tablespoons butter, and season with salt and pepper. Keep warm.

To serve, reheat all the vegetables separately and arrange on warmed serving plates. Slice the "sausage" and arrange in the center of the plates. Cut the thighs in caul fat in half and place on top of the slices. Spoon over a small amount of the sauce. Sprinkle with salt and add a grinding or two of fresh pepper. Serve at once.

Begin 2 days before

Preparation: 1½ hours

Cooking time: 2½ hours

Serves 12

—●—

3 LOBES RAW DUCK FOIE GRAS

SALT AND FRESHLY GROUND BLACK PEPPER TO TASTE

PINCH OF SALT PETER (NITRATE SALT, AVAILABLE IN SOME PHARMACIES)

PINCH OF *QUATRE-ÉPICES* (SEE NOTE, PAGE 26)

FRESHLY GRATED NUTMEG TO TASTE

3 CUPS PORT

¾ CUP COGNAC

3 QUARTS DUCK STOCK

1¾ POUNDS LEAN BEEF

1 LARGE LEEK, TRIMMED

1 CELERY RIB, FINELY CHOPPED

2 LARGE EGG WHITES

1 ENVELOPE UNFLAVORED GELATIN

¼ CUP COLD WATER

3 TABLESPOONS UNSALTED BUTTER

8 OUNCES SHALLOTS, MINCED

3 GARLIC CLOVES, CRUSHED

1 LARGE VEAL BONE

2 CARROTS

1 TOMATO, COARSELY CHOPPED

2 WHOLE CLOVES

1 FRESH THYME SPRIG

1 FRESH BAY LEAF

2 BOTTLES DRY WHITE WINE, PREFERABLY JURAÇON

¼ CUP VEGETABLE OIL

2 TABLESPOONS OLIVE OIL

3 TABLESPOON SHERRY VINEGAR

3 TABLESPOONS TRUFFLE JUICE

1¼ POUNDS LAMB'S LETTUCE (MÂCHE), TRIMMED, RINSED, AND DRIED

3 TO 4 OUNCES BLACK TRUFFLES, THINLY SLICED

FOIE GRAS WITH WINE ASPIC, LAMB'S LETTUCE, AND TRUFFLES

Place the foie gras in a large bowl and pour in enough cold water to cover. Soak for 4 hours. Remove the lobes from the water and carefully pat dry with paper towels. Cut out all traces of green gall bladder from the liver, then pull the lobes apart with your hands. With a small paring knife, remove all stringy parts, all large nerves, and any bloody veins. Work carefully; try not to destroy the original shape of the lobes and try to reserve the fine, thin skin that surrounds the exterior of the livers. Weigh the lobes and place in a large shallow bowl. Sprinkle 1½ teaspoons salt and 1 teaspoon freshly ground black pepper per pound of liver over the lobes. Add the salt peter, the *quatre-épices*, and a grating or two of fresh nutmeg. Pour in the port and Cognac, turning the livers carefully to distribute the seasonings and marinade. Cover with parchment paper and refrigerate at least overnight.

Remove the livers from the refrigerator a little in advance so that they soften slightly. Pour the duck stock into a large wide pan and bring to a simmer over medium heat. Spread a clean linen kitchen towel on a large work surface. Place the lobes in the center and roll the livers tightly in the towel to form a fat sausage; secure the ends with string. Place the rolled foie gras in the simmering stock and cook for 15 to 20 minutes. (The foie gras must be submerged during the cooking. Add simmering water if necessary to keep the roll constantly under liquid.) Remove the pan from the heat, leaving the roll in the liquid, and let cool to room temperature. Cover and chill overnight.

Remove any fat from the duck stock. Strain into a large saucepan and bring to a boil over high heat. Reduce the heat to medium and gently simmer until the liquid has reduced by half. To clarify the stock, finely chop half of the lean beef and the green part of the leek. In a separate saucepan, whisk together the chopped beef, leek green, celery, and egg whites. Whisking constantly, pour in the hot stock and bring to a boil over high heat. Reduce the heat to medium and simmer gently for 1½ hours. Ladle the clear stock through a fine sieve lined with a double layer of rinsed cheesecloth. Sprinkle the gelatin over the cold water and let stand for 5 minutes to soften. Stir into the warm strained stock.

In a large saucepan, melt the butter. Add the remaining beef cut into large cubes, the shallots, garlic, veal bone, carrots, tomato, cloves, thyme, and bay leaf. Finely chop the remaining white of the leek and add to the pan. Cook, stirring often, over medium-high heat until the vegetables are lightly browned. Bring the wine to a boil in a large nonreactive saucepan and flame. When the flames subside, pour the wine into the vegetable mixture. Season with salt and pepper, bring to a boil, reduce the heat, and simmer for 30 minutes. Season again with salt and pepper. Strain through a fine sieve and add the clarified duck stock. Cool. To test the gelatin, pour a small amount over the bottom of a large plate. Add more gelatin if the mixture is too runny.

Remove the foie gras from the towel and cut into slices. Ladle some of the aspic over the slices and refrigerate. Solidify the remaining aspic in the refrigerator, then finely chop it to serve on the side. Keep refrigerated.

Make a sauce for the salad by whisking together the two oils, the vinegar, truffle juice, salt, and pepper in a large bowl. Add the lettuce and toss well to coat.

Place 2 slices foie gras on each plate. Garnish with the dressed lettuce and chopped aspic and sprinkle with the truffle slices. Season with freshly ground pepper and serve at once.

Preparation: 1½ hours

Cooking time: 2 hours

Serves 6

—

2 LARGE PINK GRAPEFRUIT

3 CUPS GRANULATED SUGAR,
PLUS MORE TO CANDY THE PEELS

ABOUT 1 CUP COARSE OR CRYSTAL
SUGAR

1 CUP COLD WATER

6 GREEN APPLES

½ CUP CHOPPED ALMONDS

½ CUP ALL-PURPOSE FLOUR

JUICE OF 1 ORANGE

2 TEASPOONS FINELY GRATED ORANGE
ZEST

⅓ CUP UNSALTED BUTTER, MELTED

JUICE OF ½ LEMON

¾ CUP PLUS 6 TABLESPOONS
FLOC DE GASCOGNE (SEE NOTE)

GREEN APPLE GRANITÉ WITH FLOC DE GASCOGNE AND COOKIES FILLED WITH CANDIED PINK GRAPEFRUIT

With a large serrated knife, cut a slice from the top and bottom of each grapefruit. Working from the top to the bottom, cut away the zest and pith, following the curve of the fruit. (Reserve the flesh for another use.) Trim the grapefruit peel into long pieces about the size of a thick French fry. Bring a large pot of water to a boil and add the trimmed peels. Boil for 5 minutes, then refresh under cold running water. Repeat this procedure 5 times. After they have been blanched, transfer to a scale and weigh. Place the peels and an equal weight of granulated sugar in a large saucepan. Stir in a couple spoonfuls of water. Start cooking over medium-low heat and gradually increase the heat until the mixture boils. Then reduce the heat to low and simmer until the peels are transparent, about 50 minutes. Using a slotted spoon, transfer the candied peels to drain on wire racks. When cool, roll the peels in coarse sugar.

Preheat the oven to 150°F. Prepare a simple sugar syrup by combining ½ cup granulated sugar with 1 cup cold water in a small saucepan. Bring to a boil over high heat, then reduce the heat to medium. Cut one of the apples (unpeeled) into paper-thin slices on a mandoline. Plunge the slices into the syrup and poach for about 15 minutes. Drain and place on a baking sheet. Bake in the oven for 15 to 20 minutes, until the slices harden and crystallize. Keep in an airtight container until ready to serve the dessert.

Preheat the oven to 325°F. Combine 1 cup granulated sugar, the almonds, flour, orange juice, orange zest, and butter. Mix well to form a batter. Pour onto a nonstick baking sheet and spread thin. Bake for 6 to 7 minutes. As soon as the baking sheet comes out of the oven, cut into rectangles that measure 2½ inches long and 1½ inches wide and quickly roll into long, thin cylinders that resemble cigarettes.

Peel the remaining 5 apples, halve, and remove the cores. In a food processor, combine the lemon juice, the ¾ cup Floc de Gascogne, and 1½ cups granulated sugar. Add the apples and purée until smooth. Pour into a large nonreactive dish and freeze, stirring every 15 minutes with a fork to break up the crystals, until icy. Keep frozen.

To serve, fill ice cream dishes or bowls with scoops of the granité. Slip one of the candied grapefruit peels into each cookie and arrange on plates with the granité. Pour 1 tablespoon Floc de Gascogne into each dish and garnish with apple crisps.

NOTE: Floc de Gascogne is a sweet aromatic produced in the area around Armagnac. It is made of unfermented grape juice and young brandy. If unavailable, try substituting Pineau des Charentes or Calvados (apple brandy).

Preparation: 35 minutes

Cooking time: 2 hours

Serves 6

—

4½ TO 5 POUNDS SOUR CHERRIES

1½ CUPS SUGAR

2 TABLESPOONS COLD WATER

1 BOTTLE MONBAZILLAC (SEE NOTE)

4 GOLDEN DELICIOUS APPLES

1 LEMON, HALVED

5 TABLESPOONS UNSALTED BUTTER

SOUR CHERRY AND APPLE COMPOTE WITH MONBAZILLAC

Pit the cherries and place in a colander set over a large bowl to catch the juices.

In a large saucepan, combine 1 cup sugar with the cold water. Bring to a boil and cook over high heat until the sugar caramelizes. Add half of the cherries and cook 3 to 4 minutes longer. Purée the remaining cherries and add to the pan. Stir in any juices from the bowl under the colander and 1½ cups Monbazillac. Cook 2 minutes longer, then remove from the heat.

Peel the apples, rub lightly with the lemon, and dice. Melt the butter in a large skillet and add the apples. Sprinkle with ½ cup sugar and cook over medium-high heat, stirring often, until the apples are golden brown. Transfer the apples to a strainer. Return the skillet to the heat and pour in 1½ cups Monbazillac. Cook over high heat, stirring to pick up any cooked bits on the bottom of the skillet, until the wine has reduced by three-quarters. Return the apples to the skillet. Continue cooking until the apples are tender but not mushy. Cool completely.

Add a spoonful of the cherry mixture into 6 tall slender glasses. Top with 2 spoonfuls of the apples. Repeat this layering until the glasses are almost filled. Refrigerate until chilled. Just before serving, pour in a little of the remaining Monbazillac to taste.

NOTE: Monbazillac is a semisweet wine grown in a district located near Bergerac in the Dordogne. Beaumes de Venise is a good substitute if Monbazillac is unavailable.

BORDEAUX

THE WINE OF BORDEAUX IS A PRODUCT OF TRADE: A VINEYARD AROUND A CITY AND A PORT AT THE END OF AN ESTUARY FORMED BY TWO RIVERS, WHERE FOR ETERNITY THE INFLUENCES OF THE ATLANTIC OCEAN HAVE PENETRATED. BORDEAUX IS THE GREATEST VINEYARD REGION IN FRANCE, AND A CERTAIN STATE OF MIND AND ATMOSPHERE IS FOUND ONLY THERE: ALL THE NOBILITY OF AQUITAINE, GUYENNE, AND GASCONY. ITS EXTREME DISTINCTION COMES FROM ITS MIXTURE OF BRITISH AND FRENCH ROOTS; ITS SPANISH, PORTUGUESE, DUTCH, AND GERMAN BRANCHES; AND ITS SCANDINAVIAN AND SWISS TWIGS. THE WINE OF BORDEAUX IS UNIVERSAL. IT OWES THIS RENOWN AS MUCH TO ITS CELEBRATED *NÉGOCIANTS* AS TO THE VINEYARD OWNERS, WHO NUMBER AMONG SOME OF THE GREATEST ON EARTH. SOLD TO CZARS, EMPERORS, AND KINGS, BORDEAUX WINES HAVE ALWAYS ALSO PLEASED THE "BOURGEOIS." THEIR WORTH IN GOLD HAS SET A STANDARD OF VALUE. A HIERARCHY HAS EXISTED FOR MORE THAN ONE HUNDRED FIFTY YEARS. TO QUESTION THIS IS MORE SERIOUS THAN TO OVERTHROW A GOVERNMENT. FINALLY, BORDEAUX WINES ARE FOUND ON ALL TABLES. AND ALL TABLES ARE FOUND IN BORDEAUX. IT IS IMPOSSIBLE TO LIMIT THE INFLUENCES. GASTRONOMY WAS BORN FROM THE PRESENCE OF THE ESTUARY AND THE CLOSENESS OF THE PASTURES OF BAZADAIS, ENTRE DEUX MERS, THE AGENAIS, AND THE PÉRIGORD VERT. THE LANDES AS WELL AS THE GERS PLAY THEIR PART, BUT ALSO THE CHARENTES. POULTRY, GAME, RED MEATS ARE ON ALL MENUS, WHICH OFTEN GLORIFY PREPARATIONS WITH WINE. SHELLFISH AND FISH, INCLUDING SOME OF THE MOST UNUSUAL, ARE THE OPENING TO THE SEA.

Many famous places attract the wine lover in heavenly Bordeaux. To be introduced to the region in the charming city of Saint-Emilion is not a bad start for a voyage that could last a lifetime.

A GLIMPSE AT TRADITION

Lamprey à la Bordelaise

*F*inely chop 12 onions and cook in a large casserole over medium-high heat until lightly browned. Reserve 1 cup of a bottle of Médoc and bring the rest to a boil in a separate saucepan. Rinse 15 leeks and remove the dark green parts. Finely chop the light green parts of the leeks and add to the onions. Cook for 2 to 3 minutes, then sprinkle with a little flour. Stir well, cook 2 to 3 minutes longer, then pour in the boiling wine. Whisk well, then add 1 cup of stock, 3 minced garlic cloves, and 1 bouquet garni. Reduce the heat and gently simmer, for 2 hours.

Place a hook into the mouth of a sea lamprey that weighs 4 to 4½ pounds. Bring water to a boil in a large kettle and plunge in the lamprey. Boil for 10 seconds, remove, and with the back of a small knife, remove and discard the skin. Rinse well and suspend the fish over a bowl that contains the reserved 1 cup wine. Cut the tail off at the level of the anus and add this cut-off piece to the simmering sauce. Let the blood of the cut lamprey run into the bowl for about 30 minutes. Make an incision around the neck of the lamprey, above the gills, and pull out the large nerve. Use your thumb to remove the intestines, then cut the lamprey into 2-inch pieces. Place the head in the sauce.

After the sauce has cooked for 2 hours, stir in the blood, then strain through a fine sieve. Season with salt and pepper and enrich with butter. Thinly slice the whites of the leeks and blanch them.

Preheat the oven to 425° F. Oil the pieces of lamprey and arrange on a baking sheet. Season with salt and pepper and bake in the oven for about 5 minutes. Add the blanched leek whites and the pieces of lamprey to the sauce. Simmer for 15 minutes. Serve with croutons rubbed with garlic.

The Médoc manifests itself in the exotic maritime influences of the nearby ocean. In Pauillac, on the estuary, eighteen *crus classés* and three *premiers crus* crown the real capital of the Médoc. The proximity of the Atlantic gives a tragic washed-out look to the skies and an accent to the gentle lines of the vineyards. In Bordeaux, 280,000 acres are devoted to the vine and furnish an average of 132 to 158 million gallons per year.

The red wines of Bordeaux are made from three grapes: Cabernet Franc, Cabernet Sauvignon, and Merlot. Sauvignon Blanc is in the majority for dry white wines, and Sémillon dominates sweet white wines, followed by Colombard and Muscadelle.

A former student at the School of Mines and an engineer, J. M. Cazes has become in two decades a model personality of the Bordelais.

The Gironde estuary opens the region to the world and colors its gastronomy with a strong maritime nuance where wine has its place.

Lynch-Bages (Pauillac) is the cradle of a family success story that Jean-Michel Cazes represents today. The vineyard, acquired by his grandfather in 1935, is one of the loveliest illustrations of the Médoc. Since 1973, when he came to help his father, André, who tended at the same time his vineyards, an insurance agency, and his commune—he was mayor of Pauillac for forty-two years—Jean-Michel Cazes took into his hands the destiny of twelve different wine-growing properties and a trading house. He also directs an insurance agency and has opened a hotel-restaurant, Cordeillan-Bages, in an elegant seventeenth-century building near Pauillac, which has been part of the "Relais & Châteaux" chain since 1991. The innovations of Jean-Michel Cazes in wine making and in the architecture of wine buildings, in particular his ambitious renovation of Pichon-Longueville, have influenced the evolution of the profession and of Bordeaux.

JEAN-MARIE AMAT

Le Saint-James
Bouliac
Gironde

Begin the day before

Preparation: I hour

Cooking time: 2 hours

Serves 4

●

15 LARGE DUCK LEGS

2 ONIONS, COARSELY CHOPPED

1 CARROT, CUT INTO LARGE PIECES

1 CELERY RIB, CUT INTO LARGE PIECES

1 LEEK, GREENS ONLY

2 GARLIC CLOVES, CRUSHED

3 BOTTLES PREMIÈRES CÔTE DE
BORDEAUX (SEE NOTE)

SALT AND FRESHLY GROUND BLACK
PEPPER TO TASTE

2 TO 3 TABLESPOONS ALL-PURPOSE
FLOUR

¾ CUP CHICKEN BLOOD (SEE NOTE,
PAGE 138)

12 OUNCES CÈPES OR PORCINI
MUSHROOMS (*BOLETUS EDULIS*)

2 TABLESPOONS VEGETABLE OIL

4 TABLESPOONS UNSALTED BUTTER

DUCK LEGS STEWED IN RED WINE

Trim the legs of excess fat and place in a large, nonreactive bowl with the onions, carrot, celery, leek greens, and garlic. Pour in the wine, cover, and marinate overnight.

The next day, drain the legs and season with salt and pepper. Place in a large skillet without any oil and cook over medium-high heat until browned on all sides. Transfer the browned legs to a large casserole. Strain the vegetables from the marinade and add to the skillet that the legs browned in; cook, stirring, until lightly browned. Transfer to the casserole with the legs. Sprinkle the legs and vegetables with the flour. Cover and cook over medium-high heat for 15 minutes. Pour the wine from the marinade into the skillet and increase the heat to high. Bring to a boil, stirring to pick up any cooked bits on the bottom, and pour into the casserole. Reduce the heat to medium and simmer the legs for 1½ hours. The duck should be very tender and falling apart when pressed between the thumb and forefinger. Remove the casserole from the heat and cool. When the legs are cool enough to handle, skin, bone, and trim away any fat. Keep the trimmed duck refrigerated.

Strain the sauce through a fine sieve into a large saucepan. Skim off all the fat and bring to a boil over high heat. Boil until reduced by a good third. Season with salt and pepper. Pour in the blood and stir to thicken. Pour the sauce over the trimmed duck meat and gently reheat over medium-low heat.

Clean the mushrooms, then blanch in boiling water for 3 minutes. Drain, slice, and place in a large skillet. Add the vegetable oil, season with salt and pepper, and cook over medium-high heat, stirring often, until lightly browned. Add the butter, cover, and keep warm.

Arrange the stewed leg meat in a dome shape on individual serving plates. Spoon over the sauce and cover with sliced mushrooms. Serve the remaining mushroom slices on the side.

NOTE: Premières Côte de Bordeaux are wines that come from a district along the right bank of the Garonne River. These are the vineyards which face Graves, Cérons, and Sauternes. These are mostly red wines, but there are some sweet white wines produced here, too. Any pleasant, dependable red wine can be used as a substitution.

Preparation: 2¼ hours

Cooking time: 6½ hours

Serves 8 to 10

—

3 TO 3½ POUNDS DUCK BONES AND
MEATY SCRAPS

1 TABLESPOON VEGETABLE OIL

2 CARROTS, COARSELY CHOPPED

1 ONION, QUARTERED

½ CELERY RIB, SLICED

2 GARLIC CLOVES, CRUSHED

1½ CUPS SAUTERNES

1 SMALL PIECE PORK RIND

1 BOUQUET GARNI

COARSE SEA SALT

12 OUNCES LEAN GROUND BEEF

1 SMALL LEEK, FINELY CHOPPED

2 TABLESPOONS FINELY CHOPPED CELERY

2 LARGE EGG WHITES

1 ENVELOPE UNFLAVORED GELATIN

¼ CUP COLD WATER

SALT AND FRESHLY GROUND BLACK
PEPPER TO TASTE

2 TABLESPOONS BALSAMIC VINEGAR,
PLUS MORE FOR THE VINAIGRETTE

15 GLOBE ARTICHOKES

1 LEMON, HALVED

¾ CUP OLIVE OIL, PLUS MORE FOR THE
VINAIGRETTE

¾ CUP DRY WHITE WINE, PREFERABLY
BORDEAUX

1 FRESH THYME SPRIG

¼ FRESH BAY LEAF

SEVERAL WHOLE CORIANDER SEEDS

¾ CUP COLD WATER

4 OUNCES FRESH SPINACH

2½ TO 3 POUNDS RAW DUCK FOIE GRAS
IN LOBES

1 BUNCH FRESH CHIVES

1 BUNCH FRESH CHERVIL

1 BUNCH FRESH TARRAGON

LAYERED FOIE GRAS AND ARTICHOKES WITH SAUTERNES

Preheat the oven to 300°F. Chop the duck bones and scraps and place in a large casserole. Add the vegetable oil and stir over high heat on top of the stove until lightly browned. Add the carrots, onion, sliced celery, and 1 garlic clove. Cook, stirring often, until the vegetables are lightly browned. Pour off any fat and pour in 1 cup Sauternes. Bring to a boil and cook until almost all of the wine has evaporated. Pour in enough cold water to cover the bones. Bring to a boil, skim well, and add the pork rind and bouquet garni. Season lightly with coarse sea salt, cover, and bake for about 4 hours. Strain into a large saucepan and skim off all the fat. Boil until reduced by one-quarter. Keep warm.

In a separate large saucepan, blend the ground beef, leek, chopped celery, and egg whites. Whisking constantly over high heat, gradually pour in the warm stock. Continue whisking until the mixture comes to a boil. Reduce the heat to medium-low and simmer gently for 1½ hours. Ladle the clarified stock through a sieve lined with a double layer of rinsed cheesecloth. Sprinkle the gelatin over ¼ cup cold water and let sit for 5 minutes to soften. Reserve a small amount of the duck stock to prepare a vinaigrette sauce. Bring the remaining stock to a boil and stir in the gelatin. Season with salt and pepper, add the remaining ½ cup Sauternes, and 2 tablespoons balsamic vinegar. Remove from the heat and set aside.

Bend back the stems of the artichokes until they break off. With a knife, flatten the bottoms and cut away the leaves. Trim the bottoms well and scoop out the choke or stringy part of the centers. Rub well with the lemon halves. Place the bottoms in a large pot or kettle and add ¾ cup olive oil, the white wine, remaining garlic clove, the thyme, bay leaf, and coriander seeds. Pour in ¾ cup cold water, season with salt and pepper, and bring to a boil over high heat. Reduce the heat to medium-low, cover, and cook until tender.

Stem the spinach and rinse in several changes of cold water. Blanch the leaves in boiling salted water and carefully lay out on clean kitchen towels to drain. Chill.

Cut the lobes of foie gras into thick slices. Remove all nerves, veins, and any bloody deposits. Season with salt and pepper. Cook in a large skillet over high heat for about 1 minute on each side. Transfer to a wire rack to drain and cool. Do not refrigerate.

Trim the artichoke bottoms into uniform sticks about the size of a thick French fry. Reserve the scraps for another use (salad, for example).

Line a terrine mold with the clarified duck aspic. Start the layering by arranging a bed of the artichoke sticks over the bottom. Continue with the spinach leaves and slices of foie gras. Pour over the remaining aspic at the end of the layering to bind the elements. Refrigerate for at least several hours.

Unmold the terrine and cut into thick slices. Arrange a slice on individual serving plates. Garnish with the chives, chervil, and tarragon. Prepare a simple vinaigrette sauce with the reserved duck stock, balsamic vinegar, and oil. Spoon the sauce over and around the slices and serve at once.

Before harvesting, one waits for botrytis cinerea, the "noble rot," to cover the grapes. This is indispensable for the making of Sauternes.

for the ducklings and stock:

2 DUCKLINGS

2 TABLESPOONS DUCK FAT OR
VEGETABLE OIL

2 CARROTS, FINELY DICED

1 ONION, FINELY CHOPPED

1 LEEK, WHITE PART ONLY,
FINELY CHOPPED

½ CELERY RIB, FINELY CHOPPED

6 GARLIC CLOVES

2½ CUPS RED BORDEAUX,
PREFERABLY SAINT-ESTÈPHE

2½ CUPS DRY WHITE WINE

2 TABLESPOONS OLIVE OIL

for the aspic:

1¼ POUNDS LEAN BEEF

1 LARGE LEEK

½ CELERY RIB, FINELY DICED

2 LARGE EGG WHITES

1½ ENVELOPES UNFLAVORED GELATIN

½ CUP COLD WATER

3 TABLESPOONS UNSALTED BUTTER

4 OUNCES SHALLOTS, MINCED

1 VEAL BONE, ABOUT 8 OUNCES

1 GARLIC CLOVE, CRUSHED

1 CARROT, DICED

1 CLOVE

1 FRESH THYME SPRIG

½ FRESH BAY LEAF

2 CUPS RED BORDEAUX, PREFERABLY
SAINT-ESTÈPHE

½ SPLIT CALF'S FOOT

SALT AND FRESHLY GROUND BLACK
PEPPER TO TASTE

for the garnish:

10 TO 12 OUNCES COOKED FOIE GRAS

2 CARROTS, VERY FINELY DICED

2 WHITE TURNIPS, VERY FINELY DICED

½ CELERY ROOT, VERY FINELY DICE

8 OUNCES TINY GREEN BEANS

1 RED BELL PEPPER, VERY FINELY DICED

2 TABLESPOONS MAYONNAISE

SALT AND FRESHLY GROUND BLACK
PEPPER TO TASTE

8 MEDIUM TOMATOES

2 LARGE BELGIAN ENDIVES

1 BUNCH YOUNG, TENDER ARUGULA

SEVERAL TINY BAY LEAVES, FOR GARNISH

DUCKLING AND FOIE GRAS IN RED WINE ASPIC

Cut away the feet, wings, and necks of the ducklings. Remove the thighs and set aside. Keep the breasts attached to the carcasses. Heat the duck fat in a large casserole. Chop the wings, necks, and any scraps and add to the casserole. Cook over medium-high heat until lightly browned. In a small bowl, combine the carrots, onion, leek, and celery. Mince 2 of the garlic cloves and add to the bowl. Add half of this mixture to the duck bones and cook until lightly browned. Pour off any fat in the pan and add 1¾ cups each red and white wine. Increase the heat to high and boil, stirring, until the liquid has almost evaporated. Pour in enough cold water to cover the contents of the casserole. Crush the remaining 4 garlic cloves and add to the stock. Reduce the heat, and simmer for about 3 hours.

Thirty minutes before the stock is finished, place a separate large casserole over medium-high heat. Add the duck thighs and cook, skin side down, until golden brown. Turn and cook the flesh side until browned. Pour off the fat and add the remaining diced vegetable mixture. Pour in the remaining ¾ cup each red and white wine and stir well. Pour the stock through a sieve into this casserole and bring to a boil. Skim the surface, reduce the heat to medium, and simmer, for 30 minutes. Skim again and strain into a large saucepan. Increase the heat to high and boil to reduce by half.

Meanwhile, preheat the oven to 425°F. Pour the olive oil into a roasting pan and add the duckling carcass with the breasts attached. Cook for about 20 minutes, remove from the oven, and cover loosely with foil. Let rest for 10 minutes, then keep refrigerated until ready to assemble the dish.

To prepare the aspic, finely chop or grind 12 ounces of the lean beef and place it in a large saucepan. Finely chop the leek and add half to the meat. Stir in the celery and the egg whites. Whisking constantly over medium-high heat, slowly pour in the reduced duckling stock. Bring to a boil, reduce the heat to low, and simmer gently for 1½ hours. Ladle through a strainer lined with a double layer of rinsed cheesecloth. Sprinkle the gelatin over the cold water and let stand for 5 minutes to soften. Add to the warm stock, stir well, and set aside.

Melt the butter in a large saucepan. Add the shallots and cook over medium-high heat, stirring often, until lightly browned. Cut the remaining beef into large dice and add it to the pan. Add the remaining chopped leek, the veal bone, garlic, carrot, clove, thyme, and bay leaf. Cook until lightly browned. In a separate saucepan, bring the wine to a boil and ignite it. When the flames die out, pour the wine into the browned vegetable mixture. Add the calf's foot, season with salt and pepper, and reduce the heat to medium-low. Simmer for 1½ hours. Stir in 4 cups of the stock with gelatin. Bring to a boil and reduce by one-quarter. Season again with salt and pepper. Strain through a sieve, let cool, and remove any fat from the surface. Keep refrigerated.

Remove the breasts from the carcass of the duckling. Remove the skin and cut the meat into ¼-inch-thick slices.

For the garnish, cut the foie gras into slices the same size and thickness as the duckling breasts. Cover the foie gras with the duckling slices and place on a wire rack set over a large baking sheet. Keep refrigerated.

Have the aspic at the right consistency for coating. If it has solidified, gently reheat over very low heat. Ladle a small amount of the liquid aspic over the layered breasts and foie gras. Chill until firm, then repeat. Two layers are necessary for a nice glazed effect. When finished, trim into neat parcels. Chill the remaining aspic until firm, then finely chop it and return to the refrigerator.

Cook the carrots, turnips, celery root, and green beans separately in boiling salted water until tender. Refresh under cold running water and drain well. Cut the green beans into tiny dice. Combine the cooked vegetables with the red bell pepper in a small bowl. Add the mayonnaise and stir until blended. Season with salt and pepper.

Use the skins of the tomatoes to form 8 decorative roses. Remove the leaves of the endive in order to make decorative flowers for the plates. Remove the arugula leaves from the stems, rinse well, and pat dry with paper towels.

On one side of large serving plates, use 4 of the larger endive leaves per person and fill with smaller endive leaves to form a flower. Place a small flan ring in the center and fill with the vegetables in mayonnaise. Remove the ring and decorate with a tiny bay leaf. Add 2 of the duckling and foie gras slices and surround with small arugula leaves. Garnish with a tomato rose and some of the chopped aspic. Serve at once with toasted coarse-grain bread.

Preparation: 2½ hours

Cooking time: 2 hours

Serves 6

━

6 RIPE MEDIUM TOMATOES

SALT TO TASTE

PINCH OF SUGAR

FRESHLY GROUND BLACK PEPPER TO TASTE

½ CUP OLIVE OIL

FRESH THYME LEAVES

6 GARLIC CLOVES, MINCED

6 LONG, THIN POTATOES

22 TABLESPOONS (2¾ STICKS) UNSALTED BUTTER

PINCH OF SAFFRON THREADS

12 LARGE WHITE MUSHROOMS

JUICE OF 1½ LEMONS

8 OUNCES FRESH WHITE MUSHROOMS

1 SMALL BUNCH PARSLEY

2 SHALLOTS, MINCED

4 GARLIC CLOVES, PEELED

CURRY POWDER TO TASTE

18 SNAILS, QUARTERED

3¼ CUPS MILK

½ CUP POLENTA

1 LOBSTER, ABOUT 1¼ POUNDS

1 SMALL BUNCH CHIVES, SNIPPED

12 OUNCES FIRM-FLESHED POTATOES

1 SMALL MACKEREL

1 TABLESPOON MAYONNAISE

PINCH OF MIXED SPICES (CURRY, TURMERIC, GROUND GINGER, ETC.)

1 LARGE FENNEL BULB

2 SMALL CARROTS, CUT INTO THIN JULIENNE STRIPS

1 LEEK, WHITE PART ONLY, CUT INTO THIN JULIENNE STRIPS

1 CELERY RIB, CUT INTO THIN JULIENNE STRIPS

4 SMALL OR SPRING ONIONS, CUT INTO THIN JULIENNE STRIPS

1¾ CUPS DRY WHITE BORDEAUX WINE, PREFERABLY GRAVES

STUFFED VEGETABLES IN A THIN WINE SAUCE

Preheat the oven to 225°F. Peel the tomatoes and cut off a thick slice from the stem end. Set the stem slices aside. Remove the seeds from the remaining tomatoes and season with salt and a pinch of sugar. Season the interiors with freshly ground black pepper. Place in a baking pan lined with foil and drizzle with the olive oil. Sprinkle with thyme and the minced garlic. Bake until the tomatoes are very soft, 1½ to 2 hours.

Peel the 6 long potatoes and cut off the ends. Trim lightly to form the shape of a boat and scoop out the centers to make a small cavity. Melt 3 tablespoons butter in a large skillet. Add the potatoes and cook over medium-high heat, turning carefully, until lightly browned. Transfer to a saucepan filled with salted water and add the saffron. Cook over medium heat until the potatoes are yellow and tender. Drain well and keep cool but not refrigerated.

Remove the stems of the 12 large mushrooms. Flute 6 of these (see page 138). Add the juice of ½ lemon to a pan of water. Add all 12 large mushroom cups, return to a boil, add 1 tablespoon butter, and boil rapidly until tender. Remove from the heat and set the mushrooms aside in their liquid.

Clean the 8 ounces mushrooms and trim the stems. Place in a large saucepan, add enough water to cover, the juice of ½ lemon, and salt. Bring to a boil and cook until tender. Drain well and set aside. Slice one or two and set aside for garnish.

Finely chop the parsley, 1 shallot, and 3 garlic cloves together. Soften 7 tablespoons butter in a small bowl. Stir in the parsley mixture, season with salt and pepper, and set aside.

Melt 3 tablespoons butter in a large skillet. Add the remaining shallot and cook over medium-high heat until softened. Chop the reserved tomato slices and drain. Chop the 8 ounces of blanched mushrooms and add to the skillet. Cook until the water given off by the mushrooms has evaporated. Stir in the drained tomatoes and season with salt, pepper, and curry powder. Add the snails and the parslied butter. Season again with salt and pepper. Fill the cooked whole tomatoes with this mixture. Season the mushroom slices with salt, pepper, and plenty of lemon juice. Use to garnish the filled tomatoes. Set aside.

Bring 1 cup milk to a boil in a large saucepan. Gradually stir in the polenta and cook, stirring, constantly, over medium-high heat until the mixture starts to clean the sides of the pan, about 5 minutes. Set aside.

Cook the lobster in boiling salted water for about 10 minutes. Refresh under cold running water and drain well. Remove the tail and reserve, covered with a dampened kitchen towel. Dislodge the flesh from the claws and the interior of the head. Finely chop this flesh and prepare a filling in a proportion of two-thirds polenta and one-third lobster. Add the chives and season with salt and pepper. Fill the potato "boats" with this mixture and set aside.

Cook the firm-fleshed potatoes in boiling salted water until tender. Fillet the mackerel, eliminating all skins and bones. Cook the mackerel in ¾ cup milk seasoned with salt, pepper, and the remaining garlic clove, peeled. Drain the potatoes, mash with the mackerel (two-thirds potatoes to one-third mackerel), and thin with ¾ cup cold milk and the mayonnaise. Season with salt, pepper, and the pinch of mixed spices. Fill the 6 plain mushroom caps with this mixture and cover with the 6 fluted tops. Set aside.

Peel, trim, and rinse the fennel. (Reserve the fronds for garnish.) Thinly slice and cook until tender in the remaining ¾ cup milk. Transfer to a food processor and blend until smooth. Strain through a fine sieve.

Combine the julienned carrots, leeks, celery, and onions in a small nonreactive saucepan. Add a little water, salt, and pepper. Cook over medium-high heat until tender. In a separate saucepan, boil the wine over high heat until reduced to about 2 tablespoons. Pour into the cooked julienned vegetables and cover to infuse for 20 minutes. Strain through a fine sieve and place in a small saucepan. Add a spoonful of the puréed fennel and stir in 6 tablespoons butter. Season with salt and pepper. Keep warm over very low heat.

Warm the filled vegetables in a steamer. Melt the remaining 2 tablespoons butter in a small skillet. Remove the flesh from the lobster tail and cut into thick slices. Add to the skillet and cook over medium-high heat until lightly browned. Top each of the filled potatoes with one slice.

Arrange the vegetables attractively on large serving plates and spoon over some of the thin fennel sauce. Decorate with the fennel fronds and serve at once.

TURBOT COOKED ON THE BONE WITH ENDIVE AND MERLOT

Preparation: 1 hour

Cooking time: 55 minutes

Serves 8

—

1 LARGE TURBOT, 7 TO 8 POUNDS

8 BELGIAN ENDIVES

14 TABLESPOONS UNSALTED BUTTER

PINCH OF SUGAR

2 ONIONS, CHOPPED

½ LEEK, WHITE PART ONLY, THINLY SLICED

2½ POUNDS LEAN FISH BONES, PREFERABLY FROM TURBOT OR SOLE

3 CUPS MERLOT, PREFERABLY FROM BORDEAUX

1 BOUQUET GARNI

1 CLOVE

1 CUP VEAL STOCK

SALT AND FRESHLY GROUND BLACK PEPPER TO TASTE

CHOPPED FRESH THYME LEAVES

CHOPPED FRESH BAY LEAVES

Remove the head from the turbot, pull off the skin, and cut the fish lengthwise in half. Keep refrigerated.

Trim and rinse the endives, then cut lengthwise into long, thin strips. Melt 6 tablespoons butter in a large nonreactive skillet and add the endives. Sprinkle with the sugar and cook over medium-high heat, stirring often, until tender.

Melt 4 tablespoons butter in a large saucepan. Add the onions and leek. Cook over medium-high heat, stirring often, until softened. Add the fish bones and pour in the wine. Add the bouquet garni and clove. Pour in enough cold water to cover. Bring to a boil over high heat, reduce the heat to medium, and simmer for 30 minutes. Strain into another saucepan and boil until reduced by half. Add the veal stock and return to a boil. Whisk in the remaining 4 tablespoons butter, season with salt and pepper, reduce the heat to low, and keep warm.

Preheat the oven to 450°F. Season the turbot with salt, pepper, thyme, and bay leaves. Bake on a baking sheet for a few minutes, then remove and take the fillets off the bone. Cut the fillets into thick slices and transfer to a nonstick baking sheet. Season again with salt and pepper. Bake a few more minutes in the oven.

Arrange the cooked endives in the center of individual serving plates. Ladle over some of the sauce and top with the turbot. Serve at once.

Preparation: 1½ hours

Cooking time: 20 minutes

Serves 8

—

for the cakes:

14 TABLESPOONS UNSALTED BUTTER

1 CUP SUGAR

4 LARGE EGGS, SEPARATED

¾ CUP CABERNET SAUVIGNON

2 CUPS ALL-PURPOSE FLOUR

1 TEASPOON BAKING POWDER

1 TEASPOON UNSWEETENED COCOA

½ TEASPOON GROUND CINNAMON

for the figs:

8 FRSEH FIGS

1 CUP STRAINED FRESH ORANGE JUICE

½ CUP STRAINED FRESH LEMON JUICE

1 CUP CABERNET SAUVIGNON

2½ CUPS SUGAR

for the ice cream:

3 CUPS MILK

1 LARGE BUNCH BASIL, STEMS REMOVED,
LEAVES THINLY SLICED

½ VANILLA BEAN

1¼ CUPS SUGAR

11 LARGE EGG YOLKS

1½ CUPS CRÈME FRAÎCHE

SMALL BASIL LEAVES, FOR GARNISH

CABERNET CAKE WITH FIGS AND BASIL ICE CREAM

To prepare the cakes, preheat the oven to 350° F. Butter 8 small rectangular molds. In a large bowl, cream the butter with the sugar until light. Stir in the egg yolks and wine. Sift together the flour, baking powder, cocoa, and cinnamon. Gently stir into the butter mixture and blend. Beat the egg whites until stiff and carefully fold into the batter. Fill the molds and bake until a thin knife inserted into the center of the cakes comes out clean, about 20 minutes.

To prepare the figs, peel the figs without tearing or destroying their form. In a nonreactive saucepan, combine the orange juice, lemon juice, wine, and sugar. Mix well and bring to a boil. Remove from the heat and add the figs. Set aside to cool.

To make the ice cream, bring the milk to a boil in a large saucepan and add the basil leaves and vanilla bean. Remove from the heat, cover, and infuse. Mix the sugar with the eggs yolks in a large bowl. Strain the hot milk, discarding the basil leaves and vanilla bean, into the egg yolk mixture. Return to the saucepan and cook, stirring constantly, over low heat until thick enough to coat the back of a spoon. Strain, stir in the crème fraîche, and chill. Pour into an ice-cream maker and freeze according to the manufacturer's instructions.

To serve, cut the cake into thick slices and arrange in the center of individual serving plates. Brush lightly with some of the liquid from the figs and top with 2 scoops of the ice cream. Quarter the figs and arrange attractively around the cake. Garnish with small basil leaves and serve at once.

Preparation: 40 minutes

Cooking time: 10 minutes

Serves 4

—

¾ CUP GRANULATED SUGAR

½ VANILLA BEAN

¾ CUP ALMONDS, TOASTED

4 LARGE EGG YOLKS

½ CUP CRÈME FRAÎCHE

½ CUP BARSAC (SEE NOTE)

4 THIN SLICES YELLOW CAKE

4 RIPE PEARS

CONFECTIONERS' SUGAR

WILD STRAWBERRIES AND SMALL MINT
LEAVES, FOR GARNISH

PEAR GRATIN WITH PRALINE AND SWEET WINE

In a large heavy saucepan, cook ½ cup granulated sugar with the vanilla bean over medium-high heat until the sugar is golden brown. Discard the vanilla bean, add the almonds, stir well, and pour out onto an oiled heatproof surface (preferably marble). Cool completely, then break into pieces and pound to a powder using a mortar and pestle.

Beat the egg yolks with the remaining ¼ cup granulated sugar until thick enough to leave a ribbon on the surface when the whisk is lifted. Whip the crème fraîche until stiff and fold into the egg mixture. Carefully fold in the wine.

Preheat the broiler. To serve, arrange the cake slices in the center of large ovenproof plates. Cut the pears into uniform, thin slices and arrange decoratively on the cake. Spoon over some of the wine-flavored sauce and dust with some of the almond praline. Sprinkle with confectioners' sugar and place under the broiler. Broil, watching carefully, until well browned. Serve at once, garnished with wild strawberries and mint leaves, if desired.

NOTE: Barsac is a sweet Bordeaux wine from the Sauternes region. As a matter of fact, it is made from the same grape and in the same manner as Sauternes. Use any good-quality sweet or dessert wine as a substitute.

INDEX

ACKNOWLEDGMENTS

Since the photographer allows the chef to fix the ephemeral character of his creations, my thanks go first of all to Christopher Baker, whose great talent I value. We have spent much time together in the desire to put everything together to make this work a success, the joint expression of our sensibilities. My gratitude naturally goes to all those who helped us and so well received us in their vineyards, their cellars, their kitchens, and all other places—all of them passionate about their professions and the search for quality.

This work will leave us with numerous memories, some of them comical. We needed a great deal of patience to photograph, with an eye always on watch for the best light and an ear constantly listening to weather forecasts. To install ourselves on a rock in the middle of a stream in the Jura, to wait under drizzling rain with ladders, boards, and ropes in order to set up and photograph Trout Soufflé with Crayfish Sauce was not easy. In Mâcon, in the vineyards at the foot of the Roche de Solutré, to wait in the early morning for the mists to disperse to immortalize Snails with Watercress, White Beans, and Saint-Véran was a great exercise in patience. Likewise, to climb the steep vineyards above the village of Cornas in the Rhône Valley in order to execute the Layered Beef in Red Wine Sauce bathed in autumn sunlight, or to settle ourselves on a beach in the Languedoc to photograph Roasted Angler Fish with Tomato and Onion Tart in the midst of north winds—these are just a few of the experiences that we will never forget.

I would also like to warmly thank all the great creative chefs in the wine regions who offered, in respecting the spirit of the book, a *Recette de l'Amitié.*

I am also grateful to Patrick Guillemin, my close assistant in the kitchen; to the whole team that worked with me on the recipes; and to Françoise Berodier, my secretary, who helped me improve the editing of the manuscript with her practical sense and her fresh look at the cuisine of professionals.

My gratitude extends also to the whole Hachette team: Jean Arcache, Philippe Lamboley, Valérie Strauss-Kahn, Florence Lécuyer, and Michel Durand, who extended me their confidence and their precious help in the realization of this book.

Published by Clarkson N. Potter/Publishers, 201 East 50th Street, New York, New York 10022. Member of the Crown Publishing Group.

Random House, Inc.   New York, Toronto, London, Sydney, Auckland
http:www.randomhouse.com/

CLARKSON N. POTTER, POTTER, and colophon are trademarks of Clarkson N. Potter, Inc.

Originally published in French by Hachette Livre in 1995. Copyright © 1995 by Hachette Livre (Hachette Pratiques: Vie Pratique.) Photographs copyright © 1995 by Christopher Baker.

Printed in Italy

Design by Michel Durand

Library of Congress Cataloging-in-Publication Data
Blanc, Georges.
    The French vineyard table/Georges Blanc; photographs by Christopher Baker; directed by Philippe Lamboley.—1st ed.
    Includes index.
    1. Cookery, French.   2. Wine and wine making—France.   3. France—Description and travel.   I. Title.
TX719.B5875   1997
641.5944—dc21   97-12569
                                                                              CIP

ISBN 0-609-60000-1

10   9   8   7   6   5   4   3   2   1

First American Edition